Confucius

CONFUCIUS

And the World He Created

MICHAEL SCHUMAN

BASIC BOOKS
A Member of the Perseus Books Group
New York

Books published by Basic Books are available at special discounts for bulk purchases in the
United States by corporations, institutions, and other organizations. For more information,
please contact the Special Markets Department at the Perseus Books Group, 2300 Chest-
nut Street, Suite 200, Philadelphia, PA 19103, or call (800) 810-4145, ext. 5000, or e-mail
special.markets@perseusbooks.com.

Designed by Jeff Williams

Library of Congress Cataloging-in-Publication Data
Schuman, Michael.
    Confucius : and the world he created / Michael Schuman.
        pages cm
    Includes bibliographical references and index.
    ISBN 978-0-465-02551-0 (hardcover : alk. paper)—ISBN 978-0-465-04057-5 (e-book)
1. Confucius. I. Title.

B128.C8S38 2015
181'.112—dc23
                                                                            2014047092

10 9 8 7 6 5 4 3 2 1

To Eunice, my favorite Confucian

CONTENTS

INTRODUCTION

How Confucius Changed the World

I never expected a Chinese man who lived 2,500 years ago to crash my wedding.

In the spring of 2009, I married my longtime girlfriend, Eunice, who is a Korean-American journalist, and although the main ceremony was planned as a standard white-dress, Judeo-Christian affair, she also wanted to add a Korean ritual called a *paebaek*. Eunice would change into a traditional, brightly colored, flowing Korean gown known as a *hanbok*, and both of us would bow down before her parents. Then they would offer us a blessing and toss walnuts and dates into her billowing skirt as an encouragement of fertility.

When Eunice informed me about the *paebaek* I got a sick feeling in my stomach. I was extremely uncomfortable with bowing. The ritual demanded a highly stylized, obsequious, forehead-to-the-floor kind of bow. Growing up Jewish, I was taught that people should have respect for themselves and not bow down before anyone. The Bible's Book of Esther, read during every Purim celebration, tells of how a vengeful Persian official almost annihilated the local Jews because one Jewish man refused to bow before him. Even God rarely merits a full prostration in modern Jewish religious practice. More commonly, we merely bend our knees and briefly dip our heads as a sign of deference to the Almighty. But in East Asia, bowing is a regular feature of everyday life, a routine method of being polite to others, especially those in authority. People bow to older family members, bosses in the office, government officials, even seniors at universities. A friend of mine who spent many years working in Tokyo once joked that "you know you've been in Japan too long when you start bowing while talking on the phone."

Bowing to Eunice's parents was not quite the same as these other, run-of-the-mill types, however. The gesture carried greater weight and meaning. In Korea, as in the rest of East Asia, parents are often treated with a degree of reverence rarely witnessed in the modern West. By bowing to Eunice's father, I would be fulfilling my proper duty as the new son-in-law. If I refused, I'd be setting off a crisis before my wedding and instigating who-knows-what with my irate bride.

I could thank Confucius for my predicament. The famous Chinese philosopher, born in the sixth century BC and better known in China as Master Kong, or Kongzi, considered filial piety the foundation of a peaceful and prosperous society, and the continuing centrality of the concept is one of the most enduring of his legacies. According to Confucius, there is no more important relationship within society than that between father and son. The duty of a son (or in my case, a son-in-law) to show filial respect was paramount and among the most basic tenets of human virtue. The morals and rules of propriety learned within the family are easily transferable to society at large. If children acted with deference toward their parents, they would generally interact appropriately with others at school, work, or a dinner party. Confucius believed that if each member of a family understood and fulfilled his or her prescribed role, the entire world would find its proper order. In other words, by bowing to Eunice's parents, I would be reinforcing harmony in society and contributing to nothing less than the cosmic balance between man, the world we live in, and Heaven itself.

Heavy stuff indeed. With so much importance embedded in the *paebaek*, I should have just kept my mouth shut and pressed my face to the floor. Confucius always expected people to comply with such social rituals, because he thought they formed the basis for peaceful, respectful interaction between different members of a community. But I guess I'm not a very good Confucian. I decided to take a chance and express to Eunice my discomfort with the deferential ceremony. Maybe I'd catch a break.

I should have known better. Although Eunice is far from being a traditional Korean girl—she was born and raised in the midwestern United States—she can suddenly become very Confucian, especially when it comes to her parents, for whom she cares deeply. When I told her of my misgivings about the *paebaek*, her Confucian heritage—those core family values that Korean parents instill in their children all over the world—came bubbling to the surface from some rarely tapped cistern buried within her. She considered the *paebaek* so important that the issue was nonnegotiable. "Get over it," she shot back. I could practically hear the old sage rapping his cane on the floor and scolding me from the grave.

So, with difficulty, I set aside my reservations. The morning of the wedding, I asked her younger brother James for bowing lessons. I couldn't just bow any way I wanted; it had to be the right kind of bow. We found an isolated hallway at our hotel, and James gave me an emergency tutorial. While still standing, place your hands at the forehead, with the thumbs and forefingers forming a triangle between them. Then, with your hands in that position—rather than helping you to balance—lower yourself onto your knees. Next, bend over until your hands and forehead are plastered to the floorboards. Maintain that position for a few seconds, lift up your head, again without using your hands, and remain on your knees until the parents have finished speaking.

As the *paebaek* began, my heart was racing. It was easily the most nerve-wracking moment of my wedding. The fact that my closest friends were watching probably didn't help. But I got through the ceremony without embarrassing myself or insulting anyone, and it pleased Eunice's father immensely. I took a deep breath of relief—until events took an unexpected turn. Eunice's parents insisted that we repeat the *paebaek* with my own mother. Although my mother was well aware of my discomfort with the ceremony, she readily accepted and, much to my dismay, reveled in watching her son bow before her. I guess we're all Confucians at heart.

CONFUCIUS'S ATTENDANCE AT my wedding ceremony is just one very minor example of the influence the great sage still wields today. Twenty-five hundred years after Confucius first expounded his ideas, they remain ensconced within the societies of East Asia, having survived endless political upheavals, economic metamorphoses, and a torrent of foreign doctrines, religions, and cultural influences. Although in recent decades East Asia has undergone fantastically accelerated modernization, there is still simply no way to interact with a Chinese, Korean, or Japanese person without understanding, and contending with, the ancient ideals of Confucius. His teachings can be discovered in ministerial offices and parliament houses, governing how officials craft policy and relate to their citizens; in corporate boardrooms and on factory floors, guiding CEOs on business strategy and human resources; in schoolrooms, dictating how teachers educate their students; and in bedrooms, intruding on relations between husbands and wives. Confucius influences how East Asians think about democracy, raise children, choose careers, socialize at the office, and understand their own identities. You can't successfully conduct business, negotiate with a government official, make sense of the issues that arise when dating, or comprehend what motivates East Asians today without an appreciation of Confucius.

That, without question, makes Confucius one of the most important men who ever lived. His teachings shape the daily lives of well over 1.6 billion people today, nearly a quarter of the world's population—in a huge geographic swath stretching from northern Japan down to Java in Indonesia. Only Christianity can claim to hold greater sway over modern global culture. Even as Asia has been bombarded by outside influences—from the *Communist Manifesto* to the Bible to Harry Potter, from mocha lattes to McDonald's to Britney Spears, Confucius has endured, too much a part of daily life to be smothered, uprooted, or replaced. Confucius, then, ranks with Abraham, Jesus, Muhammad, and Siddhartha Gautama (better known as the Buddha), and Aristotle and Plato, as one of the founders of modern civilization.

Despite this reality, most westerners hardly know anything about Confucius. That lack of knowledge is actually quite dangerous. As Asia rises in global importance, with greater clout in the global economy and international geopolitics than the region has enjoyed in centuries, Confucius and the culture he created are rising with it. To contend with the newly empowered nations of East Asia, to understand what makes the region's businessmen, politicians, and policymakers tick, the West needs to learn, more than ever before, about Confucius, his philosophy, and his legacy. What we in the United States and Europe have to appreciate is that East Asian civilization is constructed on an entirely different philosophical basis than our own—to a great degree, the teachings of Confucius.

Scholars and politicians in the West have for centuries studied the Greek philosophers (Aristotle, Plato, Socrates), the Bible and other Judeo-Christian works, and the thinkers who laid the foundation for modern society in the West, such as John Locke, Thomas Hobbes, and Adam Smith. Not so in East Asia. Historically, academics, writers, and state officials in that part of the world have read the Confucian classics, which provided the ideological backbone of East Asia's governing institutions, the curricula of its academies, and the norms of social discourse. In China, knowledge of the Confucian canon, and the many commentaries and essays expounding on it, was traditionally a prerequisite for social and professional advancement, the basic education one had to have in order to be considered truly civilized. Chinese civil servants earned their jobs by mastering these classics for 1,900 years. In East Asia, it was Confucius, not Moses, who handed down the standards for human morality. It was Confucius, not Locke or Thomas Jefferson, who forged the relationship between citizen and state and the position of the individual in society. Confucianism has not been the sole influence on East Asian civilization. Buddhism, for instance, has played an important role. So have foreign religions and ideologies that arrived in the region over the past two hundred years, from Christianity to Marxism. And Confucius is far from Asian history's only philosopher of brilliance. Laozi, the (perhaps mythical) founder of Daoism, is just one of several important thinkers whose influence can still be felt in Asian life. Yet no individual has held more sway over East Asia for such an extended period of time as Confucius. Indeed, the history of East Asian civilization is synonymous with the development of Confucian doctrine.

MOST OF US can probably name a teacher who had a dramatic influence over our lives. Dennis Harding at Clifton High School in New Jersey inspired my enduring interest in history, which motivates me to write books like this one almost thirty years after I sat in his classroom. I still occasionally meet him for breakfast at a diner near my parents' house on my visits back home. Good teachers can do more than just get their students to balance an equation or recall the names of presidents. They can shape what people believe and how they conduct their lives; they can encourage a passion to learn and excel.

Confucius may be the greatest teacher in human history. Though at one point in his career he was a marginally successful statesman and government official, he spent most of his professional life teaching, and it was as a teacher that he left his indelible mark on Asia. The most famous text associated with him, the *Analects*, consists, for the most part, of snippets of conversations he had with his students while instructing them on virtue, good government, interpersonal relations, ethics, and history. What Confucius taught was the wisdom of Chinese antiquity, a timeless code of morality and gracious vision of humanity that can stir anyone reading his words today. His devoted students, convinced of the worth of his teachings, passed them on to another generation of students, who then repeated them to another. In every century following Confucius's death, new generations of followers studied, commented upon, and, in some cases, dramatically refashioned the sage's teachings. The result was a school of philosophy that became the dominant ethical foundation and governing ideology for East Asia. Confucius would not have become Confucius if his disciples had not propagated his ideas and nurtured his legacy.

Over the centuries, as Confucius became more and more integral to East Asian society, he also came to be seen as far more than a simple teacher. Confucius was transformed into the Supreme Sage, the founding father of

Chinese civilization, and the "Uncrowned King," one who, though he never held official sovereign authority, had been chosen by Heaven to rule. Every Chinese or Korean man who wished to be considered a true gentleman measured himself against Confucius. James Legge, the famous nineteenth-century British sinologist, wrote that in China, Confucius was "the one man by whom all possible personal excellence was exemplified, and by whom all possible lessons of social virtue and political wisdom are taught."[1] There were periods of Chinese history when Confucius was even considered something close to divine, like a superman with miraculous powers and a saintly appearance. One tale claimed that Confucius was the son of a spiritual being—a kind of Chinese Perseus. Sacrifices and ceremonies in Confucius's honor have been conducted for some 2,000 years. Every town in China of any consequence boasted its own Confucian temple. Even emperors occasionally kowtowed before his shrine. The titles bestowed upon Confucius by the royal court grew outrageously lavish. From the simple "Duke," awarded in AD 1, Confucius later became the "Accomplished Sage," the "Greatest Sage and Ancient Teacher," and then the "Classic Teacher, Accomplished, Illustrious, and Perfect Sage." His descendants were granted noble status and ample landholdings by the state.

Such lofty praise and pompous ceremonial would likely have made Confucius blush. From what we know of the historical Confucius, he at no point claimed to be more than a man, and at times, he described himself as a less-than-perfect one. The master could be surprisingly self-deprecating—downplaying his intelligence, doubting his morality, and joking about his poverty. He never considered himself a true sage, let alone some sort of superhero. "In unstinted effort I can compare with others, but in being a practicing gentleman I have had, as yet, no success," he once confessed.[2]

Uncovering the real Confucius, stripping away the myth and legend, rumors and accusations, fabrications and distortions, and the baggage heaped upon his back over two millennia, is no easy task. The Confucius of modern discourse is not the Confucius of the classical age; nor is he even the Confucius of a hundred years ago. "Every age has its own Confucius, and in each age there are several different kinds of Confuciuses," wrote twentieth-century historian Gu Jiegang. "The figure of Confucius continually changes according to whatever the people of each age think or say about him. But most people are not at all aware of this, and they ultimately don't understand what the real face of Confucius is."[3] The ability of Confucius to morph and adapt to the demands of each era has kept him a vital and engaging figure capable of withstanding centuries of change. But it has also turned him into something he probably never meant to be.

Confucius has been more a symbol than an actual man, for both his supporters and his enemies. He has been an icon of China's cultural heritage, a totem of imperial government, the archetypal human being, the face of oppression, the voice of transformation, the patron of learning, a tool for public relations, a spiritual guide, and the emblem of everything grand and everything bad about China. He has been both a reactionary and a revolutionary, a dictator and a democrat, a feudal lord and a capitalist, a brilliant scholar and a simple fraud, a xenophobe and a globalist, a pillar of authority and a dangerous dissident, a model humanist and a destroyer of souls. He has been the cause of East Asia's economic success and a cause of its economic failings, a cultural fundamentalist and a messianic visionary, the source of East Asia's strengths and weaknesses. In the West, Confucius is perceived as the personification of Chinese civilization, the sagely purveyor of the ancient wisdom of the East, appropriately garbed in flowing robes and donning the long beard of the wise man. If Confucius came back to life today, he would scarcely recognize himself.

The Confucius we know today is not the creation of the Chinese alone. The modern Confucius is "a product fashioned over several centuries by many hands, ecclesiastical and lay, Western and Chinese," said historian Lionel Jensen. By Jensen's reckoning, Confucius is in part the creation of Jesuit missionaries who arrived in China in the sixteenth century. As they tried to make sense of this new and foreign civilization in a way they could understand, they manufactured a coherent "-ism," with a great saint as its founder, in a form that the Chinese themselves had never envisioned. The name "Confucius" itself is a Jesuit invention, a strange transliteration of the Chinese *Kong fuzi*, a (rarely used) form of "Master Kong," the "Kong" being his family name. The Confucius we know, Jensen asserted, is a "figment of the Western imagination."[4]

THE DOCTRINE THAT Confucius espoused is no easier to define than the man himself, and for similar reasons. Just like the historical personality, Confucius's teachings have been interpreted and reinterpreted, elaborated upon and expanded, again and again by countless thinkers, writers, and emperors, some of whom imported fashionable ideas and practices from competing doctrines and faiths. The result is that Confucianism has become a syncretic grab bag of traditions, ideologies, ceremonies, concepts, and beliefs, with divergent strands breaking off in their own directions and rival schools engaged in heated debates and disagreements. Asian peoples living in areas outside the Chinese mainland who drafted Confucius into their own cultures, such as the Koreans and Japanese, infused their homegrown practices and beliefs into his teachings as well.

The smorgasbord nature of Confucian thought has led to a long-running (and still unresolved) debate, among both Asians and non-Asians, over what exactly Confucianism is. Very often it is bunched together with other Eastern religions, such as Daoism and Buddhism. Visit a Confucian temple in China, South Korea, or Taiwan, and you'll still find locals bowing before a shrine to Confucius in nearly the same way that they pray to the Buddha. Confucianism also offers a moral code to define and guide human behavior that is analogous to the Ten Commandments. "There is no ethical principle recognized in the West as valid that is not explicit or implicit in the Confucian teachings and no 'Christian' virtue that could not be preached from a Confucian text," the sinologist Reginald Fleming Johnston, tutor to the last emperor of China, contended.[5]

Yet delve into Confucianism just a tad deeper, and equating the tradition with other religions, of the East or West, becomes problematic. Confucianism is missing the most obvious trappings of a modern religion. There is no real clergy, no defined "church," and no central deity as a focus of worship. Although many East Asians will readily admit to being heavily influenced by Confucian philosophy, few call themselves "Confucians" in the same sense that followers of other major world religions would categorize themselves as, say, "Muslims," "Christians," or "Buddhists." Park Kwang Young, a professor of Confucianism at Sungkyunkwan University in Seoul, South Korea, estimates that at least 100,000 South Koreans consider themselves to be religiously Confucian—by no means an insignificant number, but still a tiny fraction of the country's population of 50 million. More often, East Asians will say they are Buddhists or Christians when asked about their religious affiliation, and relegate Confucianism to the realm of cultural or family traditions. From that perspective, Confucianism is not a religion, but a philosophy, a way of life, or an ethical teaching.

The role that Confucius plays in his own doctrine also muddies the picture. Unlike Moses or Muhammad, Confucius never claimed that his teachings were divinely revealed. He even appears to have purposely differentiated his teachings from religion. "The subjects on which the Master did not talk were extraordinary things, feats of strength, disorder, and spiritual beings," one ancient text informs us. Confucius did not offer answers to the deep questions of human existence that have consumed the founders of other faiths—where we came from, why we are here, and where we are going. He never wove tales about the creation of the world or the origins of man. There is no Garden of Eden, no Exodus, no capturing of Mecca to act as a founding mythology. Nor did he speculate on the afterlife. Though apparently he believed in some form of life after death—he adopted the practice of ancestor worship, which was already common in China by his day—he never explicitly elaborated a view on the fate of the soul. In fact, he studiously evaded talking about death at all. When one disciple queried him on the topic, Confucius answered: "You do not understand even life. How can you understand death?"[6]

For Confucius, exerting energy on such matters was a waste of time. He was very much a man of the here and now, focused primarily on solving real issues people faced in the real world. He sought to instill morality in man, ensure good government, strengthen the family, and bring prosperity to society. His goal was to teach people to be virtuous and put that virtue to use by building a better society. Wild speculation about the unknowable was a distraction, in his opinion, from the more important (and more practical) task of making the world a more harmonious place.

Rather than pointing his followers toward the next world, Confucius wanted them engaged in this one. He promised no personal reward, material or spiritual, to those who adhered to his teachings. There were no heavenly gates, no beautiful virgins awaiting the pious, no assurances that the soul would be released from the bonds of the flesh. Nor, however, did Confucius threaten those who ignored his exhortations with horrific punishments. There is no devil in Confucianism, and no eternal damnation; nor can you be reborn as a sea slug. As scholar Lee Dian Rainey put it: "In the Confucian tradition, if someone behaves badly, the worst you can do is say to them: 'Well, you are no gentleman!'" Confucius expected people to do the right thing because it was the right thing to do, not because they'd get paid off at some point in the future. The benefit received for a good deed was the knowledge that you had behaved honorably and perhaps done some good for the world. The Confucian experience was very much a quest for moral self-perfection. "The superior man examines his heart, that there may be nothing wrong there, and that he may have no cause for dissatisfaction with himself," explained one classic Confucian text. "That wherein the superior man cannot be equaled is simply this—his work which other men cannot see."[7]

The sometimes clinical practicality of Confucius led Legge to declare that the sage was "unreligious" and that his teachings had made the Chinese the same. "By the coldness of his temperament and intellect," Legge wrote, "his influence is unfavorable to the development of ardent religious feeling among the Chinese people generally." Yet, at the same time, Confucius did seem to believe that he was on a divinely ordained mission to spread the truth and save the world. He perceived himself as the last man alive who possessed the ancient knowledge to restore peace to China, and thus as humanity's final hope. That role, he believed, gave him a sort of godly protection. One passage in an ancient text tells us that when Confucius was under siege from hostile men from a place called Kuang, his life seemed to be in danger, but Confucius did not fret. Heaven would protect him so he could fulfill his purpose. "Is not culture invested here in me?" Confucius exclaimed. "If Heaven does not intend this culture to be destroyed, then what can the men of Kuang do to me?" He once complained that the men of his day misunderstood him and his ways, but he took solace in the hope that he was appreciated by the divine: "If I am understood at all, it is, perhaps, by Heaven."[8]

Buried within Confucius's words are seeds of something bigger than a mere moral code—a wider, grander connection between man and the universe. At the very heart of Confucius's philosophy is a belief in the power of the individual. If people act with virtue, the entire world will be at peace. Conversely, a chaotic society plagued by destitution and war is the result of selfishness and immorality. In Confucius's eyes, man does have a role to play in the cosmos—what we do every day has an impact on everything around us. We don't just wander about aimlessly bumping into each other, with no purpose or meaning. What we do determines the difference between wealth and poverty, war and peace, order and disorder, justice and injustice. The virtuous acts of one person can have an almost magical quality to change the world.

Looking over all is something Confucius refers to as "Heaven." He doesn't define what Heaven is with any clarity, but he hinted that "Heaven" is a willful force punishing wrongdoers and rewarding do-gooders, much like the Judeo-Christian God—a notion that later Confucians embraced. Borrowing a concept from Chinese antiquity, the Confucians believed that a virtuous king received the "Mandate of Heaven"—the divine right to rule—which could be rescinded if a king was cruel or incompetent. Over the centuries, other tidbits of religiosity in Confucius's words got teased out into a more complex cosmology. Confucius's often bare-bones utterances took on spiritual depth. His teachings became more than just a how-to guide for gentlemanly behavior; they were rewritten into a quest for sagehood. Perhaps Confucianism is not a religion in the same sense as the Judeo-Christian faiths or Hinduism and its outgrowths. But neither can we say that

Confucianism is sterile, devoid of spirituality, or unable to address the fundamental questions facing mankind.

Ultimately, whether Confucianism is a religion or not depends on the definition of religion. The West has tended to compare Confucius's teachings to its own religions. That began as soon as the West learned about Confucius. Those first Jesuit missionaries to arrive in China watched Chinese people bowing reverently and making offerings at Confucian shrines and wondered if they had discovered some sort of native religion, but after further investigation, they determined that the Chinese were not worshipping Confucius as a god, but merely paying respect to him as a great sage. They declared Confucian rites to be social, not religious, practices. To the Jesuits, this meant that honoring Confucius and following Jesus were compatible; Chinese converts to Christianity could both attend church and burn incense at a Confucian shrine. Other Christian missionaries from competing orders, the Franciscans and the Dominicans, came to the opposite conclusion, however. They witnessed Chinese families worshipping their ancestors and declared that Confucianism was a religion after all—worse still, a form of paganism—and, therefore, that Chinese Christian converts should have to renounce their favorite sage. The ensuing "Rites Controversy" lasted for more than a century. Eventually, in 1715, Pope Clement XI issued a papal bull ruling against the Jesuits and declaring that Chinese converts could not participate in Confucian ceremonies. An angered Chinese emperor reciprocated by banning most Christian missionaries from the country.

Those who profess to be religiously Confucian think the Western approach to understanding Confucianism is all wrong. Confucius's teachings cannot simply be compared to Judeo-Christian faiths. "Most religions have books that tell you that if you follow what is in them, you will be saved. We have books, too, but they don't tell you that," Sungkyunkwan's Park, a self-proclaimed practicing Confucian, told me outside the university's Confucian shrine. "In other religions, you need a god and ceremonies, but Confucianism is about doing your best in the world we live in. Everything is based on a self-critique of your own behavior. You believe you have to be nice, to be good to other people, to be generous. It is about following Confucius's teachings."

DESPITE HIS LOFTY stature, Confucius has not always been a beloved figure. Perhaps no other founder of a major faith or philosophy has generated as much controversy as he has. Asians and non-Asians alike have lambasted

Confucius as the source of all the ills of the civilization he created. Confucius has been blamed for suppressing women, stifling innovation, impoverishing peasants, encouraging despotism, and sparking financial crises. It is because of Confucius, his critics have claimed, that China failed to develop capitalism before the West and fell behind the United States and Europe in technology. Many modern East Asians, imbibing Western ideas on civil liberties and political freedom, have perceived Confucius as an impediment to democracy and human rights in the region.

How much of the criticism is fair? Confucius's legacy is not entirely positive, especially from a Western point of view. The societies that sprang from his philosophy are incredibly hierarchical. Those awarded a position of superiority—fathers, husbands, rulers—have used and abused Confucius's teachings to exert control over those who were condemned to subordinate status—children, wives, and citizens. Almost all East Asian governments (until recently) have been centralized and dictatorial. The inflexibility of Confucian-influenced governments has often forced the downtrodden to turn to violence as the only way to compel political change. Women, made subordinate in Confucianism's ideal social structure, have had an awful time breaking into public life. Many women in East Asia have been denied an education or a career; too many have been snuffed out at birth or while still in the womb by their own parents. Confucian corporate management practices, in which junior staffers are suppressed by a top-down decision-making structure, have impeded the ability of East Asian companies to innovate and compete. Throughout East Asian living rooms, executive suites, and schoolhouses, strict Confucian hierarchy leads to all sorts of cruel behavior. After years of getting bullied by his seniors in a Korean high school, my brother-in-law James would simply proclaim: "Confucius ruined my life."

I have personally witnessed some of the destructive behaviors that Confucianism has wrought. During the second half of the 1990s, I served as the correspondent in Seoul for the *Wall Street Journal*. With me for part of the time were two Korean women, neither of whom appeared terribly traditional. Both had lived outside of their country for long periods of time. I got fooled, however, by their outward appearance of westernization. They quickly adopted the Confucian hierarchy expected in a Korean office in the way they related to each other. The senior hazed and harassed her junior, dumped work onto her, and forced her to complete personal errands. The young reporter was too terrified to come to me for support. I sensed the tension and tried to make the bureau operate in a more relaxed American fashion, encouraging open discussion and evenhandedly applying office rules on such matters as working hours—but to no avail. I simply couldn't beat Confucius.

Nor could my female colleagues. I watched all the women who worked in the bureau suffer indignities in the normal course of doing their jobs. They had to endure condescension, browbeating, and inappropriate sexual advances. On one occasion, a staff writer rightfully seethed when two Hyundai executives inconsiderately invited us to lunch at a restaurant where scantily clad women kneeled and served the food. On another, a reporter returned to the office in a fury after (male) journalists forced her from her prized seat at the front of a briefing room to the back benches. I supported them the best I could, but discrimination against women was so widespread that it was simply part of doing business in Korea.

Confucius's reputation has been badly tarnished by such injustices. To many people today, he seems hopelessly authoritarian, misogynistic, and conservative, a man whose time came and went a long, long time ago, his ideas out of touch and out of date with modern society. Many East Asians believe the region cannot be modern with Confucius still so much a part of life, and simply don't want anything to do with his teachings. "Confucianism is an historical relic," Yan Zhang, a Chinese tech entrepreneur, told me over burgers in Beijing. "It is dysfunctional. The central tenets are in contradiction to the ideals of modern society."

Still, damning Confucius for such prejudicial social practices isn't completely justified. His teachings have been so twisted and distorted by centuries of self-interested emperors, scholars, and officials that in some cases they have deviated drastically from the sage's own positions and gotten him attacked for things he never advocated and would never support. Li Dazhao, one of the founders of China's Communist Party and a stiff twentieth-century critic of the great sage, admitted as much. "We are launching an attack not upon Confucius himself but upon the Confucius whom the past successive emperors have molded into a political idol and authority—not upon Confucius himself but upon the Confucius whom the emperors have invested with a tyrannical soul," he wrote. As a result, some modern scholars have tried to separate Confucius the man and philosopher from the Confucians who followed him, and his original teachings from the Confucianism that was created over centuries of Chinese history. Holding Confucius responsible for all of the wrongs committed in his name is akin, then, to blaming Muhammad for the 9/11 terror attacks, or Jesus for the Spanish Inquisition. "It cannot be denied that, over the centuries, Confucianism acquired a lot of dogmas and developed authoritarian tendencies," conceded

Confucian scholar D. C. Lau. "But it would be as grossly unfair to lay these at Confucius's door as to blame Jesus for the excesses of the Church in later ages."[9]

Fair or unfair, however, globalization has not been kind to Confucius. The Western ideas that have seeped into East Asian society over the past two hundred years have caused many in the region to rethink the value of their Confucian heritage. Western political and social philosophies brought in very different concepts of family and gender relationships, systems of government and education, and methods of corporate governance. Democracy has taken hold, as have American notions of gender equality, personal freedoms, and the rule of law. East Asian nations are being profoundly altered by these new ideas. Democracy movements have toppled authoritarian regimes across East Asia. Women are increasingly fighting for their proper place in politics and the corporate world. For much of the past two centuries, East Asians have equated progress with westernization, striving to copy its economic, political, and social systems. Capitalism and industrialization became the tools to end poverty and gain clout on the world stage, electoral politics the ideal for choosing leaders and navigating divisions in society. The route to success no longer passed through Confucian academies, but through Harvard and Yale. Being westernized, in language, dress, and social life, has been the mark of being modern and competitive. Politicians and reformers across East Asia have sought to uproot Confucian influence, at times violently, in their quest for life, liberty, and the pursuit of happiness. Many East Asians no longer wished to be Confucius, as they had for centuries on end. They wished to forget him.

AT FIRST GLANCE, East Asians appear to have been quite successful in that endeavor. Everywhere you look in the region today, tradition seems to be melting away in an onslaught of global culture. Japanese kimonos and Korean *hanboks* have been relegated to weddings and other occasional ceremonies; East Asians don the business suits, Nike sneakers, and miniskirts worn by everyone else in the world. Korean and Chinese pop stars rap and dance to the same hip-hop beats heard in the United States and Europe. Chinese families aspire to own Buicks and iPhones and eat KFC. My in-laws' house in Seoul looks like it could be in the Chicago suburbs. The only signs that you are in Korea are the smell of kimchi wafting from the kitchen and, during the biting winter, the traditional heated floors. Sitting next to the Christmas tree in the living room one holiday season, my brother-in-law Steve tried to convince me that Confucianism, and Asian culture more generally, are being wiped away by Western imports. "Look around," he said. "Nothing here is Asian."

My response was that looks can be deceiving. Sure, many Asians desire BMWs and Ivy League diplomas, like most people around the world. But as became apparent at my wedding, Confucius remains entrenched just under the layer of Starbucks coffee cups, *Sex in the City* DVDs, and Brooks Brothers shirts. Confucius has been so much a part of life in the region for such an astonishing period of time that, as was true with my wife, he regularly shows himself in the ways in which East Asians interact with each other and the world around them every day. Following Confucian precepts comes so naturally to East Asians that they simply consider them the ordinary features of daily life.

Moreover, the new wealth the region now enjoys is convincing East Asians to revisit their ancient culture with fresh, more confident eyes. No longer does success automatically equate with westernization; East Asians are finding new value in their old practices, teachings, and traditions. "The 200 years of Western colonization and domination of Asia was like pouring concrete slabs over Asia's history," Kishore Mahbubani, dean of the Lee Kuan Yew School of Public Policy at the National University of Singapore, and one of Asia's most influential academics, told me over lunch in Beijing. "For Asia to modernize, Asia had to reject its past. Asia's past was a burden so they focused on learning the best of the West. But now that they have succeeded, they are in a position to reengage with their past in a different way. You have to develop what I call 'cultural confidence.' What Asia is doing is finally drilling through those slabs and reconnecting back with its past. There will be a kind of cultural renaissance taking place in Asia." He calls this trend "the most significant thing happening in Asia today."

Some see the whole idea that Confucius has become irrelevant as a form of cultural imperialism, something beaten into the minds of Asians and non-Asians alike by centuries of Western dominance of global political and social discourse. If the ideas of Western philosophers, such as Aristotle or Kant, are still considered useful today, why not Confucius's? The only reason we believe otherwise, asserts Li-hsiang Lisa Rosenlee, a Taiwan-born philosophy professor at the University of Hawaii, is because of a global bias against non-Western modes of thought or traditions. "The point for me is that this sort of disparity in the treatment of Western and non-Western philosophers itself is indicative of the colonial attitude that sees the non-Western world as victims bound to their useless traditions waiting for the West to propel them into modernity," Rosenlee said in an email.

Modern history tells us there is no good reason for East Asians to feel that way. Confucian societies have been arguably the most successful in the world since World War II. South Korea, China, and other East Asian countries have registered the highest economic growth rates in history, wiping out centuries of poverty in a few decades and giving them new clout in the global economy. Confucian values such as thrift and a devotion to hard work have gotten the credit. East Asian countries have benefited from exceptionally strong governance compared to most developing nations, owing in part to a predilection among the most talented to seek public service—a preference inspired by Confucius. East Asian students are flooding into the world's best universities thanks to the obsession for learning that is very much a Confucian legacy. Companies in Confucian societies are ferocious competitors, in part because of Confucian-influenced management and labor practices. What has emerged as a result of East Asian prosperity and stability is an alternative model for a modern society—a Confucian model—that challenges the idea that the best institutions, customs, and ideas come from the West. East Asian politicians and thought-leaders are proudly asserting that copying the West isn't the only method of achieving progress and attaining global influence, and that Western ideals are not necessarily universal and appropriate for all. "In the world of tomorrow," Mahbubani told me, "we're going to move from a mono-civilization of the world, of Western domination, to a multi-civilization, of many successful civilizations."

The result is that Confucius's influence, unexpectedly, is on the rise. The Confucius who recently seemed so antiquated to many East Asians is now becoming intriguing again. In China, which has attempted to purge itself of Confucius for much of the past hundred years, Confucian ceremonies have been resurrected and Confucian education revived. Communist Party cadres now bow at Confucius's shrines just as imperial mandarins did for 1,900 years. This isn't to say that the controversies and debates about the value of Confucius have died away. His resurrection in some instances must be observed with a dose of cynicism. In China and elsewhere, those in power are attempting to again misuse Confucius to suit their own aims and justify behavior that the great sage would have found revolting. The tussle between globalization and Confucius is as fierce as ever. As East Asians rediscover their ancient culture, they are trying to decide which traditions will help in modern times and which ones will not, and how to mesh the new priorities and ideals imported from the West with the values inherited from their Confucian heritage. The fact is that the development of East Asia—politically, economically, and socially—will to a great degree be determined by how modern East Asians come to terms with Confucius.

However this happens, the consequences will be global. After 150 years of westernization, many East Asians have come to believe that their own traditions have value and wisdom that the West can no longer afford to dismiss. Citing the benefits of China's Confucian legacy, scholar Zhang Weiwei proudly proclaimed in the *New York Times* that "it may be time now for the West . . . to 'emancipate the mind' and learn a bit more about or even from China's big ideas, however extraneous they may appear, for its own benefit."[10]

I have gone through that process myself. Yes, there are aspects of Confucius's thought that today seem backward, even terrifying. But the same could be said about the Bible. What we in the Judeo-Christian tradition have done, however, is reinterpret the wisdom in the Bible so that it has meaning for us today. There is no reason we shouldn't do the same with the teachings of Confucius. In his words, too, can be found a humanistic vision of mankind applicable to any time period, political system, or culture. There is a timelessness, a universality, to the teachings of Confucius that holds meaning whatever your nationality, ethnicity, or religion. Confucius is a man who is as important for the future as he has been in the past.

Part One

Confucius Becomes Confucius

Chapter One

Confucius the Man

How can I allow myself to be treated like a gourd which,
instead of being eaten, hangs from the end of a string?
—*Confucius*

In 500 BC, Confucius notched the most impressive victory of his political career. He was then a minister in the state of Lu, located in the area of what is now Shandong Province in eastern China. Lu and its neighbor, the state of Qi, had been embroiled in a series of often bloody disputes, but after nine years of discord the two governments decided it was finally time to settle their differences. A summit between the rulers of the two states was arranged to take place in Xiagu, a somewhat untamed region along the Lu-Qi border. The ruler of Lu, Duke Ding, appointed Confucius as his master of ceremonies for the conference—a natural choice, as the learned scholar was considered the realm's ultimate expert on matters of ritual practice. One summer day, Confucius and the duke set off for Xiagu with high expectations that peace was at hand.

The leaders of Qi, however, had ulterior motives. Duke Jing, the ruler of Qi, and his advisers saw the Xiagu conference as an opportunity to grab an advantage over Lu, so, according to one historical record, they concocted a nefarious scheme. One of Duke Jing's ministers convinced him to enlist a local, non-Chinese tribe called the Lai to kidnap Lu's ruler. Confucius, he contended, was too weak and gutless to stop them. "[Confucius] is acquainted with ceremonies, but has no courage," the minister told Duke Jing. "If you employ some of the natives of Lai to come with weapons and carry off the marquis of Lu, you will get from him whatever you wish." Duke Jing set the trap in advance of Confucius's arrival.

The plotters, however, badly underestimated Confucius. Naturally wary, Confucius insisted that Duke Ding take no chances and plan for the worst by bringing the senior and junior war ministers to the summit. "I have heard that in peace men should prepare for war; in war they should prepare for peace," Confucius told the duke. Duke Ding heeded his advice and brought the ministers.

After their arrival in Xiagu, the conference began auspiciously enough. In a display of mutual respect, the two dukes bowed politely to each other, then ascended three stairs to seats placed on an earthen platform. Just as the negotiations were about to begin, however, the officials from Qi set their plot in motion. A group of well-armed Lai warriors approached the platform in a threatening manner. "Men with pennants, feathers, spears, halberds, swords and shields advanced to the roll of drums," an ancient historian recounted. Confucius immediately sensed that his ruler was in danger and boldly ordered that the Lai intruders be repulsed. Duke Ding, he reminded the Qi leadership, had agreed to attend the summit on terms of friendship, and the arrival of such barbarous tribesmen would thwart any attempts at a peace settlement. Confucius went on to scold Qi's duke for the indecency of his actions. "Weapons of war should not come near a friendly meeting," he lectured. "As before the spirits, such a thing is inauspicious; in point of virtue, it is contrary to what is right; as between man and man, it is a failure in propriety. The ruler [of Qi] must not act thus." Cowed by Confucius's reprimand, Duke Jing was compelled to call off his scheme to kidnap Duke Ding and commanded the Lai to depart.

The humiliated duke of Qi now found himself at a serious disadvantage in the peace negotiations—a position that Confucius deftly exploited. The two states inked an alliance, but in return for Lu's commitment to the treaty, Confucius bluntly demanded that Qi restore to Duke Ding's control three districts it had taken from Lu in battle. The members of the Qi delegation had no choice but to comply. In disgrace, they trudged back to their capital. Duke Jing berated his ministers for the embarrassing debacle with a nod to Confucius's wisdom. "In Lu, they use the gentleman's way to guide their prince," he complained, "while all you teach me is the barbarian way."[1]

Although the ancient historical records offer somewhat different details of what exactly transpired at Xiagu—one version adds the salacious (but improbable) claim that Confucius ordered the execution of the Lai intruders[2]—they all agree on the result: the summit was a resounding triumph for Confucius. He had employed all of his many skills and talents—his deep knowledge of state affairs, his courage and intellectual vigor, his vast learning—to the great benefit of his ruler and state. The outcome of the summit propelled Confucius to the pinnacle of his power in Lu politics.

Only three years later, however, Confucius fled Lu with a small party of supporters, never again to hold office in his home state. He was unable to convince Duke Ding to take his philosophy and its message of moral governance seriously, so, frustrated, he resigned from his ministerial post and left Lu to seek another Chinese ruler who might take heed of his advice. Years would pass, but no matter how many hundreds of miles he traveled, Confucius never found his virtuous prince. Despite his tireless efforts, he ultimately failed in his lifelong mission to reform a broken and chaotic China.

There is obvious irony here. What makes Confucius so fascinating as a historical figure is just how little impact he had on China during his own lifetime. The ideas that would come to be equated with Chinese civilization drew few adherents during his day. Confucius's real life provides barely a glimpse of the commanding role he would come to play in the history of Asia. Instead, his story offers an unexpected but telling starting point in what would prove a convoluted, controversial 2,500-year biography, replete with setbacks and successes, compromises and confrontations, reversals and revivals.

Nevertheless, the events of Confucius's life are of utmost significance. What Confucius did and said shaped Chinese civilization. In later years, both the sage's devoted adherents and his most bitter enemies dissected, analyzed, and reanalyzed his life story, searching for either nuggets of wisdom to guide them in their careers and reinforce their philosophical positions or damning evidence to attack Confucian principles and promote their own. His followers transformed Confucius's life, into a model life, his behavior into the gold standard of virtue and righteousness. What happened 2,500 years ago resonated down through the centuries to the modern day, influencing East Asians' patterns of action and thought. To understand East Asia, we have to understand Confucius the man.

DISCOVERING THE REAL Confucius is not so easy. As is the case with most figures of antiquity, all we know today about the historical Confucius is from sources that provide no more than fragments of the events of his life. Much of that information is of dubious reliability. Confucius probably left no written records of his own, much like Jesus, so everything we know about him was most likely scribbled down by others. In some cases, these accounts were written long after his death by people who could not possibly have firsthand knowledge of the man or his life. The material is in many cases highly biased, since it was compiled either by Confucius's loyal supporters, who were determined to inflate the wisdom and power of their hero, or by hostile critics, who were committed to doing just the opposite.

The first person to attempt a complete biography of Confucius was Sima Qian, one of China's greatest historians, who devoted a chapter to him in his monumental *Records of the Historian*. Yet this text was written some 350 years after Confucius's death, when his life was already clouded by myth and legend. Sima Qian, an unabashed fan of Confucius, also likely exaggerated his hero's influence in early Chinese history. Much of Sima Qian's narrative is thus considered suspect. Some biographical details can be found in the *Analects*, the text most closely associated with Confucius and considered the most trustworthy source on the sage and his ideas. Inside are tantalizing fragments about the events of Confucius's life—some attributed directly to him. But even the authenticity of the *Analects* must be questioned, as it, too, was compiled after Confucius's passing. Scholars have spent centuries scrutinizing the details spread among various ancient texts in an attempt to separate fact from falsehood, biography from hagiography, and the real Confucius from the legend.

We know quite a bit more about the times in which Confucius lived, called the Spring and Autumn Period, which lasted from 771 to roughly the mid-fifth century BC, than we know about the man himself. The violence and tremendous social upheaval that marked these three centuries shaped the course of Confucius's life, thought, and philosophy. His primary goal was to restore peace and tranquility to a country that had descended into barbarity. His teachings are dominated by theories of good government, which, if put into practice, Confucius believed would bring prosperity and stability to a dispirited and exhausted China. It is impossible to separate Confucius from the time in which he lived, or Confucianism from the age in which it was born.

The tumult resulted from the disintegration of the ruling Zhou Dynasty. By Confucius's time, the Zhou had probably been ruling China for five centuries, but the power of the Zhou royal house had greatly deteriorated. The dynasty's governing system was based on a feudal structure, meaning that lords loyal to the house administered different parts of the empire in its name. In theory, that system still prevailed during Confucius's day, with the various dukes officially proclaiming themselves to be vassals of the Zhou emperors. In reality, the Zhou empire had effectively broken apart into numerous sparring states—148 are mentioned in the ancient annals—with the emperor commanding little actual control outside of his own capital. The country descended into incessant conflicts and intrigues as the many noble families ruling the many petty kingdoms all competed for territory and riches.

However, the political disorder of Confucius's day and the two centuries that followed also sparked a flowering of intellectual debate that produced some of the most important philosophical movements in human history. Dismayed by the chaos around them, creative Chinese thinkers launched a search for answers to the many ills plaguing their nation, delving into an intense exploration of the basic questions facing human society and existence. What is the proper role of government, and how should people be governed? What is the true nature of man—good or evil? Does humanity possess a special place in the universe, and if so, what is its purpose? This intellectual development laid the foundation for a tradition of philosophy and literature that came to form the basic elements of thought in most of East Asia, a body of work every bit as influential as those that emerged from the Greek city-states and the Indian subcontinent. Confucius's teachings were a part of this blossoming of innovative thought. His voice, however, was just one of many. Others were more influential at the time and for centuries afterward. Eventually, Confucius emerged from this contest of competing philosophies as East Asia's dominant sage, but his victory was a long, slow process that lasted some 1,500 years, and that, in certain respects, was never fully complete.

CONFUCIANS HAVE TRADITIONALLY believed that the sage descended from royalty—none other than the ruling family of the Shang Dynasty, the first imperial government in China for which hard evidence survives of its existence. After the Shang fell and the Zhou rose, Confucius's distant ancestors were initially rulers of the state of Song within the new dynasty's feudal order. But the clan fell out of favor in Song, forcing his great-grandfather to flee to Lu. Some scholars argue that this distinguished lineage was probably fabricated by Confucian devotees in an attempt to link their master to historical figures of power and prestige. Whatever Confucius's distant heritage, by the time he was born, his family, the Kongs, had lost any regal status it might once have held. Confucius was a member of a class of low-ranking officials—of loftier stature than mere commoners, but well below the elite aristocracy. Sima Qian tells a story about Confucius as a young adult trying to attend a feast held by one of Lu's noble families, the Ji, but being turned away because of his lowly social standing. "The Ji clan is entertaining gentlemen,"

Confucius was curtly informed. "You are not included."[3] In an age when birth counted for more than smarts, Confucius's pedigree had a profound impact on both the events of his life and the nature of his teachings. He became an advocate of merit over birthright, a champion of the notion that being a true gentleman depended on learning and moral bearing rather than wealth, title, and family lineage. Although today he is often considered an archconservative, in his own time Confucius was on the cutting edge of social change.

Confucius's beginnings may not have just been humble, but scandalous. His father, Shuliang He, was a well-regarded war hero. His exploits (or so we're told) included a feat of Herculean strength in which, during one battle, he held a heavy gate aloft so that his fellow soldiers could escape a trap. By the time of Confucius's birth, his father was probably quite elderly. He is said to have held the relatively minor post of prefect of a small town called Zou, not far from Qufu, Lu's capital, in eastern China. According to a source of later vintage, Shuliang He had already had nine daughters with a first wife, and one son, Mengpi, with a concubine. But Mengpi was disabled or deformed—he had "a very distressed foot"—and thus he was not considered an acceptable heir. So Shuliang He, late in life, went in search of a woman who could bear him a proper son. He approached a local family, the Yan, seeking one of its three young girls as a new wife. Their father readily agreed to a match. "He has a height of ten feet and (because of) his martial prowess, I eagerly seek to establish a bond with him," Father Yan told his daughters. "While he is advanced in age and curmudgeonly, I doubt you would be unsatisfied. Of the three of you, who is able to be his wife?" The older daughters wisely kept quiet, but the youngest, Zhengzai, responded, "Since it is from you, Father, that it is fixed, why then do you ask?" Only such a dutiful daughter, her father decided, could be a suitable bride, and he chose her to marry Shuliang He.[4]

Here's where the tale becomes potentially sordid. Sima Qian leaves us with a juicy tidbit suggesting that China's greatest sage was an illegitimate child, conceived when the couple consorted "in the wilds," not in Shuliang He's bed, as a proper consummation should be. Not all scholars adhere to this common interpretation. Historian Lionel Jensen, for instance, proffers the idea that Sima Qian was attempting to infuse Confucius's birth story with an air of mysticism by placing it "in the wilds." However Sima Qian's words are to be understood, he made no mention of any formal betrothal between Shuliang He and the teenage girl from the Yan family.[5]

Later admirers of Confucius, possibly uncomfortable with his undistinguished origins, transformed his conception and birth into a miraculous event. One story, woven during the Han Dynasty (206 BC to AD 220), replaces Confucius's real father with a magical deity, in a way reminiscent of the myths of the ancient Greeks, in which Zeus consorted with beautiful women and conceived superhuman beings. "Confucius's mother, [Yan] Zhengzai, once while taking a walk happened upon the mound of a large tomb, where she fell asleep and dreamed that she received an invitation from a Black Emperor," the tale goes. "She went to him and in her dream had intercourse with him. He spoke to her, saying: 'Your confinement will take place within a hollow mulberry tree.' When she awoke she seemed to feel (pregnant) and (later) gave birth to Confucius within a hollow mulberry. This is why he [Confucius] is called the First Sage." Other literary inventions tell us that Confucius's arrival on earth was, like Jesus's, heralded by portents of the newborn's future greatness. Eclipses, dragons, and heavenly beings announced his coming. The birth was surprisingly painless, and the baby Confucius emerged with an inscription on his chest proclaiming he would become a supreme scholar.[6]

In the standard accounts, Confucius's early years were anything but glorious. Shuliang He died when Confucius was only a toddler, and his mother had to raise him on her own. Yan and her young child were shunned by Shuliang He's family after his death—perhaps more evidence that her relations with Shuliang He might have been illicit. Sima Qian tells us that Yan didn't even inform Confucius about the location of his father's grave. (When Yan died many years later, Confucius had to locate the site with the help of a stranger so he could bury his mother beside him.)[7]

We know almost nothing about Confucius's childhood. Sima Qian related that the young Confucius enjoyed playing with vessels used in ancestral sacrifices, which he lined up carefully as if preparing for a temple ceremony. The one thing that is clear is Confucius's early commitment to his studies. "At 15 I set my heart on learning," Confucius tells us.[8] That simple decision changed the history of the world.

WHAT CONFUCIUS CHOSE to study were writings and rituals that even by his time were considered ancient. In his quest for solutions to the travails of the China of his day, Confucius looked back in time to a period he perceived as a golden age, when the nation had been unified and at peace—the early years of the Zhou Dynasty. To Confucius, the founders of the Zhou, and rulers from even earlier times, were sage-kings who governed with virtue and wisdom. The reason why China had descended into chaos, Confucius believed, was that the current rulers of the nation had abandoned the ways of the Zhou. Thus he spent much of his life studying the philosophy, history, literature, and ceremonial practices of Chinese antiquity, with the aim of reintroducing those traditions into Chinese society.

Confucius may have been one of the few remaining experts on Zhou customs and culture during his time. According to Sima Qian, Confucius visited the Zhou capital to observe the ancient rites firsthand so that he would be better able to preserve and disseminate them. Confucius's political career was a long (and ultimately unsuccessful) mission to convince the kings, dukes, and ministers of China's warring states to learn from their ancient predecessors and govern based on their ideas and rituals. Confucius therefore served as a vital link between the China of distant antiquity and the China of more modern times. As a historian, he searched for the lessons of the past; as a revivalist, he strove to propagate a proud cultural legacy that was in danger of being completely obliterated. To a certain extent, he was a cultural fundamentalist, motivated by an unswerving belief that only the traditions of Chinese antiquity offered the antidote to modern evils.

In following this course, Confucius set the precedent for formal education in China for nearly 2,500 years. No man could claim to be cultured or learned without engaging in intense study of Chinese classical literature, history, and philosophy—a canon defined by Confucius and his followers. Knowledge of these subjects became the primary route to government service, and thus to social and financial advancement in the empire. For centuries on end, Chinese boys spent their youths hunched over some of the same poems and tracts that Confucius and his disciples had eagerly studied, with dreams that those texts would set them on the path to wealth, status, and power.

At the beginning of his career, however, Confucius had little opportunity to employ his extensive learning. In his first jobs, he managed the granaries of the noble Ji clan, the most influential family in Lu, and later, their livestock. Lacking money or social status, he was probably lucky to get a post in the service of Lu's nobles in the first place. "I was of humble station when young," Confucius once explained. "That is why I am skilled in many menial things." Yet he impressed his employers. "He measured the grain fairly," according to Sima Qian, and "the animals flourished." His work earned him the attention of the Lu government, and he was named minister of works—which gave him an opportunity to operate on a larger stage.[9]

That was, after all, Confucius's primary professional goal. His life was a nearly nonstop quest for senior government office and high-level influence—

a perch from which he could proselytize his ideas on good government. Many of the conversations he had with China's dukes and ministers were in essence job interviews, with Confucius attempting to impress them with his wisdom and advice. Here, again, Confucius's life laid down a path for future Confucians. Throughout the entire imperial age in China, Confucians and Confucianism became inexorably intertwined with the art of statecraft. The Confucians strove to attain positions as professional civil servants and court advisers, and when they succeeded, they crafted policy and dominated the vast machinery of the Chinese state. Being a proper Confucian, in fact, practically obligated an educated Chinese man to enter national service.

On the surface, that sounds honorable, but in practice, the Confucians' unquenchable thirst for political power—and their tremendous success in attaining it—led in the end to their ultimate fall from grace in modern times. Confucius's own life story highlights the dangers. Despite his commitment to virtue and propriety, Confucius was not above the factional contests and maneuverings in a conflict-ridden China. That stance forced him to make hard choices between his career and his convictions. In the end, the sage chose to stand by his principles, a decision that caused him to suffer privations and humiliations time and again. Not all Confucians, however, could hold fast to his example. For centuries to come, Confucians would wrangle with the same difficult choices, but too many of them lacked Confucius's inner fortitude and allowed their craving for political power to overwhelm their commitment to the sage's virtuous teachings. To maintain the ear of the emperor, they often were too quick to sacrifice their beliefs, or even worse, to twist them to suit the needs of the imperial court. The recurrent contradiction between the demands of politics and their philosophy left the Confucians morally compromised. This legacy would come to taint Confucius—with serious consequences for his standing in East Asian society.

Confucius's tireless search for positions of influence also exposed aspects of his personality that diverge greatly from his image. Confucians have often believed that he possessed boundless intelligence, unwavering conviction, and unparalleled virtue, that he was a man unmatched in human history. "Since there were living men until now, there never was another Confucius," wrote Mencius, one of China's greatest Confucian philosophers.[10] But what we find in China's ancient texts is a much more human figure, with all of mankind's usual frailties, foibles, and failings. The real Confucius comes across as something of a social climber and self-promoter, constantly networking and schmoozing in his efforts to land a good job. He at times appears as an arrogant, insufferable know-it-all who lectures and hectors those around him with irritating persistence. Confucius also has moments of weakness, when he doubts his abilities and courage.

Confucians have tended to give their Uncrowned King a pass on these imperfections. His goal—the restoration of peace in China and the advancement of virtue in society—was just and noble, so it is possible to see his ends as justifying his means. Yet it also becomes clear that one reason why Confucius ultimately failed in his grand mission was that he had an abrasive personality. Rather than endearing himself to those in authority and winning them over to his thinking, he alienated people in power and fomented resistance. For a man so committed to politics, he was a singularly poor politician. This tendency may have been obvious to some of his contemporaries. According to a story from Sima Qian (considered apocryphal by historians today), Confucius met Laozi, the elderly founder of Daoism, while on his visit to the Zhou capital, and the experienced philosopher warned him about his confrontational approach. "Let me offer you a few words of advice," Laozi told Confucius. "A shrewd observer, prone to criticize others, risks his own life. A learned man who exposes the faults of others endangers himself. A filial son must never thrust himself forward, and neither may a good subject."[11] If this meeting did happen, Confucius ignored Laozi's advice, and he landed in hot water again and again as a result.

This shortcoming became abundantly clear as Confucius's stature grew. When Confucius was thirty years old, Duke Jing of Qi (the same who later schemed against Confucius at the Xiagu summit) visited Lu, and upon meeting Confucius, asked him how one small Chinese state, called Qin, had once managed to become a major regional power. (Duke Jing hoped to follow Qin's example.) Confucius embarked on a historical lecture about meritocracy. The Qin ruler, he noted, had placed a freed slave in charge of his government, purely because he thought the man was the most capable. "Judging by this," Confucius said, "he was worthy to be a king—being a conqueror was not good enough for him."[12] A story with noble sentiments, perhaps, but one suspects that in imparting this tale, Confucius was angling for a job.

Confucius's lobbying continued in Qi five years later. A political dispute in Lu forced its ruler to flee to Qi, and Confucius joined him. There the conversations between Confucius and Duke Jing continued. Impressed by Confucius's wisdom, Duke Jing wished to grant him a fiefdom in Qi. But Confucius had alienated Qi's chief minister, Yan Ying—not surprisingly, since the sage was plotting for his job—and this rival worked to undermine him at court. Confucius, Yan Ying told the duke, was not suited for high office. "A beggar who roams the land talking is not a man to entrust with affairs of state. To adopt his way of reforming the state would not be putting the common people first." Duke Jing thereafter cooled on Confucius, their discussions on government ceased, and the sage never received his fiefdom. Eventually, the duke flatly informed Confucius that he had no future in Qi. "I am old," the duke said. "I cannot make use of your services."[13]

Confucius was compelled to return to Lu, where his luck wasn't much better. Unable to secure a government post, he spent the next several years teaching. By this time, Confucius's knowledge of history and culture had attracted numerous students—the people who would become his cherished disciples. They were a diverse bunch, hailing from a wide range of backgrounds and social classes, and some were quite poor. But they shared a common interest in advancing their education and a firm belief in Confucius's wisdom.

How many disciples Confucius had over the course of his life has been a subject of great debate. Sima Qian tells us that Confucius amassed 3,000 students, though modern scholars believe this figure is almost certainly inflated. Mencius mentions 70, which is a more likely estimate, but scholar D. C. Lau, in his study of the *Analects*, counted only 25 in the text, and even some of those merit only a passing mention. What we do know is that a small coterie of these students became fiercely loyal to Confucius. They believed that his philosophy was the best way to solve China's political and social problems, and they committed themselves to his cause. The conversations they had with their teacher, recorded and handed down to us in the *Analects*, are the primary source on Confucius's ideas today. These disciples remained devoted to Confucius until his death, and after he passed on, they carried on his message and his work, leading to the creation of Confucianism.[14]

Of all Confucius's disciples, his obvious favorite was Yan Hui. Confucius admired this student's austerity, eagerness to learn, and tireless pursuit of self-improvement. Others only rarely merited the praise he lavished on Yan Hui. Confucius once said that Yan Hui "did not vent his anger upon an innocent person, nor did he make the same mistake twice." The sage even seems to have considered Yan Hui his equal—and in some respects, his superior. "Neither of us is as good as [Yan Hui] is," Confucius once told another follower. When Yan Hui died, tragically quite young, Confucius was distraught and wailed in grief. "Alas! Heaven has bereft me! Heaven has bereft me!" he lamented.[15]

Another distinguished disciple was Zigong. He was likely a skilled merchant—Confucius takes note of his talent at making money in the *Analects*—and would turn out to be a successful statesman. Confucius considered

Zigong highly intelligent, but of more questionable moral character than Yan Hui. In one conversation, Zigong told Confucius, "While I do not wish others to impose on me, I also wish not to impose on others." Confucius responded harshly: "That is quite beyond you." Perhaps no other disciple tested Confucius's patience, though, more than the hardheaded and outspoken Zilu. Probably closer in age to Confucius than most of his other disciples, Zilu was more a man of action than a thoughtful scholar, and although Confucius considered him to be capable and just, he also criticized him for his brashness. Zilu, Confucius once said, "has a greater love for courage than I, but is lacking in judgment." (The statement proved prescient. Zilu met his end in battle after a needless display of bravado.)[16]

Confucius enjoyed teaching and debating with his disciples. However, it wasn't enough to satisfy his ambition. The longer he went without a government post, the more desperate he became—to the point where his resolve began to weaken. Confucius's will was put to the test by tumult in Lu politics. A rebellion was afoot in the state, led by a man named Yang Hu, who was a steward in the service of the Ji family. Confucius, it seems, had some knowledge of the plot. One of Yang Hu's protégés summoned Confucius, apparently in the hope that the out-of-work civil servant would join the rebel cause. At first, Confucius was eager to go. Perhaps this was the big break that would finally win him a top government job. Yet his disciples were appalled by their master's willingness even to communicate with the upstarts. Yang Hu and his coterie were traitors, and Confucius would potentially sully his upright reputation by associating with them. Zilu protested: "We may have nowhere to go, but why must we go to [the rebels]?" Confucius attempted to justify himself. If he could team up with the rebel leaders to reform government and usher in a new golden age, would he not be remiss in rejecting their cause? "The man who summons me must have a purpose," Confucius responded. "If his purpose is to employ me, can I not, perhaps, create another Zhou?"[17]

In the end, Confucius decided rebellion was not for him, and he studiously kept his distance from Yang Hu's clique—which proved a smart decision. Yang Hu's rebellion was crushed, and the rebel leader was forced to flee. But Confucius's dalliance with Yang Hu highlights another aspect of his life that would come to shape the Confucian attitude toward authority throughout Chinese history. Confucians tended to follow Confucius's example and strove to reform governments by participating in them, rather than by protesting as an opposition. Like their master, Confucians were no rebels. That doesn't mean they were always sycophants—on the contrary, Confucians often bluntly criticized the emperors, sometimes at great personal risk. But they generally preferred to support the existing authorities in the hopes of making them better rulers and, in the process, maintaining political influence.

That's exactly what happened to Confucius. His decision to shun Yang Hu proved politically astute. Duke Ding, the new ruler of Lu, named him magistrate of a district, which, as Sima Qian boasted, became a model of good government within a year. Confucius's commendable performance convinced the duke to reappoint him to the Lu administration, first as minister of works, then as minister of crime, akin to a chief justice. Confucius's star rose even further after his masterful diplomatic coup at the Xiagu peace summit. Sima Qian gushed about the near-magical impact Confucius had on Lu's politics and society. "Vendors of lamb and pork stopped raising their prices," he wrote. "Men and women walked on different sides of the street, no one picked up anything lost on the road, and strangers coming to the city did not have to look for the officers in charge, for everyone made them welcome."[18]

Confucius gained so much influence that he decided to pursue a major reform of Lu's government. In 498 BC, he unleashed an assault on the power of Lu's three noble clans in order to centralize control in the hands of Duke Ding, whom Confucius considered the rightful authority in the state. The families had by this time usurped much of the duke's power. They acted as semi-independent ruling bodies, with their own fortified towns and military forces. An edict went out that the families had to dismantle the walls around their towns. Sima Qian handed full credit to Confucius for initiating the move by personally convincing Duke Ding to order the nobles to destroy their defenses.[19]

At first, the noble families went along with the edict. It was not long, however, before Confucius encountered stiff resistance. As the Ji clan attempted to tear down the defenses of their town, called Bi, their stewards revolted and led a counterattack against Lu's capital. Duke Ding fled to the palace of the Ji, where he ascended a tower for safety as the battle raged around him. Confucius saved the day by sending fresh soldiers to his rescue. The insurgent leaders retreated, and the walls of Bi were destroyed. The duke, however, had less success in a campaign against the Meng clan, the last of Lu's major noble families to resist his authority. When the Meng refused to comply with Confucius's demands, Duke Ding laid siege to the family's stronghold of Cheng in an effort to force them to heel, but he was unable to take the town. Confucius's attempt to overhaul the governing structure within Lu ended with the siege. The power of the noble clans and their grasping retainers was far from broken.[20]

Instead, it was Confucius who seems to have lost the power struggle. In 497 BC, the year after he launched his assault on the nobles, Confucius suddenly resigned from his coveted government post and left Lu. His departure is usually attributed to a conspiracy hatched by the unscrupulous leaders of Qi, who were probably still smarting over Confucius's triumph at the Xiagu peace conference three years earlier. According to Sima Qian, the Qi ministers fretted that Lu would become more and more powerful under Confucius's wise management, so they plotted to undercut his influence. Qi's leaders collected eighty of the prettiest dancing girls they could find and sent them as a gift to Duke Ding of Lu. The troupe of beauties waited outside the city gate of his capital. Duke Ding's chief minister, Jihuanzi, donned a disguise and went to see the girls; impressed, he convinced the duke to take a look for himself. Duke Ding, evidently enthralled, began to neglect his official duties. For three days, no court was held. Confucius was so disappointed by Duke Ding's dalliance that he picked up and left Lu. As he departed, he chanted a song:

> A woman's tongue
> Can cost a man his post;
> A woman's words
> Can cost a man his head;
> Then why not retire
> To spend my last years as I please?[21]

Sima Qian's tale is highly entertaining, but is it true? Could a group of dancing girls really defeat the grand master? In certain respects, we can see how the girls would have convinced a frustrated Confucius to give up on Duke Ding. Confucius was, without question, sincerely committed to his responsibilities. Why would a reform-minded professional like him waste his time serving a ruler so easily distracted from the important affairs of state? By flouting the sacrificial rites, Duke Ding exposed his inadequacy as a ruler. The story shows just how seriously Confucius took political reform. Like any disgruntled employee, Confucius may have thought he could find a more appreciative and competent employer elsewhere.

Yet, at the same time, the tale seems too simplistic. Confucius, who at this point was in his mid-fifties, had spent his entire life striving for the exact type of ministerial post he had attained in Lu. Would he so impulsively walk away from his hard-won position? Mencius offers a different version of the story that contains a few enlightening details. Confucius, Mencius explained,

left Lu because he was not offered some of the meat from a temple sacrifice. Proper ritual practice dictated that he should receive this honor, and
the slight was a serious infraction in Confucius's eyes—a blatant disregard
of the dictates of propriety. Even more to the point, though, it was a measure
of Confucius's declining influence in Lu. For Duke Ding, Mencius informed
us, "came not to follow his counsels." In other words, Confucius was losing
the ear of the duke and being edged out of his inner circle of advisers, and so
he took the sacrificial snub as an excuse to make his exit. "The fact was, that
Confucius wanted to go away on occasion of some small offence, not wishing to do so without some apparent cause," Mencius explained.[22]

But it seems that this still isn't the whole story. Mencius mentioned that
Confucius "went away even without taking off his cap of ceremony." Simply
put, Confucius fled. Why would he be in such a rush? Confucius must have
made an army of enemies during his tenure in office, the three noble families
and their retainers, whom Confucius had tried to marginalize, probably chief
among them. Having lost his struggle with the nobles, he must have become
highly vulnerable. If Duke Ding, who had supported his efforts, withdrew
his favor, as Mencius suggested, Confucius might well have found himself in
serious trouble. When he didn't get his sacrificial meat, he took it as a signal
that he had lost the protection of the duke. If these assumptions are accurate,
then it was not a pack of dancing girls who ruined Confucius. Confucius
ruined himself. His reform efforts earned him too many powerful enemies.
His ideas were so difficult to implement or caused so much upheaval that
Duke Ding soured on his advice. In the rough-and-tumble political world of
the China of his day, Confucius wound up on the losing end. So Confucius
collected a small handful of his closest disciples, including Zilu, Zigong, and
Yan Hui, and departed from Lu. He was not to return for thirteen years.

IT IS REVEALING THAT Confucius traveled not with his family, but with his
disciples. Though he put family at the center of his vision of a harmonious
society, we know surprisingly little about his personal life. He never even
mentions his parents in the *Analects*. At some point, Confucius married,
though there is no record of his wife's name. In one text she is simply described as "the daughter of the Qiguan family in the state of Song." She bore
Confucius a son, Boyu, and two daughters, neither of whom come down
to us with proper names. One of the daughters may have died as a child.
None of his children figure prominently in early sources on his life. By the
time Confucius left Lu, his family responsibilities seem to have come to an

end—he had likely divorced his wife while in his forties; his son had his own household, and his remaining daughter was married. The *Analects* informs us that Confucius gave this daughter in marriage to a man who had been in jail—as much a stigma then as now—but he believed his son-in-law had been wrongfully imprisoned. That decision was just one of many examples that showed how passionately Confucius believed that merit should trump social status.[23]

The *Analects* is much more generous in its descriptions of Confucius the man. Its compilers were intensely interested in every aspect of his behavior, which became a model of manners for proper gentlemen. An entire book of the *Analects* is devoted to describing what he did in court, in the village, at meals, and in other common social settings—sort of an ancient Emily Post how-to guide for cultured Chinese. What emerges from its pages is an image of Confucius as an uptight fuddy-duddy, a tireless stickler on points of propriety. He always strove to adhere to the rituals appropriate to the people around him, from those in authority to the ordinary man on the street, and to the circumstances in which he encountered them.

Confucius was careful to show the proper solemnity at official ceremonies, for example. At the ancestral temple or at court, "he did not speak lightly," the *Analects* tells us. "When summoned by his lord, he would set off without waiting for horses to be yoked to his carriage," and once he was before his superior, "his bearing, though respectful, was composed." If he was acting as an usher at a formal audience, "his face took on a serious expression and his step became brisk," and "when he bowed to his colleagues, stretching out his hands to the left or to the right, his robes followed his movements without being disarranged." The compilation also offered some fashion advice based on Confucius's habits: he "avoided using dark purple and maroon colored silk for lapels and cuffs," and "when in the heat of summer, he wore an unlined robe made of either fine or coarse material, he invariably wore it over an underrobe to set it off." The *Analects* even describes Confucius's dinner etiquette. "He did not eat his fill of polished rice, nor did he eat his fill of finely minced meat," we're told. "He did not eat food that was not properly prepared nor did he eat except at the proper times. He did not eat food that had not been properly cut up, nor did he eat unless the proper sauce was available." Such fussiness was evident in every aspect of Confucius's life. "He did not sit, unless his mat was straight," the ancient text explains.[24]

Since Confucius demanded such strict adherence to the dictates of propriety in his own actions, he showed little patience for others who flouted them. On one occasion, Confucius encountered a young man who was sitting "with his legs spread wide." Confucius disapproved: "To be neither modest nor deferential while young," he said, "that is what I call a pest." The master then rapped the youngster on the shin with his cane. Nevertheless, the *Analects* does not portray Confucius as a saint. Even he was not capable of behaving perfectly under all circumstances, and he would occasionally let his passions get the best of him. Sometimes, he could be very human— arrogant, bossy, even outright rude. For instance, a man named Ru Bei once visited Confucius at his home, but the sage did not care to see him and feigned illness. As soon as the man departed, however, Confucius "took his lute and sang to it, . . . in order that Bei might hear him." Devising an excuse was probably considered an appropriate method of avoiding an unwanted meeting, but by making his lie so obvious, Confucius was likely being pur- posefully insulting.[25]

Yet Confucius wasn't an irrepressible curmudgeon. In the *Analects*, we discover a man who could also be approachable and fun-loving. Although he endured the trials of professional disappointment and, in some instances, even deprivation, he tried to find happiness in what little he had. "In the eating of coarse rice and the drinking of water, the using of one's elbow for a pillow, joy is to be found," he once said. Confucius is often portrayed in good spirits—singing with friends, playing the lute, laughing and joking. He once told a disciple that he should be described as "so full of joy that he forgets his worries." On another occasion, Confucius asked his disciples to tell him what their goals would be if they earned the eye of a ruler. One pledged to fix a broken state, another to bring prosperity to the people, and a third to serve in the ancestral temples. Then the disciple Zeng Dian spoke. "Dian, pausing as he was playing on his lute, while it was yet twanging, laid the instrument aside," the *Analects* recounts. "'My wishes,'" he said, "'are different from the cherished purposes of these three gentlemen. In this, the last month of spring, with the dress of the season all complete, along with five or six young men who have assumed the cap, and six or seven boys, I would wash in the Yi [River], enjoy the breeze among the rain altars, and return home sing- ing.'" Confucius then "heaved a sigh and said, 'I give my approval to Dian.'"[26]

Whatever his foibles, to his disciples, Confucius was the wisest of men and the greatest of teachers, and they defended him with passion. "The tal- ents and virtue of other men are hillocks and mounds which may be stepped over. [But Confucius] is the sun or moon, which it is not possible to step over," Zigong protested to a critic of his master. Even as Confucius stumbled in his own career, his loyal students maintained absolute confidence in the rightness of his teachings. "Were our Master in the position of the ruler of a state or the chief of a family, we should find verified the description which has been given of a sage's rule," Zigong once said. "While he lived, he would be glorious. When he died, he would be bitterly lamented."[27]

Confucius may not have agreed with this assessment. Perhaps the most intriguing aspect of his personality was how honest he was about himself. He never considered himself a great sage. In fact, Confucius didn't even believe he was the truly virtuous person he implored others to be, and he admitted to his lapses in adhering to his own teachings. "It is these things that cause me concern," he once said. "Failure to cultivate virtue, failure to go more deeply into what I have learned, inability, when I am told what is right, to move to where it is, and inability to reform myself when I have defects."[28] His struggles, both in his personal quest for self-perfection and in his professional mission to reform the world, caused him to suffer bouts of despair. Yet he continued to keep faith that his ideas would bring peace and prosperity to China. As he left Lu and embarked on a long, punishing journey across the country in search of opportunities to turn his vision into reality, that faith would be tested more than ever before.

CONFUCIUS'S TRAVELS TOOK him through much of central China. His exact itinerary is hard to determine, since there are conflicting versions of events. He likely visited at least six Chinese states—one of them, Wei, probably more than once—and sometimes remained in the same place for years at a time. Throughout this period, Confucius tirelessly sought out a ruler who would employ him and adopt his teachings. With his reputation for learning preceding him, he had no trouble attracting the attention of one ducal court after another, and he had many conversations with rulers and their advisers. We can envision Confucius's long journey as a thirteen-year marketing campaign of Confucian principles of government and societal reform. Mencius suggested that Confucius may have landed at least one job during this period. To his endless frustration, however, Confucius seems never to have earned the influence in government that he so earnestly desired. Every time a position came within reach, somehow his hopes were dashed. In one typical example, the king of Chu wanted to grant Confucius a fiefdom, but his chief minister spoke against the plan. "If Confucius with such able disciples to help him were to have land of his own, that would not be to our advantage," the minister warned. Chu's ruler dropped the idea.[29]

There were moments when his misfortune weakened his conviction. Early in his journey, a steward employed by a noble family in the state of Jin staged a revolt and asked Confucius to join him. As he had when presented with Yang Hu's plot in Lu, Confucius at first wanted to do so, but again, Zilu protested, throwing Confucius's own words back at him: "I heard it from you, Master, that the gentleman does not enter the domain of one who in his own person does what is not good," Zilu said. "How can you justify going there?" Confucius acknowledged that he had taught just that, but nevertheless tried to defend his interest in joining the uprising. A truly virtuous man, he said, wouldn't be tarnished by associating with an evildoer, and a chance to finally hold influence over government was too important to pass up, no matter who was offering it. "Has it not been said: 'White indeed is that which can withstand black dye?'" he asked Zilu. "Moreover, how can I allow myself to be treated like a gourd which, instead of being eaten, hangs from the end of a string?"[30] In the end, however, Confucius rejected the steward's offer.

This wasn't the only time his growing despondency seemed to cloud his judgment. On one of his visits to Wei, for instance, he got tangled up with Nanzi, the controversial wife of its ruler, Duke Ling. She had earned herself a reputation for illicit sexual exploits—just the sort of morally suspect person Confucius usually preferred to avoid. Sima Qian tells us, however, that Nanzi sent Confucius a very blunt summons. "When gentlemen from other lands honor our lord [Duke Ling] with their friendship," the note read, "they always call on his lady." Initially, Confucius demurred, but then he reconsidered. Nanzi had left Confucius in an awkward position. If he wanted a job in Wei, her note made clear, he would require her support. Yet by submitting to her request, Confucius would be involving himself with a person of dubious propriety. Eventually, he came to believe that he had little choice but to make an appearance. The meeting went pleasantly enough. Nanzi, appropriately, remained behind a curtain during his visit. Confucius bowed before her, and, as she returned the courtesy, "her jade pendants tinkled."[31]

Nevertheless, the mere fact that Confucius called on Nanzi became a point of contention among his followers. Perhaps they feared that a private session with Nanzi would sully Confucius's reputation and be a subject of gossip. Or maybe they believed he was groveling too much in an attempt to get ahead in Wei. After Confucius's return from Nanzi's lair, Zilu was displeased, and the master felt compelled to defend his honor. "If I have done anything improper, may Heaven's curse be on me! May Heaven's curse be on me!" the master declared. His encounter with Nanzi didn't improve his career prospects anyway. Sima Qian says that Nanzi, or Duke Ling's unhealthy obsession with her, prompted Confucius to depart from the state "in disgust." The great historian has Confucius complaining: "I have yet to see the man who loves virtue as much as he loves feminine beauty."[32]

During his long journey, there were moments when Confucius faced grave danger, even death. While passing by a place called Kuang, the local residents, mistaking Confucius for a man who had mistreated them, detained him. They became so hostile that his disciples were terrified. Fortunately, the Kuang residents came to their senses and set Confucius and his followers free. Then, in Song, the state's war minister tried to assassinate Confucius by toppling a tree onto him while he was delivering a lecture to his disciples. He narrowly escaped. The small party sometimes became bedraggled and impoverished. When Confucius arrived at one walled city and became separated from his traveling companions, a local citizen saw him outside the gate and remarked: "Lost as a stray dog he looks!" When Confucius heard about the man's comment, all he could do was laugh. "That is certainly true!" he exclaimed.[33]

The lowest point of the entire journey came around 489 BC, when Confucius was traveling through a remote part of the state of Chen. He had resided in Chen for three years, but the start of a war there had convinced him to leave. Confucius and his disciples found themselves in a desolate wilderness and in increasingly dire straits. Their food supplies dwindled, and they faced the real possibility of starvation. Even the usually austere *Analects* paints the situation in the gravest of terms: "When the provisions ran out, the followers [of Confucius] had become so weak that none of them could rise to their feet." How Confucius got himself into such a predicament is unclear. Sima Qian informs us that the authorities of Chen and neighboring Cai, hearing that Confucius might have a job prospect in the rival state of Chu, became fearful that he might help Chu gain power, and sent men to block his way. Yet it is also likely that the party simply got lost. This moment is one of the most important in Confucius's life. On empty stomachs, after years of wandering, with no prospects, Confucius and his disciples appear to have reached the limits of their endurance, both physically and emotionally.[34]

Not surprisingly, it was the argumentative Zilu who whined the loudest about their fate. "With resentment written all over his face," the *Analects* says, he confronted Confucius. Why, he questioned, were men who were striving to follow a moral path rewarded with such deprivations? "Are there times when even gentlemen are brought to such extreme straits?" Zilu asked. Confucius answered that a virtuous person finds his true strength when faced with misfortune. "It comes as no surprise to the gentleman to find himself in extreme straits," the sage said. "The small man finding himself in extreme straits would throw over all restraint." Writing two centuries after these events, the great Confucian thinker Xunzi handed down a different version of Confucius's response, which sharpens his commitment to doing what is right no matter what hardships life may bring. In this account, Confucius tells Zilu that the proper gentleman is just like beautiful flowers hidden in a deep forest. "That no one is there to smell them does not take away their fragrance," he explained. "The same applies to the learning of a gentleman; he does not learn in order to be known. Thus, in extreme straits, he will not be vexed; in times of anxiety, his purpose will not diminish." Confucius's message was clear and simple: a good man must maintain his commitment to virtue under all circumstances, and not expect any recompense in return. This idea is one of the defining tenets of Confucianism, and also one of its most endearing.[35]

Zilu's bitterness, though, is understandable. In his exchange with Confucius, he was acknowledging the unfairness of their predicament: Confucius and his disciples, despite their dedication to justice and benevolent social reform, were the ones starving to death, abandoned in the middle of nowhere, while less honorable men were ensconced comfortably in their stately offices and luxurious homes, well fed and powerful. Zilu's devotion to Confucius and his philosophy had won him neither material well-being nor political influence. As they suffered in the wilderness, Sima Qian recounted, Confucius and his loyal followers examined what had gone wrong and how they could resurrect their fortunes. Confucius, beginning with a rare expression of doubt, asked Zilu: "Is our way wrong? Is that why we have come to this?" Zilu found fault with himself and Confucius. "Maybe we lack humanity and therefore men do not trust us," he said. "Or perhaps we are not intelligent enough for them to follow our way." Confucius disagreed. He named other learned men from Chinese history who had come to tragic ends, pointing out that the most knowledgeable do not always gain the public's support.

Confucius then posed the same question to Zigong, who blamed the difficulties any man would face living up to the lofty standards of Confucius's teachings. "Master, your way is too great for the world to accept," Zigong said. "You should modify it a little." Again, Confucius refuted this suggestion. It would be misguided, he said, to compromise virtue for the sake of winning popularity. "A gentleman can cultivate his way, draw up principles, recapitulate and reason, but may not be able to make his way accepted," he told Zigong. "Now your aim is not to cultivate your way but to please others. Your ambition is not high enough." Finally, Confucius asked Yan Hui for his opinion. Yan Hui did not share the misgivings of his companions. He thought they should pursue what they believed to be right to the best of their abilities, even if others failed to heed their wisdom. "We are at fault if we do not cultivate the true way," he told Confucius. "Yet if we cultivate it fully and it is not adopted, it is the rulers who are at fault."[36]

How Confucius and his followers escaped from the wilderness is not entirely clear. Sima Qian wrote that Confucius sent Zigong ahead to the state of Chu, which dispatched a rescue party, though many scholars doubt this tale is true. Somehow Confucius ended up in Chu, alive and as determined as ever to pursue his mission. Yet at this point in the story, it seems that others had begun to realize what Confucius had not—his cause was a hopeless one. The *Analects* tells us about a man named Jie Yu, known as the "Madman of Chu," who passed by Confucius singing a song:

> *How thy virtue has declined!*
> *What is past is beyond help,*
> *What is to come is not yet lost.*
> *Give up, give up!*
> *Perilous is the lot of those in office today.*

Confucius jumped down from his carriage to talk to the Madman, but he had already run off.[37]

The Madman, it appears, was attempting to lure Confucius into setting an entirely different course. Jie Yu was suggesting that the master had wasted enough of his life in a fruitless quest and that any man of his moral convictions and tough-mindedness who entered the brutal politics of the day was risking his life. The Madman was advocating that Confucius give it all up— and perhaps follow Jie Yu's example: instead of engaging with the world, he should withdraw from the flawed society that would never appreciate him. Confucius may have been intrigued—thus his rush to converse with the Madman. But Confucius could never bring himself to turn his back on the world. The *Analects* makes that clear in the next entry, in which Confucius states: "One cannot associate with birds and beasts. Am I not a member of this human race?"[38]

WHY WERE CONFUCIUS's ideas, so highly regarded in later centuries, so thoroughly ignored in his own day? At first glance, Confucius's failure may seem surprising. As emperors and officials in China and much of the rest of East Asia would later come to appreciate, many aspects of Confucius's teachings provided a useful ideological basis for imperial rule. He aimed at reinvigorating, reforming, and reinforcing traditional Chinese social and political institutions, not overturning them. Confucius's preferred form of government was the standard of his day: monarchy, with a strong king at its apex. In his model society, the king deserved and received great reverence from his officials and subjects. For Confucius, only a mighty emperor—called the "Son of Heaven" by Confucians—in full command of his realm could govern effectively. "When good government prevails in the empire, ceremonies, music, and punitive military expeditions proceed from the Son of Heaven," he said. "When bad government prevails in the empire, ceremonies, music, and punitive military expeditions proceed from the princes. When these things proceed from the princes, as a rule, the cases will be few in which they do not lose their power in ten generations."[39]

The ruler, in Confucius's thinking, sat at the top of a hierarchy that dictated clearly defined social responsibilities. Confucius believed that order could be restored to China only if each member of the community fulfilled specific duties based on his or her station in the world, from the ruler down to the common farmer. Confucius explained this most basic concept of his teachings in a conversation with the strong-headed Zilu, who asked Confucius what he would do first if he were put in charge of administering a government. "What is necessary is to rectify names," Confucius responded. The cryptic answer baffled even his disciple. "So! Indeed!" said Zilu. "You are wide of the mark!" Confucius, slightly annoyed, had to spell the matter out for him: "How uncultivated you are," the sage shot back. "If names be not correct, language is not in accordance with the truth of things. If language be not in accordance with the truth of things, affairs cannot be carried on to success. . . . The people do not know how to move hand or foot. Therefore a superior man considers it necessary that the names he uses may be spoken appropriately, and also that what he speaks may be carried out appropriately."[40]

What Confucius is trying to say here is actually quite simple: everyone had to do what they were supposed to do. A minister in a government, for instance, should adhere to the duties of a minister—to administer the government wisely and serve his ruler loyally. If he shirked his responsibilities, acted for his personal gain rather than the public good, or usurped the power of the sovereign, then he was not living up to his ministerial duties, and thus could not honestly be called a minister. Citizens, too, had to fulfill their required responsibilities—to pay taxes, serve in the armed forces, and be respectful to the sovereign. If they did not behave in this way, they could not be proper citizens. If names did not match reality, then the resulting confusion and uncertainty would spark conflict within the government, discontent among the people, and an unruly society. By "rectifying" names, Confucius would ensure that all people met their given responsibilities, thus minimizing disagreements and bad practices and bringing order to society.

So far, so good, if you're a king. Confucius handed rulers ultimate authority over their realms—just what the kings and dukes of his day sought. But there was an important catch. In Confucius's perfect world, the ruler could not govern however he wished. He had his designated part to play in society as well. The ruler was supposed to be benevolent toward the people, governing in their best interests and caring for their welfare. When one official asked him how to instill reverence in the people, Confucius said: "Rule over them with dignity and they will be reverent; treat them with kindness and they will do their best; raise the good and instruct those who are backward and they will be imbued with enthusiasm."[41] If a king did not honor these responsibilities—if he lazed about all day in luxury, or amassed great wealth at the expense of the common man, or fooled around with dancing girls and ignored state affairs like Duke Ding of Lu, then he had no right to call himself the king. Even though Confucius believed that a dominant monarch was best, his vision of good government did not award that sovereign unlimited power or the right to abuse his position. Confucius advocated for the *constraint* of authority, not absolute authority.

That constraint was morality. Confucius believed that every person—the king included—should strive to attain a lofty ethical standard in his or her behavior. The basis of that standard was similar to Christianity's: "Do not impose on others what you yourself do not desire," Confucius said.[42] He thus professed the equivalent of the Golden Rule five hundred years before Jesus. The most fundamental of virtues a gentleman possessed was "benevolence," and he attempts to teach his disciples what benevolence is and how to practice it throughout the *Analects*. Confucius once said that benevolence was characterized by five traits: respectfulness, tolerance, trustworthiness in word, quickness, and generosity. On another occasion, he simply said: "Love your fellow men"—a statement also very similar to Jesus's philosophy. Confucius called the person who was capable of upholding benevolence, and the many other qualities he held dear—righteousness, wisdom, and sincerity, to name just a few—a "gentleman," or *junzi*, and the path he pursued "the Way," or *dao*. He acknowledged that following the Way was a difficult road to take. "I have no hopes of meeting a sage," he once said. "I would be content if I met someone who is a gentleman."[43]

Confucius expected even more of the king than an ordinary person. In addition to strictly adhering to these moral precepts, the king carried the heavy responsibility of acting as a paragon of virtue for everyone else in the country to emulate. He could rule only by perfecting himself, and in that process, he would perfect society overall. "Encourage the people to work hard by setting an example yourself," Confucius once said when asked about governing. On another occasion, he told an official that "if you set an example by being correct, who would dare to remain incorrect?" Even more importantly, he believed that a king could retain his authority only by being virtuous. The people would then follow him willingly. His kingdom would become populous and rich—he would conquer China through benevolence, not arms. "The rule of virtue can be compared to the Pole Star which commands the homage of the multitude of stars without leaving its place," Confucius once said. The point of Confucius's message was that moral power was true power.[44]

It is easy to understand the logic behind this thinking. A virtuous, selfless king, who runs a sound administration and looks after the well-being of the little guy, will win broad support, whereas a ruler who imposes unreasonable taxes, spends lavishly, and does nothing while the common man struggles to feed his family can maintain his authority only through coercion, which will come to turn the people against him. Confucius makes the rational case that good, honest policies can earn a king the all-important support of the masses more readily than laws and punishments can. He hoped that by following this path, the rulers of his day would become like the ancient sage-kings, restoring virtuous rule in China and ushering in a new age of peace and prosperity.

Perhaps here we find Confucius's most radical idea. The rulers of his time were obsessed with armies, conquests, and treasure. They worried about how many soldiers they could muster compared to their neighbors, and how much money was crammed into their vaults. Confucius was trying to tell them that they were going about nation-building the wrong way. Swords and shields would not win an empire; burdensome taxes and military servitude would not woo loyal subjects. Benevolence was the correct and only route to power and prestige. Yet in the Spring and Autumn Period, when so many petty kingdoms were vying for territory, revenue, and survival, Confucius's message fell on deaf ears. When the dukes and kings of China sought out Confucius's advice, they wanted to talk about military tactics and geopolitical strategy. Instead they got lessons on ethics, history, and poetry.

The fact that China's rulers did not find his message appealing is made obvious in the *Analects*. When Duke Ling of Wei asked Confucius for advice on military formations, the master answered: "I have, indeed, heard something about the use of sacrificial vessels, but I have never studied the matter of commanding troops." After that, Confucius departed from Wei. China's ambitious leaders wanted a hard-nosed Machiavelli; instead they got an old man pontificating about court ceremonies and quoting ancient odes. Rulers wanted to maximize their power, not fetter it in moral dictates and ancient doctrines. Confucius simply expected too much from the men then ruling over China. Once he was asked about the officials in his day, and he retorted, "Oh, they are of such limited capacity that they hardly count." Confucius was a man ahead of his time. China would have to undergo a thorough political reformation before the nation's elite would discover the worth of his teachings.[45]

IN 484 BC, Confucius received a handwritten note from Lu. A new duke was summoning him home. The invitation was likely the work of Ran Qiu, one of Confucius's disciples, who had achieved high office and great influence back in his native state. Confucius, weary and despondent after so many fruitless years on the road, accepted and returned to Lu. Yet when he arrived, no official post was waiting for him, and, more interestingly, Sima Qian says he didn't seek one.[46]

Conditions in Lu were deplorable. The noble families had sidelined the new ruler, Duke Ai, and were running the state in their own selfish interests. Confucius found he had little influence, even with his own followers. On one telling occasion, Ran Qiu sought out Confucius for his advice on a plan by his employers, the rich Ji family, to raise more revenue by imposing a land tax. Confucius tried to dodge, probably because he knew Ran Qiu wouldn't care for what he had to say. He simply stated that he knew nothing of the matter. After the Ji clan made four unsuccessful attempts to get a proper response from Confucius, the sage approached Ran Qiu privately and laid out his opinion that the tax was inappropriate—an unnecessary burden on the common men that would be imposed only to feed the ravenous appetite of the nobles. "The conduct of a superior man is governed by the rules of propriety," Confucius lectured. "If [the Ji] be not governed by the rules of propriety, but by a covetous daring and insatiableness, though he enact this taxation of the lands, it will still not be enough. If you wish to act in an irregular manner, why do you consult me?" Ran Qiu ignored him and collected the new tax anyway. Confucius was furious. "He is no disciple of mine," he groused.[47]

Confucius withdrew from the public sphere and focused his energies on teaching and writing. In her biography of the great sage, Annping Chin suggests that Confucius had finally come to terms with his destiny, that he had moved past his desire for political triumphs and found peace with his life as it was.[48] Perhaps he tried his best to accept his disappointments and shed himself of regret. Yet it must have been very difficult. The world around him was no less chaotic, the suffering of the Chinese people no less heartbreaking, the greed and selfishness of their leaders no less troubling. Confucius remained convinced that he held the answers to China's many problems, but no one wanted to listen. We can only imagine his frustration. Confucius entered old age a deflated man, rejected and ignored.

Yet this same broken man became, for later generations, the father of Chinese civilization. His life story begs questions about what part the historical Confucius really played in Chinese history. The real-life Confucius can be characterized as no more than a classicist, a teacher who regurgitated ideas and propagated literature conceived long before he walked the earth, who ultimately had minimal impact on the China of his day, rather than as the founder of a flourishing doctrine that shaped the political and social development of China and much of East Asia. Seen in this light, Confucius the man did not create a formal doctrine called "Confucianism," and the defining and epoch-making role that was later awarded to him was a retrospective rewriting of history undertaken by later followers to exaggerate his importance. Even Confucius admitted that he was primarily passing on the teachings and traditions of an earlier era, rather than inventing an entirely new doctrine. "I transmit but do not innovate," he once said.[49]

Confucius, though, was being modest. The failures of his life do not diminish his importance in world history. There have been many people throughout time who have come to wield tremendous influence over global civilization only after they passed from the scene—think Jesus here. Though few beyond his most loyal students recognized it at the time, Confucius had created something of great power—a coherent philosophy steeped in Chinese history that offered a clear vision for a peaceful society and a guide for human behavior. He rescued the wisdom of China's sages, reformed it, reimagined some of its concepts, and passed it down to future generations as a unique doctrine.

The challenge, however, is figuring out exactly what Confucius meant to preach. Confucius left his many future disciples very little to go on. Chinese scholars traditionally held that Confucius wrote, edited, or compiled most or all of what are known as the Five Classics—the foundational texts of Confucianism. They include *The Book of Changes* (a work of divination), *The Book of Rites* (a dissertation on ritual practice), *The Book of Documents* (a text on history), *The Book of Odes* (a collection of poetry), and the *Spring and Autumn Annals* (the historical record of the state of Lu). Sima Qian, for instance, informed his readers that Confucius carefully pared 3,000 ancient songs down to the 305 he considered to have "moral value" and collected them into *The Book of Odes*, in the process ensuring that the ancient rites "became widely known, to the enrichment of the kingly culture."[50] Some scholars have argued that Confucius assembled these works to use as textbooks for teaching his disciples. In other words, there were no Five Classics before Confucius. Scholars of imperial times believed that Confucius was doing much more than just binding together a bunch of old verse and scripture. For centuries, Confucians believed that the sage wrote the *Spring and Autumn Annals* as a how-to booklet for successful government, infused with secret messages that had to be decoded to reveal the hidden wisdom of Confucius's teachings. The Five Classics have had an incalculable influence over Chinese civilization. These works, and Confucian works such as the *Analects*, became the basis of Chinese education and government for almost all of the imperial age—a full 2,000 years.

Modern scholars have questioned Confucius's connection to the Five Classics and other works attributed to him. Some have claimed that he may have had nothing to do with them at all, others that Confucius and his disciples represent merely a handful of the intellectuals who drafted and compiled the classics over a long period of time. Certain material was very likely written before his time, in some cases long before, while other components were written or edited after his death, at least in the form in which we know them today.[51]

Even the text most closely associated with Confucius and Confucianism, the *Analects*, was almost definitely not written by his own hand. Confucians usually credited his immediate disciples with writing the *Analects* from what they remembered of their conversations with him and from his lectures, though it is now widely accepted that it was more likely the next generation of Confucians—the disciples of his disciples—who were responsible for the text. This isn't to say that the *Analects* and other works don't contain any material that originated with the man himself—many of the sayings attributed to him, especially in the *Analects*, are considered at least somewhat reliable. But (again, much like Jesus) what we know today about Confucius and his teachings comes to us secondhand, and perhaps not in its original form, and thus we can never be fully sure of its accuracy. Still, the mere existence of the

Analects tells us a lot about Confucius's standing and reputation in scholarly circles during Chinese antiquity. Books were rare items, and only the most respected of men had their thoughts recorded in writing. The fact that we have any material at all directly attributed to Confucius is an indication of how important some scholars considered his teachings to be.

IN 479 BC, Confucius fell ill. One of his most loyal disciples, Zigong, traveled from the distant state of Chu to visit him. The two close companions had not seen each other in nearly a decade. Zigong had been away from Lu, successfully pursuing a diplomatic career. When Zigong approached Confucius's house, the sage, elderly and frail, was pacing by the door with a stick. The reunion had every reason to be a joyous and emotional one. But Confucius was in poor spirits. He complained to Zigong that he had come too late. Then he began to chant a few lines from one of his cherished ancient poems—lines that perfectly evoked the trauma of decline and the inevitability of death:

> *Mount Tai crumbles,*
> *The great beam breaks,*
> *The wise man withers away.*

Tears filled Confucius's eyes. "The world has long strayed from the true way," he said to Zigong, "and no one can follow me."

A week later, Confucius died. He was seventy-three.[52]

Perhaps Zigong's presence at his side in those final hours was a comfort to Confucius. At this point in his life, he might have been almost totally alone. His son had already passed away; so had Zilu and Yan Hui. At least, as he drifted away, he had Zigong there to watch over him.

Or Zigong's presence might well have been an irritant. Zigong had excelled in public service, while his master had been sidelined and forgotten. Zigong symbolized what Confucius wanted in his life and had never achieved. It may be uncomfortable for us to think of the great sage drifting into the next world with his thoughts fixated on regret, envy, and disappointment. We can only hope that, as the end drew near, he was able to judge his life not as a failure, but as an unwavering quest to repair a broken society. Perhaps, he could tell himself, he gave life his best shot.

Confucius had reason to be hopeful, though he may not have realized it. Zigong represented something else, something Confucius probably could never have foreseen in 479 BC. Zigong represented a future for Confucius and his teachings. What may be the greatest legacy of Confucius the man is the group of loyal disciples he left behind—learned men every bit as committed to Confucius's ideals and goals as the sage himself. It would be these followers, and the many more to come, who would transform Confucius from a failed statesman into the most influential individual in East Asian history.

Chapter Two

Confucius the Sage

[Confucius] came to comprehend the principles of a
hundred kings and to accord with Heaven's course from
beginning to end.
                                        —Dong Zhongshu

"I am left alone in the world, full of grief and sorrow," Duke Ai, the ruler of
Lu, lamented after Confucius's death. "Oh, master, to whom shall I look for
guidance now?" Tradition has it that the distraught duke, in an unusual show
of respect, ordered a temple to be erected and sacrifices offered in the name
of Confucius. He was the first in what was to become a long line of Chinese
rulers who would honor Confucius over the next 2,500 years.[1]

Yet Duke Ai's sudden outpouring of emotion rang hollow. He was lavish-
ing far more attention onto Confucius in death than he had during the sage's
life, and the hypocrisy of the duke's display did not go unnoticed in Lu. "Not
to employ the master during his lifetime but to mourn him after death runs
counter to true ceremony," Zigong bitterly complained.[2] The fact remained
that, despite Duke Ai's melodramatic farewell, Confucius and his ideas held
no more appeal to the governing elite of Lu, or of any other state in China, in
the years after his death than they had during his life.

Confucius's disciples grieved over him with much greater sincerity. They
gathered at his grave on the outskirts of the city of Qufu (where it remains
today) and, following the sage's teachings for family deaths, spent the next
three years in mourning, as if Confucius were their real father. Then they
went their separate ways. "On entering to take their leave . . . , as they looked
towards one another, they wailed, till they all lost their voices," Mencius
later recounted.[3] Zigong opted to remain. He built a hut next to Confucius's
grave and mourned his master for an additional three years. Then he, too,

departed. Confucius lay in his grave, alone. The great sage's mission came to an end. But the story of Confucius was just beginning.

CONFUCIUS WAS GONE, but not forgotten. Zigong and the other disciples may have lost their master, but not their dedication to his ideas or his cause. Much in the same way that the apostles Peter and John propagated the teachings of Jesus after his crucifixion, Confucius's disciples continued preaching his philosophy to a new generation of students. And those students then acquired disciples of their own. As the decades passed, more and more young men became educated in Confucian ideals. This expanding group of followers began to record the sayings of Confucius that were passed down to them—what became recorded in the *Analects*—and wrote their own treatises on Confucius's thought, elaborating on his ideas and enlarging the scope of his teachings. That process kept Confucius alive, in a sense, and, even more, turned his ideas into an increasingly complex and comprehensive school of philosophy.

The most important of these early thinkers was Mencius. No one in history did more to advance the development of Confucianism, aside from Confucius himself, than Mencius, whom the Chinese have enshrined as the "Second Sage." The main text that contains his teachings, the *Book of Mencius*, a collection of his sayings and conversations that is similar in style to the *Analects*, is lauded as one of the most important of all books in the Confucian canon.

Much of Mencius's life reads like a replay of Confucius's own. "What I wish to do," Mencius once said, "is to learn to be like Confucius." Scholars are not certain exactly when Mencius lived, but he probably spent most of his years in the fourth century BC. Born not far from his hero's hometown of Qufu, Mencius, just like Confucius, lost his father at an early age. He was raised by a hardheaded, education-minded mother. Too poor to pay school tuition, Mother Meng sat her son outside the schoolhouse window so he could absorb whatever he could hear, until the teacher, impressed by Mencius's tenacity, invited him inside. Sima Qian tells us that Mencius was tutored by Confucius's grandson, Zi Si, but, based on our understanding of when the two men lived, that is highly improbable. It was likely a story invented to link Mencius as directly as possible to Confucius.[4]

Like Confucius, Mencius wanted to enter public service and reform China's government from within. The situation in China during Mencius's time was just as violent and unstable as it had been in Confucius's day. The age is aptly named the Warring States Period, and it lasted from roughly 475 to 221 BC. Those centuries were characterized by almost constant conflict between various kingdoms that were all ambitiously seeking to unify China under their own royal houses. Mencius believed, as Confucius had, that he was on a divinely ordained mission to end this terrible chaos. Once, lamenting that no true sage-king had emerged for centuries, Mencius said: "Heaven does not yet wish that the kingdom should enjoy tranquility and good order. If it wished this, who is there besides me to bring it about?"[5]

So Mencius, following in the footsteps of his favorite sage, traveled between the country's squabbling states—perhaps for as long as forty years—seeking employment and trying to convince self-aggrandizing rulers of the wisdom of adopting Confucian principles of government. His style mimicked Confucius's—both were direct and often abrasive. "I am not fond of disputing," he once said, "but I am compelled to do it." Although he seems to have held a senior position in the state of Qi at one point, ultimately Mencius was no more successful than Confucius in winning adherents among the Chinese elite or gaining long-term employment. "The whole realm was divided into alliances . . . and fighting was held in high regard," Sima Qian lamented. "Mencius . . . could not get on with these rulers."[6]

Mencius, though, tried not only to spread Confucius's teachings, but to build upon them. He delved into subjects the sage himself had barely discussed. Most notably, Mencius was willing to wrestle with one of the more hotly debated issues of the time—the nature of man. Chinese thinkers of the era, dismayed by the turmoil around them, wondered what motivated man's actions. Was humankind inherently evil? It is on this grand question that Mencius made his most important contribution to Confucian thought, one that would shape much of the doctrine's development over the following two millennia. He asserted that man was by nature good—or, more specifically, that people innately have the potential to be good. This was an extension of Confucius's ideas, but Mencius was the first of his followers to make that belief explicit.

Mencius attempted to prove his case by showing how, in a time of crisis, people tend to follow their most positive and compassionate instincts. "When I say that all men have a mind which cannot bear to see the sufferings of others, my meaning may be illustrated thus," Mencius explained:

> Even nowadays, if men suddenly see a child about to fall into a well, they
> will without exception experience a feeling of alarm and distress. They
> will feel so, not as a ground on which they may gain the favor of the

child's parents, nor as a ground on which they may seek the praise of their neighbors and friends, nor from a dislike to the reputation of having been unmoved by such a thing. From this case we may perceive that the feeling of commiseration is essential to man, that the feeling of shame and dislike is essential to man, that the feeling of modesty and complaisance is essential to man.

Yet to fully realize their inherent good nature, men must cultivate and educate themselves; otherwise, they can become corrupted by earthly desires, forget their true nature, and end up greedy, violent, and evil. "Let them know to give (innate aspects of goodness) all their development and completion, and the issue will be like that of fire which has begun to burn, or that of a spring which has begun to find vent," Mencius said. "Let them have their complete development, and they will suffice to love and protect all within the four seas. Let them be denied that development, and they will not suffice for a man to serve his parents with."[7]

Mencius was making a bold statement here, especially in a time of such strife. He was saying, in essence, that all people are inherently the same. The only difference between the evil tyrant and a great sage was the amount of effort each expended to cultivate his inherent potential to be benevolent and righteous. In another bit of folksy wisdom to prove his point, Mencius compared people to barley seeds. All seeds are the same and should grow into the same stalks, but they don't because of the way in which they are nurtured. "In good years the children of the people are most of them good, while in bad years the most of them abandon themselves to evil." Mencius explained:

It is not owing to any difference of their natural powers conferred by Heaven that they are thus different. The abandonment is owing to the circumstances through which they allow their minds to be ensnared and drowned in evil. There now is barley. Let it be sown and covered up; the ground being the same, and the time of sowing likewise the same, it grows rapidly up, and, when the full time is come, it is all found to be ripe. Although there may be inequalities of produce, that is owing to the difference of the soil, as rich or poor, to the unequal nourishment afforded by the rains and dews, and to the different ways in which man has performed his business in reference to it. Thus all things which are the same in kind are like to one another; why should we doubt in regard to man, as if he were a solitary exception to this? The sage and we are the same in kind.[8]

Mencius, however, did not speak for all the followers of Confucius. In the period after Confucius's death, there was no such thing as "Confucianism," or a single set of beliefs and principles associated with Confucius. Different scholars interpreted the sage's ideas in different ways and debated over the true meaning of his teachings. The most important of these arguments was between Mencius and another great Confucian thinker, Xunzi. A native of the state of Zhao in north-central China, Xunzi's exact birth date is unknown, though it was likely in the late fourth century BC. Like Confucius and Mencius, Xunzi also sought a top government position, and he appears to have been somewhat more successful, serving for many years as a magistrate in the state of Chu. Even the usually verbose Sima Qian provided only the scantiest description of him: we're told simply that Xunzi "hated the governments of his corrupt generation, its dying states and evil princes, who did not follow the Way, but gave their attention to magic and prayers and believed in omens and luck."[9]

Although he is not as famous today as Mencius, Xunzi, or "Master Xun," was much more influential in the Confucian circles of his day and for centuries following his death. He had the same goal as Confucius and Mencius— to restore order to a disorderly world by correcting the wanton ways of China's rulers. Like Mencius, Xunzi believed that Confucius had been equal to the sage-kings of ancient times. Confucius, Xunzi wrote, "was benevolent, wise, and free from obsession."[10]

Yet, in key ways, Xunzi and Mencius didn't agree at all. They scrutinized the same classic literature, but arrived at very different conclusions, with far-reaching consequences for the history of Confucianism. Most notably, while Mencius argued that man was inherently good, Xunzi took the opposite position, writing that "man's nature is evil; goodness is the result of conscious activity." He contended that Mencius had not "really understood man's nature nor distinguished properly between the basic nature and conscious activity." Xunzi employed the same sort of commonsense examples as Mencius had to bolster his position. "It is the nature of man that when he is hungry he will desire satisfaction, when he is cold he will desire warmth, and when he is weary he will desire rest," Xunzi wrote. "This is his emotional nature. And yet a man, although he is hungry, will not dare to be the first to eat if he is in the presence of his elders, because he knows that he should yield to them, and although he is weary, he will not dare to demand rest because he knows that he should relieve others of the burden of labor. . . . Acts such as these are all contrary to man's nature and run counter to his emotions. . . . If men follow their emotional nature, there will be no courtesy or humility." The debate over human nature between Mencius and Xunzi wasn't fully resolved within Confucian circles for another 1,500 years.[11]

THOUGH CONFUCIUS'S FOLLOWERS could not agree among themselves, they did still have one goal in common: to defend their favorite sage from the virulent attacks of rival schools. An important motivation driving the philosophical exertions of Mencius and Xunzi was their desire to prove that Confucius's teachings were superior to those being propagated by other thinkers. If the vile doctrines of false prophets were not squashed, Mencius said, "and the principles of Confucius not set forth, then those perverse speakings will delude the people, and stop up the path of benevolence and righteousness."[12] Confucius had earned enough fame and his teachings sufficient attention to make him a primary target of criticism from competing schools. Some of it was surprisingly nasty. Confucius's enemies not only lambasted his doctrine, but savaged him personally, portraying him as a traitor, a hypocrite, or worse.

Perhaps the most vicious smear campaign was launched by Mozi, or "Master Mo," who founded a school called Mohism. Mozi's philosophy, though almost forgotten today, was actually much more popular in China than Confucius's during the late first millennium BC. Mozi may have been born around the time Confucius died, so he would have been active during the period when Confucius's disciples and their students were spreading their master's ideas around China. In an indication that they may have scored some early successes, Mozi and his followers devoted long tracts to assaulting the sage. In one passage, he recounted a tale about Confucius's attempts to land a government post in the state of Qi. In Mozi's story, a minister warned the ruling duke against hiring Confucius by painting the sage as a charlatan, too impractical to be of help to the ruler and too obsessed with ceremony. "Confucius dresses elaborately and puts on adornments to mislead the people," the minister said. "[He] promotes music and dancing to attract the multitudes, performs elaborate ceremonies of going up and coming down the steps, and practices the etiquette of rushing and soaring to dazzle the multitudes. With all his extensive learning he cannot plan for the world; with all his laborious thought he cannot help the people." Elsewhere, Mozi described Confucians as parasites feeding off the lives of others. The Confucian "causes poverty, and lives in idleness," and "is indolent and proud," Mozi ranted. "He behaves like a beggar; grasps food like a hamster, gazes at things like a he-goat, and rises up like a wild boar. The gentlemen all laugh at him. . . . He depends on others' houses for his wealth and uses others' fields to uphold his dignity."[13]

Confucius also figures prominently in the writings of Zhuangzi, an important early interpreter of Daoism, who likely lived around the same time as Mencius. His approach to Confucius is somewhat kinder than Mozi's, but still, on many occasions, Zhuangzi portrays the great sage as well-intentioned but misguided. Under Zhuangzi's brush, Confucius is inappropriately obsessed with status and fame, too arrogant to understand the world, and incapable of solving its problems. In several passages, Confucius is shown as the student, not the master, being instructed by some other, wiser figure. In one story, an Old Master (perhaps Laozi, the founder of Daoism) summons Confucius, who is described as a man "with a long body and short legs, his back a little humped and his ears set way back," and then proceeds to berate him. "Get rid of your proud bearing and that knowing look on your face and you can become a gentleman!" the master lectures. "You can't bear to watch the sufferings of one age, and so you go and make trouble for ten thousand ages to come!"[14]

In one especially vitriol-infused story, Zhuangzi tells of how Confucius tried to convince a criminal who was rampaging across the country, known as Robber Zhi, to give up his evil ways and use his talents for the good of society. The tale gives Zhuangzi an opportunity to heap abuse on Confucius through the mouth of a disdainful adversary. After Confucius politely states his case, Robber Zhi blasts him as a bumbling fool whose ideas have been rejected throughout the nation: "With your peculiar robe and narrow girdle, with your deceitful speech and hypocritical conduct, you delude the lords of the different states, and are seeking for riches and honors," Robber Zhi rages. "There is no greater robber than you are. . . . You have done no good either for yourself or for others—how can your doctrines be worth being thought much of? . . . Your Way is only a wild recklessness, deceitful, artful, vain, and hypocritical." Having failed in his mission, Confucius hurriedly flees, frazzled and disoriented. His "eyes were dazed," according to Zhuangzi: he "could not see; and his color was that of slaked lime." Once Confucius reaches his carriage, "he lays hold of the crossbar, holding his head down, and unable to draw his breath."[15]

As the Warring States period came to a close, the enemies of Confucius seemed to get the upper hand. After five centuries of disarray and war, China was finally reunified under a new dynasty, the Qin, when its king, Ying Zheng, defeated the last of the Warring States in 221 BC. Seeking to mark the immensity of his accomplishment, he proclaimed a new empire and awarded himself a new title—emperor. King Zheng became forever known as simply the First Emperor, or Qin Shihuangdi.

The First Emperor was not overstating the historic importance of the moment. The empire he forged became the basic model for imperial China for the next 2,100 years. Tossing aside the Zhou practice of ruling through feudal lords, the Qin created administrative provinces managed directly by professional bureaucrats. The government became much more centralized than ever before, with decision making dominated by the capital, Xianyang (near modern Xi'an). The Qin had seemingly fulfilled Confucius's dream of a unified China overseen by a strong government able to restore order and peace.

But the order imposed by the Qin was not Confucius's sort of order. The Qin were adherents of a rival school to the Confucians—the Legalists. Ironically, the Legalists and the Confucians had common roots. One of the founding fathers of the Legalists, the third-century BC scholar Han Feizi, was a student of Xunzi. Yet the Legalists devised radically different views from the Confucians on good government and the ideal society. Although Han Feizi retained some respect for Confucius, admiring his commitment to principle, he also believed the sage was hopelessly idealistic. Confucius's conviction that peace could be maintained through benevolence and rightness alone was foolish, Han Feizi contended. People were incorrigibly self-interested and could never live up to Confucius's lofty standards of moral behavior. The only way to bring order to society was to impose it through tough laws; the only way to preserve government authority was to maximize state power.

To prove his point, Han Feizi mocked Confucius by highlighting how few Chinese had adhered to his cause during his lifetime. "The people are such as would be firmly obedient to authority, but are rarely able to appreciate righteousness," Han Feizi explained:

> [Confucius], who was a sage of All-under-Heaven, cultivated virtuous conduct, exemplified the right way, and travelled about within the seas; but those within the seas who talked about his benevolence and praised his righteousness and avowed discipleship to him, were only seventy. For to honor benevolence was rare and to practice righteousness was hard.... And there was only one person really benevolent and righteous—[Confucius] himself! ... Now, the learned men of today, when they counsel the Lord of Men, assert that if His Majesty applied himself to the practice of benevolence and righteousness instead of making use of victory-ensuring authority, he would certainly become ruler of All-under-Heaven. This

is simply to require every lord of men to come up to the level of [Confucius] and all the common people of the world to act like his disciples. It is surely an ineffectual measure.[16]

For Han Feizi, the Confucian emphasis on studying the classics and revering antiquity was not sufficient for the purpose of managing a state. Confucius, in his view, failed to understand that his teachings would undermine public order rather than strengthen it. If the rulers followed the way of Confucius, the government would disintegrate and the nation would again descend into chaos. "To enact the law is to lead the people, whereas if the superior esteems literary learning, the people will become skeptical in following the law," Han Feizi argued. "To reward for merit is to encourage the people, whereas if the superior honors the cultivation of virtuous conduct, the people will become lazy in producing profits. If the superior holds literary learning in high esteem and thereby causes doubt in the law, and if he honors the cultivation of virtuous conduct and thereby causes disbelief in meritorious work, to strive after the wealth and strength of the state is impossible."[17]

Such thinking was of obvious appeal to a power-crazed strongman like Qin Shihuangdi. The most influential official in the Qin, outside of the emperor himself, was the chief minister, Li Si, who, like Han Feizi, was a student of Xunzi who turned on the Confucians. After the Qin conquest of China, the emperor and Li Si created China's first centralized, dictatorial state. Decrees and orders flowed out of the Qin capital and were enforced through the might of the army. To fund this giant military establishment, the Qin slapped burdensome taxes on the common people. The government conscripted hundreds of thousands of laborers to build the first Great Wall of China to keep out persistent nomadic intruders from the northern steppe. Citizens were encouraged to spy on each other. Offenders were regularly executed, mutilated, or condemned to forced labor.

The Confucians were appalled. By deviating so drastically from the ways of the ancients, the First Emperor, they believed, was leading China to ruin. Their displeasure turned into public dissent at a banquet the emperor arranged for seventy "scholars of broad learning" at his palace in the capital in 213 BC. The dinner, as Sima Qian tells it, started off pleasantly enough. The chief administrator of the scholars, Zhou Qingchen, showered the First Emperor with compliments and praised his "divine power and brilliant sagacity." "Since high antiquity Your Majesty's authority and virtue have not been matched," Zhou flattered him. But then the evening went awry. Another scholar, Chunyu Yue, stepped forward and sharply criticized the First Emperor in front of his guests. The regime was doomed to fail, Chunyu Yue predicted, since the emperor was ignoring the lessons of China's history. The reason the dynasties of antiquity "reigned for more than 1,000 years was because they [gave fiefdoms to] their sons and younger brothers and successful officials to provide branches and supports for themselves," the scholar said. "Now although Your Majesty possesses all within the seas, your sons and younger brothers are private individuals. . . . If there is no one to offer support and assistance, how will you rescue each other? That an enterprise can survive for long if it is not modeled on antiquity is not anything I have heard about." Yue's argument could easily have come straight from Confucius's mouth. Confucius judged the rulers of his day against the standard he believed had been set by the sage-kings of antiquity; Yue, and many Confucians to follow, would do the same again and again.

Dismayed by what he had heard, the First Emperor asked Li Si about the scholar's protest. Li Si was quick to censure the Confucians. "Your Majesty has created a great enterprise and constructed an achievement which will last for 10,000 generations, which is certainly not something which a foolish Confucian would understand," Li Si said. "All the scholars do not take the present as a model but study antiquity, and thus they reject the present generation." Echoing Han Feizi, Li Si warned the First Emperor of the dangers of allowing the Confucians to continue their historical studies and literary pursuits. "Those who have studied privately collaborate with each other to reject the laws and teachings, and when people hear ordinances promulgated everyone criticizes them in accordance with his own studies," Li Si told the emperor. Such dissent would eventually lead to the fall of Qin, Li Si predicted, and could not be tolerated. "Disagreement they regard as noble, and they encourage all the lower orders to fabricate slander," he said. "If such things are not prohibited, then above the sovereign's power will decline, and below factions will form."

Then Li Si made a fateful suggestion. To stifle further opposition, he recommended that the Qin place education and information at the service of the state. The Confucians would no longer be permitted to study their old books and use that knowledge to criticize the government. All privately held copies of the classics and the histories (save those of the Qin) should be turned over to government officials and "indiscriminately burnt," Li Si said. Even mentioning the classics in private conversation should result in execution, he suggested. Anyone still possessing such books after thirty days "should be branded and sent to do forced labor on the walls." Finally, "those who, using the old, reject the new will be wiped out together with their clans." Li Si had hit upon the sinister idea that in order to control the people, the government had to control their minds.[18]

Sima Qian related the unfortunate consequences. "Approving his proposals," he wrote, "the First Emperor collected up and got rid of the *Songs*, the *Documents*, and the sayings of the hundred schools in order to make the people stupid and ensure that in all under Heaven there should be no rejection of the present by using the past."[19] The event became known in Chinese history as the "Burning of the Books."

The Confucians and other scholars, however, were not so easily cowed. Some took great risks to save their cherished classics from destruction. Tradition has it that the descendants of Confucius hid the *Analects* and other texts in the walls of the Kong family home in Qufu. Two brave scholars, Master Hou and Master Lu, were daring enough to speak out against the First Emperor and his tyrannical ways. "The Supreme One enjoys using punishments and executions as a sign of his authority, and since all under Heaven hang on to their salaries in fear of punishment, nobody dares to fulfill his loyal duties," they protested. "Since the Supreme One does not hear about his faults, he grows daily more arrogant." Then the two men fled.

The First Emperor flew into a rage. "I collected together the writings of all under Heaven and got rid of all which were useless," he insisted. "I called together all the scholars and magicians, an extremely large gathering, intending to promote an era of great peace by this means." The emperor then asked the imperial secretary to investigate the scholars. The outcome was grisly. "Although [the scholars] tried to exonerate themselves," Sima Qian recounted, "more than 460 who had infringed the prohibitions were all buried alive at Xianyang, and the whole Empire was made to know about this to serve as a warning for the future."[20]

Modern scholars believe that these tales of death and destruction were exaggerated by later scholars (like Sima Qian) to vilify the Qin. More likely, they say, the government controlled access to the classical texts. Li Si believed that a unitary state required a unitary political ideology, so he may have rounded up copies of the classics that were in private hands, stored them in an imperial library, and permitted only those with government approval to read them. The Qin court was not completely opposed to classical learning, either. The First Emperor consulted scholars on matters of ritual, and some of his inscriptions contain citations from the old texts. In all, the Qin may not have been the arch enemies of Confucian scholarship that they were painted to be.[21]

Still, Li Si's efforts at thought control could not save the Qin. As Confucius would have predicted, the Qin's overbearing tactics and harsh punishments fueled opposition to the regime. Rebellions broke out. The unraveling began soon after the sudden death of the First Emperor in 210 BC. His court descended into political intrigues that eventually claimed Li Si himself. Accused of plotting a coup, a political rival "had him flogged more than 1,000 times and, since he could not bear the pain, he made a false confession," according to Sima Qian. Li Si was condemned to be cut in two at the waist in the marketplace of the Qin capital.[22] In 206 BC, Xianyang was conquered by rebel forces. Four years later, one of the rebel commanders, a former low-ranking Qin official named Liu Bang, proclaimed a new empire—the Han Dynasty. With the rise of the Han, the fortunes of the Confucians changed forever, as did the course of Asian civilization.

THE NEW EMPEROR of China is usually portrayed as an uneducated soldier of peasant stock who was unfamiliar with Confucius's favorite classics. It is more probable, however, that Liu Bang (also known as Gaozu, or Emperor Gao) had some education—otherwise, he would likely not have earned even the minor government post he had held under the Qin.[23] Still, he was no Confucian. One story has it that when a group of scholars approached Liu Bang dressed in full traditional costume, he suddenly snatched a cap off one of their heads and urinated into it.

When the rebel became emperor, the realities of ruling a vast domain forced him to reconsider his attitude. The Han inherited the centralized state built by the Qin and had no desire to significantly diminish its authority. But ruling as the Qin had done was out of the question as well. Despite the Qin's military prowess and vast resources, the new empire had collapsed like a house of cards. Clearly, the First Emperor and his heirs had done something terribly wrong. If Gaozu intended his new Han Dynasty to survive for generations to come, he had to devise a superior form of government.

But what should that be? Although Gaozu and his comrades-in-arms had no clear idea about how to rule an empire, the Confucians did. By the time the Han took charge, the Confucians possessed experience in administration, deep knowledge of Chinese history, and, most importantly, a well-defined vision of government and a doctrine of governing principles. Looking for ways to control an increasingly large and complex empire, and anxious to legitimize its newly proclaimed dynasty, the Han court began to see the followers of the old sage as the keepers of a philosophy that could both provide the ideological justification for imperial rule and serve as a guide to state policy. In this way, the Confucians now benefited tremendously from the real-world sensibility of Confucius himself.

The Confucians, meanwhile, proved tremendously adept at marketing their ideas to the Han court. They used the sudden downfall of the Qin to bolster their own theories on government, arguing that the severity of Qin rule was its fatal flaw. The people could not be coerced into supporting the regime indefinitely; instead, coercion fostered resentment and rebellion. By this reckoning, the Qin Dynasty had evaporated because its sovereigns had never won the hearts of the common man; they lost power because they lacked humanity. Influential statesman Jia Yi expressed just such a view in an essay he wrote during the early decades of the Han. "Qin, from a tiny base, had become a great power, ruling the land and receiving homage from all quarters," he observed. "Yet after they had unified the land . . . , a single common rustic could nevertheless challenge this empire and cause its ancestral temples to topple and its ruler to die at the hand of others, a laughingstock in the eyes of all. Why? Because the ruler lacked humaneness and rightness, because preserving power differs fundamentally from seizing power." In other words, the Qin emperors failed because they ignored one of Confucius's most central principles—moral power trumps physical power.[24]

The Confucians with access to Gaozu pressed home this very point. Around 195 BC, during a meeting with the emperor, a well-regarded Confucian scholar and diplomat named Lu Jia started quoting from the classics, but the new emperor expressed disdain for such archaic literature. "I got the empire on horseback," Gaozu told him. "Why should I bother with the *Book of Odes* or the *Book of History*?" Lu Jia had the perfect reply. "You got it on horseback, but can you rule it from horseback?" the scholar asked. Gaozu evidently took notice. He requested that Lu Jia produce a treatise on "why the Qin failed and the Han succeeded, and also on the merits of rulers throughout history."[25]

The resulting text, called *New Discourses*, was a thoroughly Confucian affair, in that it stressed that the fate of regimes depended on their virtue. "Actions that do not combine humaneness and rightness are doomed to failure," Lu Jia wrote. "Those who maintain the country with humaneness are themselves secure." Lu Jia also made sure to tell Gaozu that it was Confucius who had set down the correct path for rulers. "When rights and rightness were not practiced and regulations and disciplines were not maintained, succeeding generations became weak and decadent," he wrote. "Thus the later sage [Confucius] defined the Five Classics and taught the Six Arts, following the principles of Heaven and Earth, all the while exhaustively pursuing the minutest ways of things and events." Confucius did this in order "to correct decay and disorder," so that "the wise would maximize their minds." The sage "curbed extravagance, rectified customs and extended true culture." Lu Jia supposedly read Gaozu each chapter as it was completed.[26]

STILL, GAOZU NEVER fully committed himself to Confucian doctrine, and neither did his court. In the early decades of the Han, its rulers experimented with a variety of philosophies—Confucius's wasn't even the most influential. The Legalists, left over from the Qin and entrenched in the bureaucracy they had created, remained a force in government, and the Han did little at first to uproot them. The Daoists also held great sway. After the heavy hand of the Qin, the more live-and-let-live sensibilities of Daoism seemed especially appropriate for a new age. Hundreds of years would pass before Confucius would become China's most important sage.

That process began in earnest during the long reign of Emperor Wu. The young ruler, who claimed the Han throne in 141 BC, set in place policies on education and the civil service that would—over the course of time—come to embed Confucianism within the very structure of the Chinese imperial state.

Why did Emperor Wu choose Confucius? Part of the reason might have been palace politics. Although he was formally the emperor, he found himself under the thumb of the empress dowager, Dou, his grandmother, who was a devoted Daoist. Emperor Wu might have tried to promote the Confucians at court in an attempt to sideline the overbearing old lady. The status of Confucius during Emperor Wu's first few years on the throne might have been influenced by the contest between him and his grandma.

Emperor Wu's initial attempt to change the philosophical basis for Han rule came shortly after his ascension, when he moved against the discredited Legalists. He issued an edict banning experts in Legalist doctrines from government service. The decision has been interpreted by some scholars as an effort by Emperor Wu, under the guidance of a group of Confucian advisers, to purge non-Confucians from his administration. But a year later, the decree was revoked by the empress dowager. That wasn't the only time she foiled the Confucians. Emperor Wu had collected a group of learned Confucian scholars around him who proposed to revive ancient court rituals and construct a ceremonial hall of the type used by the Zhou court. The emperor, a sucker for pomp, found these policies appealing and planned to implement them, but the empress dowager would have none of it. "Before any of these plans had been put into effect," Sima Qian wrote, "Empress Dowager Dou, who . . . had no use for Confucianism, sent men in secret to spy on [the Confucian officials] . . . and gather evidence to show that they were deriving illegal profit from their posts." Two of the accused committed suicide. Emperor Wu had no choice but to abandon the Confucians' proposals.[27]

Political shifts within the imperial court eventually made it possible for Emperor Wu to elevate Confucius to a more prominent position. After the empress dowager fell ill and died in 136 BC, the chief impediment to greater Confucian influence passed away with her. By this time, Daoist principles were losing their appeal anyway. The more laissez-faire approach to governing that Daoism engendered was not active and forceful enough to be a sound basis on which to build an empire. The Confucians were finally free to infuse their beliefs into the system of imperial government.

No SINGLE PERSON deserves more credit for convincing the Han to adopt Confucius's teachings than a scholar named Dong Zhongshu. Though he is usually not ranked with the greatest of the great Confucian thinkers, such as Mencius and Xunzi, Dong was nevertheless one of the most influential scholars in Chinese history. He was Confucius's most successful publicist, and his adaptations of Confucian thought and efforts to market them to the Han elite were instrumental in turning Confucianism from one school among many to the paramount philosophical tradition in China. "During the long period of the influence of Dong Zhongshu, the teaching of Confucius was spread throughout the country and was understood by all men," an ancient history of the Han Dynasty tells us, though with some embellishment. "Scholars were developed, schools established, and learning was patronized by the state. Dong Zhongshu was the cause of all this."[28]

Dong, who lived between 179 and 104 BC, was, in classic Confucian fashion, both a scholar and a public official; at one point he served as a palace courtier. Sima Qian took note of his somewhat eccentric teaching techniques. "He used to lower the curtains of his room and lecture from within them," the historian wrote, "and his older disciples would pass on what they had learned to the newer ones, so that some of his students had never seen his face. Three years he taught in this way and never once took the time even to look out into his garden, such was his devotion to his task."[29]

That task was first and foremost studying the *Spring and Autumn Annals*. Dong considered that history of the state of Lu the most important of the five classics—so much so that his writings come down to us today in a collection quaintly called *Luxurious Gems of the Spring and Autumn Annals*. The *Annals* are, to the casual observer, little more than a scant, dry, and rather cryptic list of events. As one modern historian quipped, they have "about as much intrinsic literary merit as the New York City telephone book."[30] During Dong's time, however, it was widely held that Confucius had written the *Annals*, and Dong believed that the sage had implanted within the sparse entries of this work the moral lessons of history. A careful study of the *Annals* would reveal the course a ruler must follow to ensure that the world would prosper and remain at peace. By Dong's reckoning, that code of behavior was handed down to man by Heaven itself, which, in his writings, became a spiritual power that rewarded do-gooders and punished the wrongheaded. Failing to heed the wisdom of the *Annals* meant acting contrary to the will of Heaven and would only lead to disaster.

In connecting these streams of thought, Dong greatly elevated the role of Confucius in human history. Since ignoring the wisdom of the *Annals* was equivalent to acting against Heaven, and Confucius wrote the *Annals*, then refusing to heed Confucius meant disregarding Heaven's wishes. Dong turned Confucius into the ultimate sage, the only one who fully understood the will of Heaven, and therefore the final arbiter of right and wrong, good and evil. He wrote that Confucius "came to comprehend the principles of a hundred kings and to accord with Heaven's course from beginning to end."[31] By extension, those who followed Confucius (Dong himself, for instance) were the only scholars who possessed the depth of understanding needed to determine what Heaven wanted the emperor to do and to guide him in crafting proper state policies. In making these arguments, Dong was not only stating the case for Confucianism but being a smart politician. By awarding the Confucians the right to interpret the divine, he was attempting to sideline adherents of other philosophies in the real world of court politics.

Dong's analysis expanded Confucian thought. He made tremendous strides in transforming Confucius's teachings from an ethical tradition focused very much on the here-and-now issues of morality, good government, and proper human relationships into a more universalistic philosophy connecting man with the workings of the cosmos. In doing so, he nudged Confucianism toward something more like what we would consider a religion. Historians have called Dong Confucianism's first theologian. He updated Confucius's teachings for the emerging culture of the Han by mixing into it ideas of other schools and traditions that were popular at the time. Most notably, Dong absorbed the concept of *yin* and *yang*—a system based on two, counterbalancing forces that govern the pattern of change in the world—which was already well established in Chinese thought by his day and mentioned by the Daoists and Mohists. With Dong's help, Confucianism took on a syncretic character that made it more attractive to Han society. Dong started the process of turning Confucianism into a basket able to hold varied elements of traditional Chinese thought and culture.

In another important expansion of Confucian teachings, Dong unequivocally awarded man a special role in the universe. In the cosmological system Dong created, man played an indispensable role in bringing order to the world. By following the will of Heaven—which meant Confucian moral principles like filial piety and benevolence—man could ensure peace not just on earth, but also throughout the universe. Man was part of a triumvirate with Heaven and Earth, and these three components were so firmly connected that they could not function properly without each other. "Heaven, Earth and humankind are the foundation of all living things," Dong wrote. "Heaven engenders all living things, Earth nourishes them, and humankind completes them. . . . These three assist one another just as the hands and feet join to complete the body."[32] If man did not play his proper role, then the world would degenerate into chaos.

Man, however, was not capable of fulfilling such weighty responsibility all by himself. Humankind possesses the potential for good, in Dong's view, but in order to realize that potential, man requires training and guidance. In a political masterstroke, Dong, expanding on Confucius's own ideas, awarded the king the role of super-teacher, the only person who could help man follow Heaven's way and ensure prosperity on earth. "The nature of man is like a silk cocoon or an egg," Dong explained. "An egg has to be hatched to become a chicken, and a silk cocoon has to be unraveled to make silk. It is the true character of Heaven that nature needs to be trained before becoming good. . . . Therefore it sets up the king to make it good. . . . The people receive from Heaven a nature which cannot be good (by itself), and they turn to the king to receive the training which completes their nature. It is the duty of the king to obey the will of Heaven and to complete the nature of the people." For Dong, the ruler "is the pivot of all living things" and "Heaven's agent," and the fate of human society and the stability of the universe depend on the king's virtuous behavior. "The king is the beginning of man," Dong wrote. "If the king is correct, then the original material force will be harmonious, wind and rain will be timely, lucky stars will appear, and the yellow dragon will descend. If the king is not correct, then strange manifestations will take place in heaven above, and bandits will appear." Dong placed the imperial government into a new, expansive Confucian vision of the world. In effect, he gave empire a sort of divine sanction, awarding the Han Heaven's blessing.[33]

Dong had an opportunity to market his revised Confucian doctrine to Emperor Wu soon after he ascended the throne, when the emperor requested that the top scholars of the day make suggestions on how to improve the Han government and solve the empire's problems. Repeatedly quoting the *Analects*, Dong told the emperor that the secret to good government was ruling with righteousness. "The principle of government is to follow the action of Heaven by governing with uprightness, for the ruler must act as Heaven acts," he asserted. "These five virtues, benevolence, righteousness, correct behavior, wisdom and faith, should be practiced by every ruler; and if you do this, you will receive blessings from Heaven . . . while your good administration will spread to the four corners of the world."[34]

Dong also had more practical advice for the emperor, submitting a series of proposals that came to have great influence on Emperor Wu, the fate of Confucianism, and the course of Chinese history. To improve the quality of the functionaries running the Han administration, he recommended that the emperor establish a national university to train scholars to serve in the state bureaucracy. "Among the things paramount for the upbringing of scholars, none is more important than a university," Dong asserted. "A university is intimately related to virtuous scholars and to the foundation of education. . . . Your servant desires Your Majesty to erect a university and appoint illustrious teachers for it."[35]

Most importantly, Dong pressed the emperor to place Confucian teachings above all other philosophies. Dong believed that to maintain consistent policies and solidify the support of the people, China needed "unity" of thought. In this regard, he was not so different from Qin minister Li Si. But whereas Li Si tried to impose a single ideology by force, Dong was more subtle, maneuvering to elevate Confucianism by making it the dominant doctrine in China's royal court and education system. "The teachers of today have different doctrines, and men expound diverse theories; the various schools of philosophy differ in their ways, and their principles do not agree," Dong told the emperor. "The laws and institutions undergo frequent changes, and the people do not know what to honor. Your unworthy servant considers that whatever is not encompassed by the Six Disciplines and the arts of Confucius should be suppressed and not allowed to continue further, and evil and vain theories be stamped out. Only then will unity be achieved, the laws be made clear, and the people know what to follow."[36]

Emperor Wu was so impressed by Dong's suggestions that he followed them. In 136 BC, he made study of the Five Classics a prerequisite for attaining official academic posts in the government. In 124 BC, he opened an Imperial University to train civil servants with a curriculum based on the classics. With those decisions, the emperor began the process of making knowledge of Confucian doctrine mandatory for anyone hoping to attain an influential government position. These decisions, in effect, turned Confucianism into something close to state orthodoxy. With Dong's memorials (written submissions to the royal court), "Confucius was elevated and the other schools of philosophy were degraded," the annals of the Han Dynasty tell us. Confucian thinker Fung Yu-lan went even further. "From this time onward, if one wished to gain official position, one had to be an advocate of Confucianism, and this Confucianism furthermore had to be of a sort conforming to that decided upon by the government," he asserted. "The atmosphere of complete freedom of speech and thought . . . completely disappeared."[37]

FUNG YU-LAN's assertion is an exaggeration. Emperor Wu may have set in place the policies that promoted Confucius over other philosophers, but the great sage did not become the dominant force in Chinese thought during his reign. It would be far too simplistic to assume that a few edicts from the emperor, no matter how powerful he might be, could instantaneously convert the members of an entire government—let alone an entire society—into devotees of any one philosopher. In fact, modern scholars believe that Confucius's influence during Emperor Wu's reign remained marginal. Although it is true that the students at the new Imperial University had to specialize in the Five Classics, their Confucian instruction must have been limited, because they attended the university for only a year. At the beginning, only a small fraction of the government's civil servants actually attended the university, and its early classes graduated a mere 50 students. Historians also believe that no more than a handful of Emperor Wu's most important advisers and officials were committed Confucians—by one count, a meager 6 out of 76.[38] Nor is it clear that Wu intended to transform China into a Confucian society. With his love of war, grand ceremony, and self-aggrandizement, he never fully adhered to Confucian principles or policies, and he seemed to lose interest in Confucianism over the course of his reign.

We also have to be careful in reading the historical records composed at the time. Scribes like Sima Qian might have elevated the sage's importance during this early period of the Han. By categorizing all classical scholars—known as the literati, or *ru* in Chinese—as the followers of Confucius, writers of Chinese history have tended to overstate the role of the Confucians in the first centuries of imperial rule. But although it is true that the Five Classics were closely associated with Confucius's teachings and beloved by his later supporters, these texts, the founding books of Chinese civilization, were also read by all sorts of scholars who may or may not have identified themselves as "Confucians."

Nor is it clear that Confucius had much support among the general public. The industrious Sima Qian visited Confucius's hometown of Qufu on a research trip and found that a community of the sage's devotees had collected around his grave, where they formed a town that came to be known as Confucius Village. They sacrificed at his tomb site on festival days and held village feasts and archery tournaments there. Confucius's home had been turned into a temple, and his clothes, hat, lute, carriage, and books were kept there.[39] However, there is no reliable evidence that Confucius was venerated outside of Qufu, nor any record that the early Han emperors ever honored him with sacrifices and ceremonies in the capital. In the end, the picture we have of the importance of Confucius during the first two hundred years of Han rule is a confused one.

What is clear is that the Han Dynasty became more Confucian over time. During the Eastern, or Later Han, Dynasty, formed in AD 25, when the royal house was restored after one of its officials briefly usurped the throne, Confucianism became more and more entrenched in the imperial system. By mandating that all students passing through the Imperial University study the ancient classics, Emperor Wu ensured that, over time, a larger and larger proportion of government officials would be educated in the Confucian tradition, especially because the number of students who attended that institution each year swelled dramatically, to 30,000 by the second century AD. A larger and larger share of the most senior officials became identified with Confucianism as well. Some 70 percent of the top ministers serving in the Later Han court were confirmed Confucians, by one estimate.[40]

The Later Han emperors, too, turned more Confucian. They began to worship their ancestors as stipulated by Confucian ritual. Confucius himself became an object of imperial veneration. The official histories record that Later Han emperors on three occasions traveled to Qufu to personally offer sacrifices to the sage at the memorial temple there (the origins of which are

Contra Costa County Library
Prewett
6/10/2017 2:31:45 PM

- Patron Receipt -
- Charges -

ID: 21901023094844

Item: 31901055988044
Title: Confucius : and the world he created /
Call Number: 181.112 SCHUMAN
Due Date: 7/1/2017

Item: 31901044896480
Title: Lives of Confucius : civilization's greatest
Call Number: 181.112 NYLAN
Due Date: 7/1/2017

All Contra Costa County Libraries will be
closed on Tuesday, July 4th. Items may
be renewed online at ccclib.org or by calling
1-800-984-4636, menu option 1.
Book drops will be open.

----- Please keep this slip -----

a bit murky). The Later Han court also mandated in a decree issued in AD 59 that the sage be honored by sacrifices in government schools.

Some modern scholars see a critical turning point in the "Confucianization" of the imperial court with the reign of Emperor Guangwu, the first of the Later Han sovereigns. Up until his time, the Confucians at the Han court had had to lobby the emperors to adopt Confucian ideas and practices; with Guangwu's ascension, an emperor for the first time turned to Confucianism to legitimize his regime. Guangwu propagated a body of texts known to us today as the "Confucian apocrypha" as proof that Heaven had passed on its mandate to rule, namely, by giving it to him. These texts, now effectively purged from the Confucian canon, were highly prized at the time—in fact, they were heralded as Confucius's "secret classics," works supposedly written by the sage himself but kept hidden for later generations to discover. In reality, the texts were likely of more recent vintage, probably originating in the early years of the first century AD. Some Confucians during this period believed that Heaven sent down omens and portents to signal its pleasure with or disapproval of imperial action, and the apocrypha were heavy on prognostication. Guangwu had these texts promulgated nationwide and punished those who questioned their validity.

Confucius was also transformed into much more than a mere mortal during the Later Han. This was when he became known as the "Uncrowned King," a man who was meant to reign over China, even though he never actually sat upon the imperial throne. This idea was based on a theory floated by Dong Zhongshu, who interpreted an entry in the *Spring and Autumn Annals* regarding the discovery of a unicorn in Lu in 481 BC as proof that Confucius had been awarded the mandate to rule by Heaven shortly before his death. One Han Dynasty tale reads that "a small red bird . . . became a piece of yellow jade carved with an inscription which said: 'Confucius, holding (Heaven's) Mandate to act, created these governmental institutions in accordance with the laws.'" To writers of the apocrypha, Confucius was no longer a sage with great knowledge, but a legendary being with mystical powers. Even his appearance was superhuman. Confucius "was over ten feet high," boasted one Han-era text. "He had a head shaped like a hill, a square face, a moonlike protuberance on the right side of his forehead, a solar nose, eyes that are straight and long, a dragon-like forehead, lips like the Dipper, a bright face, an even chin, a supportive throat, joined teeth, a dragon frame, a tortoise's spine, and tiger paws. . . . When standing he looks like a phoenix perched bolt upright; when sitting he is like a crouching dragon. On his chest there are words that say 'The talisman of creating regulations to stabilize the world.'"[41]

Five centuries after his death, Confucius reigned supreme, possessing far more power and influence than he had ever dreamed of during his lifetime. Yet there were still many more twists and turns to come in his long biography.

Chapter Three

Confucius the King

Great art thou, O perfect sage! Among mortal men there
has not been thine equal.
—*Prayer offered to Confucius during imperial ceremonies*

Confucius's position at the top of China's intellectual hierarchy was not as
secure as it seemed, however. Beset by internal power struggles, natural di-
sasters, and peasant rebellions, the Later Han Dynasty came to an end in AD
220 with the abdication of its last emperor. That event dealt a heavy blow to
Confucius. The sage had become so closely associated with the Han that its
collapse undercut his stature in Chinese society. China once again fractured
into contending fiefdoms and mini-kingdoms, depriving the Confucians of
the strong, central patrons they had found in the Han rulers.

Meanwhile, Buddhism had filtered into China from its Indian birthplace,
probably during the first century AD, and steadily grew in popularity. Although scholars such as Dong Zhongshu had infused Confucius's teachings
with some aspects of religious faith, Confucianism remained at heart too
practical a philosophy to compete for the sympathies of Chinese villagers.
The Buddha's spiritual message of eternal salvation appealed to them much
more. For seven centuries after the fall of the Han, the development and expansion of Buddhism dominated Chinese religious culture. Temples popped
up throughout the country, and the number of monks proliferated. Daoism
also flourished. Confucianism fell into a dark period of stagnation. Little intellectual advance in the philosophy occurred, and few great commentators
or original thinkers emerged.

This isn't to say that Confucius was forgotten. His teachings remained the
backbone of government ideology, and Confucians continued to serve as advisers to the various thrones that emerged after the demise of the Han. More

importantly, Confucian thought became entrenched even more firmly in the country's education. In AD 587, the Sui Dynasty (581–618) introduced China's famed civil service examination system, through which the government began recruiting professional administrators for the imperial bureaucracy. Following in the footsteps of Emperor Wu, the Sui enshrined the Confucian Five Classics as the official curriculum for the exams. This decision was one of the most important in Confucian history. These exams became a critical method through which Confucian thought was disseminated throughout the populace.

This period also saw the emergence of an imperial cult to the great sage. In AD 241, the emperor of the state of Wei, one of the kingdoms that succeeded the Han, ordered a sacrifice to Confucius at the Imperial University—the first confirmed record of such an official state ceremony in the capital. Two centuries later, the short-lived Liu-Song Dynasty built the first state temple to Confucius. The founding emperor of the Tang Dynasty (618–907) greatly expanded the cult by ordering schools across the empire to open temples devoted to the sage where regular sacrifices would be made to him.

Still, the Tang court wasn't nearly as supportive of the Confucians as the Han had been. The open-minded Tang royals dabbled with all sorts of diverse traditions and fashionable foreign habits that drifted into China over the trade routes from Central Asia and India, including Buddhism. The Confucians were horrified. To them, Buddhism was an imported intrusion that undermined and contradicted China's native traditions. One Confucian labeled Buddhism "no more than a cult of the barbarian peoples"; another blasted Buddhist practice as "a corruption that eats into and destroys men." In 819, when a civil servant, Han Yu, one of the most influential Confucian thinkers of the entire first millennium, heard that the Tang emperor was planning to welcome a relic of the Buddha to the capital, he protested in a blistering memorial to the throne. "The common people are ignorant and dull, easily misled and hard to enlighten, and should they see their emperor do these things they might say that Your Majesty was serving Buddhism with a true heart," he wrote. "Then will our old ways be corrupted, our customs violated, and the tale will spread to make us the mockery of the world." That tirade earned Han Yu exile in southern China.[1]

It is easy to see why the Confucians disliked the Buddhists so much. The two doctrines—and the philosophers who founded them—were like oil and water. Confucius was very much a man of the here and now. He spent a lifetime engaged in public affairs, intent on building a better world, and studiously ignored cosmic questions about the afterlife and the origins of the universe. But the Buddha preached the insignificance of the world and fixated his followers on escaping from it. Confucians thought society could be perfected and advocated a program to achieve that; the Buddhists believed the world was ephemeral and people should avoid becoming attached to it. The Confucians had nothing but disdain for Buddhist monks. They believed the monks were shirking their responsibility to serve society and were instead parasitically feasting off of it.

As the Tang weakened in the eighth century and disorder again gripped China, the Confucians blamed the proliferation of Buddhism for the ills facing the nation. The problem, the Confucians believed, was that Buddhism had clouded the minds of men; the wisdom of Confucius had been forgotten. "When believers took these men [Buddha and Laozi] as their masters and followed them, they despised and defamed Confucius," wrote Han Yu. "And those of later ages who might wish to hear of the teachings on humaneness and rightness, the Way and its power, had no one to listen to. . . . Today we elevate barbarian practices and place them above the teachings of our former kings. How long will it be before we ourselves have all become barbarians?"[2]

THE RISE OF a new dynasty gave the Confucians new hope. In 960, the Song took hold of the nation, and its leaders embraced Confucianism with a fervor unmatched since the days of the Han—and perhaps by any rulers up to that point in China's history. What emerged from the three centuries of Song rule was an imperial government, educational system, and national ideology that shaped every succeeding dynasty in China with Confucius and his teachings as the dominant force and unquestioned heart of the country's political culture. Once the Song Dynasty restored the Uncrowned King to his throne, he wasn't forced down from it until the end of imperial rule itself in the early twentieth century.

The Song claimed power in a very un-Confucian way—with a military coup. Zhao Kuangyin, an adviser to the beleaguered Later Zhou Dynasty, a short-lived empire that emerged after the fall of the Tang, pretended to march out of the capital with his troops, ostensibly to defend the nation from threatening barbarians on the frontier. Instead, he turned them on his royal employer and forced the six-year-old emperor to abdicate. Zhao then proclaimed the birth of the Song. After his death, he was given the name of Taizu, or "Supreme Progenitor."

Taizu proved to be one of the most able, ingenious, and determined emperors in China's long history—and as his new dynasty was finding its footing, he needed all of his skills to keep it alive. Northern tribes had claimed a chunk of territory in the northwest that had formerly been controlled by the Chinese, and they continued to covet China's heartland. Taizu still had to complete the unification of a country that had been in chaos for decades. Moreover, he worried that his military commanders would turn traitorous and claim pieces of his new empire for themselves. If Taizu was to solidify his new dynasty, he needed a clear program to follow and a strong ideology to support his rule.

The Confucians were standing at the ready. The solution to the country's ills, as Han Yu had argued, was to restore the long-ignored methods of the ancient sage-kings—the Way that had been taught by Confucius and enshrined in his classics. With Confucius reinvigorated, his followers contended, the country would return to peace and prosperity. "Foolish persons of recent times have all declared that times are different and things have changed, so that [the Way] can no longer be practiced," influential Confucian thinker Cheng Yi wrote in a 1050 memorial to the Song court. "This only shows how deep their ignorance is, and yet time and again the rulers of men have been deceived by their talk."[3] The problems facing China could be resolved by reconnecting the Chinese citizenry to the genius of Confucius and his ancient wisdom.

Taizu and his immediate successors were a willing audience. Many currents in China at the time played a role in directing them toward Confucius's teachings.[4] In part, the old sage won by default. The Tang Dynasty and the short-lived kingdoms that had succeeded it had been heavily influenced by Buddhism and Daoism, but the disorder of the previous century had tarnished these doctrines as the basis of a governing ideology. The otherworldly dreaminess of Buddhism seemed ill-suited to the task of tackling the very real challenges facing the Song court. The Confucian thinkers, in contrast, had at their fingertips a store of historical precedent and defined governing principles that could become the foundation of state policy. What developed between the Song emperors and the Confucians was a partnership so close that the dynasty became almost jointly managed by the emperors, who inherited their authority by birth, and the professional scholar-officials, who attained their influence through their knowledge of Confucian doctrine. This model of government would persist for the next nine hundred years of imperial rule.

This bond had tremendous implications for the future of Confucius. Once his teachings (finally) became the unchallenged governing ideology of the imperial regime, the Confucians were able to push their many rivals to the sidelines once and for all. Although Daoism and Buddhism continued to hold their appeal at a popular level, Confucianism firmly took hold of government and education and made deeper inroads into the daily lives and family practices of the Chinese. That achievement fixed Confucius himself as the most influential individual in China's civilization, the man who devised the philosophy that distinguished the Chinese from the other cultures that surrounded them, which, in Chinese eyes, were barbaric. However, the lofty position Confucius attained would come to haunt him. He became a symbol of imperial rule and the Chinese social system that developed under it—and, in modern times, when that traditional system came under attack from new ideas from the West, it was the sage himself, along with the society that had been created in his name, that became tarnished as backward.

But that fall from grace was still centuries into the future. As Taizu was forging his Song Dynasty, the new emperor immediately endeared himself to the Confucians. Although he had won the empire by force, he quickly moved to defang the military by shrewdly offering his most senior commanders the governorships of provinces. That decision simultaneously reduced the risk that one of these hardboiled generals would contend for the Song throne and won over the Confucians, who preferred civilian over military authority (which they called putting the "civil principle" over the "military principle"). One Song history proudly boasts that "when the Cultivated Progenitor [Taizu] changed the mandate, he first employed civil officials and took power away from the military officials. Esteeming the civil principle by the Song had its origin in this."[5]

Next, Taizu introduced a policy that permanently tied the imperial system and the Confucians together. The new emperor reinstated the civil service examinations and greatly expanded their scope and influence. Before the Song, most government jobs had still been filled by members of established elite families who received their posts through political connections, not by passing examinations. The Song changed that by elevating the exam system into the primary route to lucrative and respected government service. Far more officials earned their employment by excelling at the tests during the Song than ever before. In 973, Taizu further linked these men directly to the Song court by adding a final, prestigious step in the exam system called the "Palace Examination," which he oversaw personally.

These reforms served three critical purposes. First, they enhanced the power of the centralized imperial government by creating a civil service filled with young men who were more loyal to the emperor than to their own familial and local interests. Second, the Song reform professionalized the civil service by basing admission on education instead of pedigree. Finally, because of Taizu's promotion of the exams, Confucius's teachings were able to penetrate even more deeply into Chinese society and culture. The curriculum for the exams, as before, consisted solely of the Confucian classics. That meant that the best way to win a government post was to focus first and foremost on studying Confucius's doctrine. Historian Dieter Kuhn has said that, as a result of these and other changes, the transition to the Song "marks the most decisive rupture in the history of imperial China."[6]

The early Song emperors also presented themselves as devoted Confucian kings. Emperor Zhenzong, the third to reign in the Song, prided himself on being the model hardworking sovereign—already engaged in his first meeting with his counselors at dawn and listening to reports from his finance, military, and administrative chiefs through breakfast and beyond. The early Song emperors propagated Confucian learning with the aid of new technology. Advances in printing, including the eleventh-century introduction of movable type (some four centuries before Gutenberg), made books cheaper to produce and more widely available. Zhenzong oversaw the completion of a new, authoritative compilation of the Confucian classics in 1011.

The emperors made sure to pay the proper respects to Confucius as well. An official Song history carefully records Zhenzong's visit to the sage's hometown of Qufu. "The temple was decorated with yellow banners and hangings, and the clan of Confucius [the Kong family] assisted at the sacrifice," it tells us. "The emperor wore the robes and boots of state. . . . In former times the officials prepared the sacrifice, and the emperor merely bowed [before the altar], raising his folded hands, but on this occasion, the emperor performed the kowtow as an expression of his reverence for Confucius and the canonical learning. He wrote an ode, which was engraved on a stone monument placed in the temple. After this he visited the grave [of Confucius], riding on a horse, not in his palanquin, where he offered a libation of wine, and kowtowed twice."[7]

THE CONFUCIANS NOW acquired what they had always craved most of all: political power, which had eluded even their master. Thousands of new, motivated civil servants, indoctrinated with Confucian ideals, the Confucian view of history, and Confucian policy preferences and methods of state-craft, flooded into the government machinery. The Confucians thus gained a stranglehold on the formulation of policy in imperial China—a grip that they would not relinquish until the collapse of the last imperial dynasty, the Qing, in the early twentieth century.

And now that they had finally grasped the political clout they had long desired, the Confucians fully intended on wielding it. Some 1,500 years after the great sage first pleaded with China's wayward rulers, the Song-era Confucians strove to put his ideas into practice at court. The Confucians believed that they, and only they, knew the right path to virtuous rule, and they expected the emperor to listen to them. In a memorial to the throne, philosopher and scholar Cheng Yi made it perfectly clear that the emperor may be the emperor, but he would fail if he didn't heed his Confucian advisers. "Since ancient times," Cheng Yi said, "it has never happened that sagely virtue could be achieved by one who failed to respect worthies and stand in awe of his ministers." Cheng Yi, who personally instructed the emperor on Confucian ethics, was so stern that the supposedly all-powerful ruler of China was a bit afraid of him. One time, when Cheng Yi was advised to be more respectful to his sovereign, he responded: "I am a commoner. As the teacher of the Emperor, I must maintain my self-respect and dignity."[8]

The crusty Cheng Yi was not the only scholar-official to speak his mind to the Song rulers. In 1071, for instance, when the emperor said that his reforms were for the benefit of the people, his chief statesman, Wen Yanbo, remarked: "You govern the nation with *us*, the officials, not with the people." Such comments "reflected a new interpretation of imperial authority and revealed a remarkable independence of mind and self-esteem among Song scholar-officials—not unlike that of Confucius himself," historian Kuhn commented. Another historian, Peter Bol, proffered the idea that this new relationship between emperor and professional official altered the very nature of the imperial regime by creating a political system that he called a "scholar-official government."[9]

Although the Confucians finally got control over government policy, they didn't always agree on what that policy should be. As usual, they were far from unified in their interpretations of Confucius's teachings and how they should be transformed into a policy platform. That led to massive, and often nasty, ideological battles within the imperial court. Each faction in these rabid debates liberally invoked the Confucian classics and Confucius's sayings to bolster their respective positions. Simply put, policymaking in imperial China became a battleground among persnickety, *Analects*-toting

Confucian scholars arguing over the fine points of Confucian doctrine. The debate over what kind of government Confucius really intended to create, and what a true Confucian ruler ought to do, goes on to this day.

Perhaps no contest of wills was more heated or divisive than the one that emerged in an eleventh-century showdown between two titans of Chinese scholarship and statecraft—Wang Anshi and Sima Guang. Wang was a brash, argumentative, hyper-intelligent technocrat who had risen up through the exam system, and he held radical ideas on how to interpret Confucius and reform the empire. He saw government as a tool that could be used to perfect society and was determined to refashion the institutions of state and the economic system to that end. Sima was a respected historian and long-serving court official who favored a more traditional approach. In his view, the ideal society would be achieved by focusing on maintaining order, strengthening the Confucian hierarchy, and continuing in the ways set down by the sage-kings. To Sima, Wang's activist agenda was a dangerous deviation from Confucian political thought.[10]

The clash erupted after the nineteen-year-old emperor, Shenzong, took the Song throne in 1067, bursting with youthful energy, eager to make his mark, and open to ideas for drastic reform that could strengthen the military and help him recapture the lands lost to northern "barbarians," which continued to be a court obsession. The new emperor was immediately drawn to the bold Wang Anshi. During their first meeting, he asked Wang for his assessment of the Tang Dynasty founder. Wang responded that the young man would be better off following the path of the sage-kings of antiquity. Their principles were "very easy to put into practice," he told the impressionable emperor. "It is only because scholars of recent times do not really understand them that they think such standards of government are unattainable."[11] Wang talked himself into a job. The emperor appointed him vice chief councillor in 1069.

Wang unleashed a torrent of reforms called the "New Policies" that impacted education, the military, and large swaths of the economy. Under the Green Sprouts Act of 1069, the state offered farmers low-interest loans twice a year in an attempt to sideline loan sharks and boost agricultural productivity. To improve the quality of civil servants, Wang altered the exams to include an essay on the "meaning" of the classics, to test candidates' understanding of the texts. "The most urgent need of the present time is to secure capable men," Wang once told the throne. "Only when we get capable men in the government will there be no difficulty in assessing what may be done."[12]

To support his overhaul, Wang was always quick with an example from history or a snippet of the classics, to show that his policies were modeled on the ways of the sage-kings. China suffered from political and economic difficulties "because most of the present body of law does not accord with the government of the ancient kings," he contended in a 1058 memorial to the throne. "Now our own age is far removed from that of the ancient kings, and the changes and circumstances with which we are confronted are not the same. . . . Yet they never differed as to their underlying aims in the government of the empire, the state, and the family."[13]

Wang's aim was to strengthen the government, enhance prosperity, and decrease inequality through direct state action. His New Policies stemmed from a paternalistic strain of Confucian thought that expected scholar-officials to employ their wisdom to fix the problems plaguing mankind. But in intervening so aggressively and on such a wide scale, Wang was also breaking with precedent. Traditionally, the Confucians believed they shouldn't dirty their hands selling grain or granting loans, for example, but should focus on the ethical training of the common people. Once the minds and hearts of the masses were filled with benevolence, the empire would be set right on its own. The opposition to Wang's reforms was fierce and widespread. Led by Sima Guang, the factions engaged in bitter debates right in front of the emperor. Wang ruthlessly used his influence within the imperial court to purge officials who were opposed to his reforms. In 1070, frustrated and disgusted, Sima resigned from his government post in protest.

Both Wang and Sima claimed that Confucius was on their side. "The sages looked after the interests of the common people simply by lightening taxes, imposts and other burdens," Sima wrote to Wang in a blunt 1070 letter. "In your opinion, this is conventional Confucian blather, not worthy of attention. . . . Confucius said that a man of virtue should seek the fault in himself. . . . You cannot lay all the blame on everyone else." Wang's response was equally confrontational. "What Confucian scholars strive so hard to attain is a correspondence between what things are called and what they in fact are," he wrote to Sima. "I have adopted the policies of the ancient kings to bring about prosperity and relieve distress. . . . Your argument that what we need today is a policy of doing nothing at all and merely preserving the old ways is something I cannot accept."[14]

Ultimately, Wang lost this dispute. Under consistent and ferocious attack, he retired from the court despite the pleas of Emperor Shenzong to remain in office. After the emperor died in 1085, Wang's opponents got the upper hand. They called an aged and sickly Sima Guang out of retirement long enough for him to reverse most of the New Policies. The essence of their debate—the contest between traditionalism and reform—would resurface again and again, even in modern times. But although Wang Anshi and other Confucian progressives often found themselves at the losing end of these battles, they would become the model for a scholar-official in the twentieth century—a new breed who worked tirelessly to make East Asia a better, more prosperous society.

DEBATES AMONG CONFUCIANS during the Song period were not limited to the details of public policy. An equally lively exchange took place on issues of great doctrinal importance. The Song was among the most vibrant periods of development and experimentation in Confucian thought, a time when scholars delved deeply into all sorts of questions of philosophical heft—how to become a sage, the nature of humanity, and the connections among man, the universe, and everything else. What emerged from these musings was a radical break with the philosophy's past. Not for the last time, Confucius's thought got pulled apart and put back together again in a different form to suit the fashions and demands of a new age. In fact, the Song-era thinkers so drastically altered Confucius's teachings that the old sage would probably not have recognized them. What emerged was a new form of Confucianism known to us today as Neo-Confucianism.

When the Song first came to power, the dynasty inherited a Confucius who had been crafted by preceding dynasties. This Confucius was the patron saint of the literati, the preacher of good government, and the founder of a coherent code of ethics. Young boys were still required to study the *Analects*, and exam candidates had to master the same Five Classics that had been enshrined by Emperor Wu more than a millennium earlier. Students of Confucianism learned the sage's teachings on moral government, gentlemanly behavior, and ritual propriety. The followers of the sage during the Song period, however, created a different Confucius. The eager Confucian reformers of this era rejected the Confucianism that had existed since the Han as a gross distortion of the meaning of their master's teachings. In fact, they believed that the understanding of the true Way had ceased with Mencius, and that the faithful implementation of it had stopped even further back in China's past. To truly understand Confucius's wisdom, the Song scholars believed, they had to look upon his words with fresh eyes. These cultural revivalists revisited the original classics and other Confucian writings and reinterpreted them. Their approach took time to gain hold—Neo-Confucianism didn't become widely accepted until late in the Song period. But once it did, the revamping of Confucian thought forever changed the doctrine, and with it, Chinese history and society.

What the Neo-Confucians did was bring Confucius to the people. They infused his teachings with an enhanced universality and spirituality in order to challenge the appeal of Buddhism and Daoism. No longer would Confucius remain confined to the stodgy hallways of academies and ministerial offices; now he would reach out to touch every Chinese in every household across the empire. After the Song metamorphosis, Confucians would not have to fixate on winning the ear of the emperor to change the world. The Neo-Confucians believed that any individual could exert a positive impact on society simply by practicing benevolence and adhering to Confucius's Way. Confucius and his followers had always taught the transformative potential of moral cultivation; the Neo-Confucians elevated that theme into a realizable program of self-improvement. "Until this time Confucianism had focused on the Way of the sage kings or Way of the noble person as social and political leader," noted one study of Chinese philosophy. "The Neo-Confucians aspired to a spiritual ideal of sagehood for everyone."[15]

There were several thinkers whose ideas and personalities propelled this movement, from the haughty but brilliant Cheng Yi to the eccentric Shao Yang, who lived as a hermit, tilled his own vegetables, and called himself "Mr. Happiness." The towering figure, though, was unquestionably Zhu Xi. In the long history of Confucianism, perhaps no individual has had more influence over its development, outside of the two great masters, Confucius and Mencius. Zhu Xi "gave Confucianism new meaning and for centuries dominated not only Chinese thought but the thought of Korea and Japan as well," wrote scholar Chan Wing-tsit in his classic anthology of Chinese philosophy. "Virtually every cardinal Confucian concept was brought to a higher peak by Zhu Xi."[16]

Zhu Xi never attained such stature during his lifetime, however. Born to a police officer in 1130 in Fujian Province, he passed the civil service exams and became a scholar-official in the Song Dynasty. But he preferred the cerebral life of writing and studying to slaving away in the bureaucracy and served for only nine years. Even that stint was rocky: Zhu Xi followed Confucius's example of lecturing his superiors—and alienated them in the process. In 1181, he was demoted to a minor post after complaining to the emperor about the incompetency of his officials. In scholarship, though, Zhu Xi had no equal during his age. A prolific writer, he authored commentaries on the Confucian classics as well as original works. Zhu Xi's book *Family Rituals*, a must-have how-to guide for respectable families, played a key role in spreading Confucian household customs throughout East Asia. Historian Kuhn praised Zhu Xi's 1176 treatise *Reflections on Things at Hand* as "the first and best-organized presentation of Chinese philosophical knowledge up to that time."[17] Much of Zhu Xi's teaching, though, did not originate with him. His major contribution was synthesizing the varied ideas of previous Neo-Confucians into the "Learning of the Way"—a coherent Confucianism that was more unified than it ever had been before.

The focus of Zhu Xi's Confucianism was understanding the "principle," or *li*, both in one's self and in all other things. Everything possesses *li*, which comes from Heaven and thus connects each individual to the universe and to everything else. Principle is both universal and distinct, part of a whole but in specific things holding individual characteristics. Zhu Xi called principle in its universal form the "Supreme Ultimate." "There is only one Supreme Ultimate, yet each of the myriad things has been endowed with it and each in itself possesses the Supreme Ultimate in its entirety," Zhu Xi explained. "This is similar to the fact that there is only one moon in the sky, but when its light is scattered upon rivers and lakes, it can be seen everywhere."[18] In humankind, principle is one's moral nature, Zhu Xi said, and following Mencius, he believed it was inherently good. The *li* cannot be readily perceived by the physical senses, however, since it has no form, and one can discover it only by engaging in intensive study and self-cultivation—that is, through "the investigation of things." A sage is one who is able not only to see his own *li* but also to understand how it connects to other *lis*—in other words, to comprehend the unity between man and all things in the cosmos.

Standing between man and sagehood, however, is the *qi*. All things in the universe are made of *qi*, and the shape *qi* takes is determined by its *li*. But the *qi* also obscures the *li*. By creating human passions, the *qi* distracts man from perceiving the true *li*. Only by overcoming these worldly desires can a man become a sage. The goal is to enhance one's benevolence, since through the pursuit of that most important of virtues, one purges oneself of the selfishness that blocks the mind from understanding principle. Through extreme self-discipline and cultivation, the individual was to strive to reach a state of consciousness that would enable him to discern good from evil instantaneously and then act based on that judgment in a way that was just as natural as seeing or hearing. One method of achieving this state was "quiet-sitting"—a fancy Confucian term for meditation—which could produce in the dedicated a revelatory experience. "The learner, as he comes upon the things of this world, must proceed from principles already known and further fathom them until he reaches the limit," Zhu Xi said. "After exerting himself for a long time, he will one day experience a breakthrough to integral comprehension. Then the qualities of all things, whether internal or external, refined or coarse, will all be apprehended and the mind, in its whole substance and great functioning, will all be clearly manifested."[19]

In forging these ideas, Zhu Xi and his Neo-Confucian colleagues borrowed liberally from the Buddhism they so detested. The practice of meditation as a route to discovering the truth, the idea that a sort of enlightenment can be attained by understanding the workings of the cosmos, and the belief that suppressing desires is the route to personal betterment were all adopted from their rival religion. But unlike Buddhism, Neo-Confucianism retained the very worldly purposefulness emphasized by Confucius. This Neo-Confucian enlightened man was not supposed to withdraw from society, as the Buddhist monks did, but to fulfill his destiny by employing his knowledge in solving the problems of society. Just as Confucius in his own life resisted calls from recluses to renounce the world, the Neo-Confucians insisted that the path to true sagehood could be found only in the real world through intensive learning matched to social activism. The quest to be the proper Neo-Confucian involved cultivating the self in order to perfect the world. "The sagely ideal was meant to inspire heroic self-sacrifice on the part of all," one modern study of Chinese philosophy explains. "Neo-Confucianism reasserted in an even more far-reaching manner what Confucius and his followers had always taught—that the human sense of order and value does not leave one alienated from the universe but is precisely what unites one to it."[20]

Zhu Xi's version of Confucianism may seem to deviate greatly from what Confucius himself had taught. But that's not how Zhu Xi and his Neo-Confucian colleagues saw it. They were convinced that they had rediscovered the long-lost true teachings of Confucius. "As for our master Confucius, though he did not attain a position of authority, nevertheless his resuming the learning of the past sages and imparting it to later scholars was a contribution even more worthy than that of [the sage-kings]," Zhu Xi commented. Not all of his Confucian colleagues at the time agreed with him, however. Zhu Xi was widely vilified during his own day. Other reformers, echoing Confucius himself, thought his metaphysical musings of little practical relevance. "In a situation where the peace of the world depends on taking great revenge for ruler and father, they [Zhu Xi's followers] simply raise their eyebrows and, their hands in their sleeves, talk about human nature and destiny," complained one court official in an 1178 memorial to the throne. "They do not know what human nature and destiny are really like." Zhu Xi was accused of propagating "false learning." He and his ideas were banned by the Song in 1196; there was even a call for Zhu Xi's execution.[21]

Zhu Xi, though, had the last laugh. In the decades after his death in 1200, his teachings gained in popularity, mostly within private academies. Zhu Xi's influence redirected Confucian scholarship to a different set of core texts. The basis of Confucian education since the Han Dynasty had been the Five Classics; Zhu Xi selected a smaller subset of writings that he believed offered the best guidance for those hoping to achieve the moral self-cultivation so crucial to the Neo-Confucian project. Called the Four Books, they include the *Analects*, *Mencius*, and two chapters excised from *The Book of Rites* and awarded independent stature: *The Great Learning* and *The Doctrine of the Mean*. All four were much more directly linked with Confucius and his disciples than the original Five Classics. Zhu Xi's elevation of Mencius is what firmly established his views within the Confucian orthodoxy. (Mencius had finally won his long-running argument with Xunzi over the nature of man.) Along with Zhu Xi's doctrines, the popularity of the Four Books also rose over time, and today they are considered the most important Confucian texts.

Persistent admiration for Zhu Xi led the Song to partially rehabilitate him after his death, but he was no more than tolerated within the dynasty's official circles. It took a change of regime to elevate Zhu Xi and his teachings to the forefront of the Confucian movement. Ironically, that new dynasty was formed by the northern "barbarians" that Zhu Xi and his Neo-Confucians had tried so desperately to keep out of China. After losing China's northern heartland to invading Jurchens, the Song's southern bastion was overrun by Genghis Khan's grandson Kublai, who proclaimed the Yuan Dynasty in 1271.

As an outsider ruling China, Kublai Khan had no choice but to rely on the Song's Confucian bureaucracy to manage his new empire. Confucian scholar-officials at the Yuan court began agitating for a reinstatement of the national civil service exams, which had been suspended in the later years of the Song. But they advocated for a reformed version of the exams based on Zhu Xi's Learning of the Way. "The proper method for the recruitment of scholars is through classical studies that fulfill the Way of Self-discipline for the Governance of Men," one official told the throne in 1313. Under the traditional exams, he said, "scholars have become accustomed to superficiality. Now what we propose . . . will emphasize virtuous conduct and an understanding of the classics. If scholars are chosen in this way, they will all be the right kind of men."[22]

The Yuan emperor at the time was convinced, and that same year, the court ordered the reintroduction of exams, with the Four Books to be given special prominence alongside the Five Classics. Zhu Xi's commentaries were also designated as the standard interpretation for the purpose of judging the candidates' answers. Thus the Mongols made Zhu Xi's version of Confucianism effectively the state orthodoxy, a stature it would retain until the end of the imperial age six hundred years later. Zhu Xi's supporters were triumphant. One proclaimed that the court's decision was nothing less than "the greatest blessing that has come to scholars throughout the ages."[23]

THE INFLUENCE OF Confucius spread well beyond the borders of China. Confucian ideas may have started to infiltrate China's neighbors way back in the days of the Han Dynasty, but it was the Neo-Confucian movement that caused the sage's teachings to become more firmly ingrained throughout East Asia, especially from the fourteenth century. In some cases, Confucianism was transplanted by Chinese immigrants who carried their family rituals and ceremonies with them to their new homes in Thailand, Indonesia, Malaysia, the Philippines, and elsewhere in the region. Yet it was not only the Chinese who were attracted to Confucius. His teachings traveled far and wide in the region on their own account and affected government policy, education, social mores, family practices, philosophical development, and moral standards.

The expansion of Confucianism beyond China's borders is part of the wider influence Chinese culture has had on the rest of Asia. China was the biggest, richest, most powerful, and advanced society in East Asia for much of recorded history, and what happened there naturally spilled over its borders into its neighbors. The art, architecture, languages, literature, governing systems—and, of course, philosophies—of other East Asian societies were heavily influenced by Chinese styles, preferences, and ideas. Both Japan and Korea adopted Chinese characters in their writing systems, for instance. Political scientists call this sort of clout "soft power"—the method by which a country or society can exert its sway over others without direct diplomatic engagement or use of force. Confucius has long been China's chief soft-power practitioner, an ambassador for his country. In promoting Chinese culture, he posthumously crafted an image of China as an advanced, even superior society, enhancing the weight that China carried in regional and global affairs.

Perhaps no other nation has been shaped by Confucius more than Korea. The doctrine may be more entrenched there today than in China itself. Confucius's teachings may have first traveled to the Korean Peninsula during the reign of Emperor Wu.[24] The ambitious monarch planted a colony of Chinese in what is now Pyongyang, and its occupants may have brought Confucian texts with them. Confucian doctrine seems to have already held sway with the Korean imperial regime in the first century AD. King Taejo of the Goguryeo (Koguryo) Dynasty, whose long reign supposedly lasted from AD 53 to 146, proclaimed in his "Ten Rules of Governing" that the court should be guided by benevolence and the Confucian "kingly way." The Goguryeo also opened a Confucian college, perhaps as early as the late fourth century. But Confucianism was something of a fringe philosophy in Korea during the first millennium AD. Buddhism dominated, and Confucius's teachings were confined mainly to academies and government offices and had minimal impact on greater society.

That changed with the arrival of Neo-Confucianism in the thirteenth century. The person credited with carrying the doctrine to Korea—literally—is a scholar-educator named An Hyang. One old Korean history tells us that An "was solemn and composed, and everyone held him in awe. . . . He always held the promotion of learning and the nurturing of worthies to be his duty."[25] An was introduced to Neo-Confucianism in 1286 while on an official visit with the king of the Goryeo (Koryo) Dynasty, then the dominant state on the Korean Peninsula, to the court of Kublai Khan in Beijing. Ironically, the Mongol conquest of China had opened Korea up to Chinese culture more than ever before. Although Goryeo had not been conquered by the Mongols, it was forced to become a tributary state to the khans after a series of devastating wars. The courts of the Yuan and Goryeo, at its capital of Kaesong, became linked more closely than any previous Chinese and Korean dynasties.

On this diplomatic mission, An Hyang read Zhu Xi's writings for the first time, and he was instantly enthralled. "When An first got to see them [Zhu Xi's works], he absorbed himself in them and respected them greatly," according to an ancient biography. "He recognized that they represented the true tradition of Confucius and Mencius, whereupon he copied them by hand . . . and brought everything back home."[26] Upon his return to Korea in 1289, he started propagating Zhu Xi's brand of Confucianism within the court and the academies. The consequences for Korea were momentous.

The Koreans were attracted to Neo-Confucianism for many of the same reasons that Chinese scholars were, especially its combination of a practical program of national reform with the spiritual pursuit of human perfection. The philosophy arrived in Korea at an especially auspicious moment. By the thirteenth century, the Goryeo Dynasty was becoming wobbly, and the Korean Confucians, like all Confucians in times of disarray, were eager to find a way to restore order and strength to the country. They were no more enamored of the Buddhists and their hold on religious life in Korea than the Chinese Neo-Confucians were, and Zhu Xi's metaphysical synthesis provided a possible Confucian alternative. The Korean Neo-Confucians were also discovering China's ancient sage-kings in the pages of the Confucian classics, and, much like their Chinese counterparts, they were mesmerized by them. Following in the footsteps of Wang Anshi, they were inspired to try to re-create that society in the Korea of their times through an active and aggressive reform agenda. A group of Neo-Confucian scholar-officials set about to "Confucianize" Korean society from the top down.[27]

These officials had a bit of success forcing through reforms during the last years of the Goryeo, but it was only after a new dynasty emerged that they got a real opportunity to implement their plans. In 1388, Yi Seong Gye, a military commander, turned his army on Kaesong and effectively claimed power over the government. Four years later, he deposed the last Goryeo king and ruled in his own name, shortly thereafter proclaiming the Joseon (Chosun) Dynasty, which would endure for five hundred years. The new king and the Neo-Confucians forged a partnership from the earliest days of the dynasty. The number of scholar-officials committed to Confucian reform was relatively small, but some of their leading figures held key positions at court and commanded Yi's ear. The interests of the royal house and the Confucian scholars dovetailed nicely. Yi Seong Gye needed to restore vitality to the government and required an ideology with which to justify his rule. The Confucians not only sincerely believed that Confucianism, applied with vigor, could save the nation, but also saw government promotion of Confucian reforms as a route to solidifying their own stature and power. Much like Cheng Yi and his peers in the Song court, the Korean Confucians considered themselves the guardians of wisdom on good government, and they believed that gave them the right to dominate state policy.

With the support of the new dynasty, the Confucians were able to exert their influence not only over the government, but also Korean society generally. What followed was a torrent of new laws and regulations that altered nearly every aspect of life in Korea. The legislation was carefully crafted, or so the Neo-Confucians thought, to copy the practices of the ancient sage-kings of China as recorded in the Confucian canon. In the process, many practices

common to Confucian China—but unfamiliar to Korea—were forcibly installed by Joseon lawmakers. Ancestor worship, not practiced previously, was
mandated for government officials by Confucian reformers in 1390, during
the waning years of Goryeo, and reinforced in the first Joseon legal code,
promulgated in 1397. Obsessed with forging Confucian-style patrilineal
families, policymakers instituted a series of measures that, combined with
other economic factors, altered existing patterns of inheritance and the suc-
cession of family leadership, so that power and wealth became passed down
through eldest sons. There was no question as to the government's commitment to the Confucian agenda. In 1421, a royal edict was issued commanding the crown prince himself to worship at the Confucian shrine.

Not all of these reforms were welcomed by Koreans. The Confucians,
for instance, were frustrated that government officers were slow to build
the halls necessary for ancestor worship. But over the centuries, under relentless pressure from the scholar-officials, Confucian marriage, mourning,
inheritance, and other rituals took root. Known today as "traditional" Korean culture, such rites and practices are, in reality, foreign imports, imposed
by Confucian reformers who were obsessed with the supposed golden age
of a foreign civilization. The result was a country transformed into what its
creators intended to be a model Confucian world. As the scholar Martina
Deuchler has noted, "the scholar-officials [in Korea] succeeded in reshaping
the sociopolitical environment to an extent the Song Neo-Confucians would
never have dreamed possible."[28]

CONFUCIANISM ALSO CROSSED the Sea of Japan. Traditionally, the Japanese
have believed Confucianism was introduced to their islands by a Korean
scholar named Wang In who, probably in the early fifth century, carried a
copy of the *Analects* with him when he arrived to tutor a prince. This tale
is disputed by some scholars who suspect that knowledge of Confucianism drifted to Japan earlier than that. Whenever they arrived, the teachings had minimal impact on the country for much of its history. Not even
the Neo-Confucian reformation registered in Japan. Although Zhu Xi's
Neo-Confucian synthesis was known in Japan in the thirteenth century, its
study was confined mainly to Zen Buddhist temples, where the monks reveled in the similarities it shared with their own practices.

The prospects for Confucianism in Japan improved significantly with the
formation of the Tokugawa shogunate in 1603. Tokugawa Ieyasu, its military founder, has been painted by Japanese historians as a natural Confucian

who was committed at an early stage to the sage's teachings. "Ieyasu had conquered the nation on horseback, but being an enlightened and wise man, realized early that the land could not be governed from a horse," the *True Tokugawa Records* tell us, in an account reminiscent of the lesson learned by the first emperor of the Han Dynasty. "He had always respected and believed in the Way of the Sages. He wisely decided that in order to govern the land and follow the path proper to man, he must pursue the path of learning."[29]

Ieyasu's interest in Confucius was inspired by many of the same factors that had led Emperor Taizu of China's Song Dynasty to embrace the sage. Ieyasu had unified Japan after years of war and disorder, and he was looking for ways to enhance the legitimacy of his shogunate and restore stability to the country. Confucianism, with its long, successful history as part of China's imperial system, could, he believed, achieve both aims. Ieyasu thus sought out Confucian scholars, most notably Hayashi Razan, a former monk who had taken the unusual step of renouncing Buddhism to devote his life and studies to Neo-Confucianism. During a 1605 audience, the new shogun peppered Hayashi with questions about China. Whereas Ieyasu's confused Buddhist attendants could offer only vague or incomplete responses, Hayashi easily provided the shogun with precise answers. "This youngster knows a lot," Ieyasu exclaimed, and he hired Hayashi as one of his advisers.[30]

Hayashi would serve the first four Tokugawa shoguns, and he relentlessly promoted the sage's teachings against his numerous Buddhist rivals inside the new Tokugawa court. His efforts bore fruit. The third shogun, Tokugawa Iemitsu, allocated funds for Hayashi to open an academy in the capital, Edo (today's Tokyo), which became the primary center for Confucian learning in Japan. Over the course of the 1600s, Confucianism became a primary source of guidance for the Tokugawa shoguns. Tokugawa Tsunayoshi, the fifth ruler, routinely lectured his ministers on Neo-Confucianism at court.

It is likely, however, that the story of Confucius in Tokugawa Japan had much more complicated beginnings. Much like the tale of Emperor Wu's Confucian conversion, the story of Ieyasu's devotion to Confucianism was probably highly exaggerated by Hayashi and his later followers to elevate the influence Confucius commanded during the early years of the shoguns. Modern scholars believe that Confucianism was just one doctrine among several in the Tokugawa court. Ieyasu and his successors maintained advisers from the Buddhist establishment and the local Shinto faith and lavished them with more funds and support than anything given to Hayashi.[31]

As in China, the influence of Confucius in Japan likely seeped into government and society slowly, propelled by many historical factors and urged on by many officials. Historian Kiri Paramore concluded that Confucianism only became firmly embedded into the Tokugawa state almost two centuries after Ieyasu's reign, a result of a Confucian-inspired policy program that came to be called the Kansei Reforms.[32] These policies were spearheaded by a feudal lord named Matsudaira Sadanobu after he became the shogunate's chief counselor in 1787. Matsudaira, who was well-read in Confucian philosophy and Chinese history, believed that a strict dose of Confucian ethics could restore strength to the challenged shogunate and uplift sagging national morale. He exhorted the samurai class to engage in serious Confucian study, curtailed excessive government spending, and launched a puritanical campaign to bolster public morality by banning pornography and mixed-sex bathhouses.

Matsudaira, though, is best known for his attempt to suppress intellectual debate in Japan, which he believed was leading people astray. "Who shall support scholarship if this superfluity of scholars—one could count them by the dozen and ship them by the cartload—continue to argue and abuse one another with their various theories, like the bubbling of boiling water or the twisting of strands of thread," he once complained.[33] With that in mind, he issued an edict in 1790 to the headmaster at Hayashi's Confucian school, banning "heterodox" teachings and mandating that only Zhu Xi's version of Confucianism be studied at the academy. The edict stamped Neo-Confucianism as something of an "official" ideology for the shogunate. This standardized Neo-Confucian education became the backbone of a new, Chinese-style civil service examination system, introduced in 1792, which aimed to breed professional bureaucrats for the regime's expanding administration.

Confucianism, though, never received the sort of state largesse in Japan that it had in China, and the scale of the Japanese exam system never matched that of its Chinese counterpart. Nevertheless, Confucianism managed to penetrate Japanese society, its literature, family traditions, religious life, and intellectual discourse.

BY THE EIGHTEENTH century, Confucius's position in government and society was unassailable across much of East Asia. Students and intellectuals around the region were hunched over the *Analects*, *Mencius*, and Zhu Xi's commentaries. Households operated on the strict rules of hierarchy and separation of the sexes that formed the cornerstone of Confucian family practice. Government officials sacrificed to the sage in countless temples. Confucius had truly become the "Uncrowned King."

The court of China's Qing Dynasty, founded in 1644, was itself a symbol of Confucius's dominance. The royals were not Chinese, but Manchus, a northern tribe the locals would consider "barbarians." But the new emperors embraced Confucius with an ardor every bit as strong as that of their subjects. In fact, the early Qing went to great lengths to support Confucius in an effort to appeal to the Chinese elite, supporting Confucian scholarship and undertaking massive projects to collect and publish compendiums of traditional texts. Sinologist James Legge handed down to us a description of a typical Qing ceremony honoring Confucius in which the emperor himself would kneel before the sage's shrine at Beijing's Imperial University, touching his forehead to the floor. "Great art thou, O perfect sage!" he would declare. "Thy virtue is full; thy doctrine is complete. Among mortal men there has not been thine equal. All kings honor thee. Thy statutes and laws have come gloriously down." At this point in the ceremony, with the spirit of Confucius believed to be present, offerings were made and a prayer was read by an attending official. "I, . . . the emperor, offer a sacrifice to the philosopher Kong [Confucius], the ancient Teacher, the perfect Sage, and say,—O Teacher, in virtue equal to Heaven and Earth, whose doctrines embrace the past time and the present, thou didst digest and transmit the six classics, and didst hand down lessons for all generations!"[34]

Yet even as the Qing engaged in these tributes, Confucius's position in East Asia was not as secure as it appeared. In fact, cracks were beginning to appear in the pedestal on which so many emperors had placed the great sage. The Chinese empire, once so advanced, had fallen behind nations that its elite had perceived as hopelessly uncivilized. New foreign technologies and ideas began to threaten China's political and social system—and the stature of the man who created them.

Chapter Four

Confucius the Oppressor

Confucius lived in a feudal age. The ethics he promoted
is the ethics of the feudal age.
—*Chen Duxiu*

Rarely had China endured such humiliation in its thousands of years of history. In April 1895 in the town of Shimonoseki in Japan, Chinese and Japanese negotiators signed a treaty ending a brief but costly war between the two Asian nations. The conflict was barely a contest. What began as a dispute over hegemony in Korea a year earlier had left China's armed forces in tatters and its expensive new navy at the bottom of the ocean. The Japanese had easily invaded Manchuria in China's far northeast, steamrolling over an army that was supposed to have been modernized and equipped with the latest weaponry. In the embarrassing peace agreement, China gave up all claims over Korea, which Beijing had long considered a vassal state; agreed to pay a massive indemnity; and ceded the island of Formosa (today called Taiwan) to Japan. A haughty Beijing had always seen Japan as a backward civilization; now the great Chinese empire was humbled by people they considered barbarians. How far China had fallen.

The ignominious settlement generated horror, shock, and confusion in China, and for some Chinese, reinforced the belief that the country had to change to survive. One was a Confucian scholar named Kang Youwei. For him, the defeat was just more proof that the drastic reform he had been preaching for years was more critical to the nation's future than ever before. The defeat to Japan was just the latest in a long series of humiliations that the once mighty empire had suffered at the hands of foreigners. For Kang, it was the final straw. In Beijing at the time of the peace treaty, he convinced 1,300 civil service exam candidates to sign a petition to the Qing court protesting against it. Then Kang and his supporters launched a "study society" to mobilize the educated into a more coherent movement to agitate for reform.

Kang believed that China's elite, buried in their classics and studying for old-fashioned exams, had their minds too fixated on the distant past to confront the pressing problems of the day. "Our enfeebled China has been lying in the midst of a group of strong powers and soundly sleeping on the top of a pile of kindling," he wrote. "Her scholars specialize in the study of antiquity, not in the understanding of the present. . . . O you closed-door scholars, are some of you coming to the point of speaking about respecting the emperor and rejecting the barbarians? If you do, not only the teachings of the sacred Qing dynasty, the two emperors, the three kings, and Confucius, but also the four hundred millions of the people will have something to rely upon." If steps were not taken, and quickly, Kang worried, the Chinese would fall prey to imperialist powers, as had other peoples around the world. "It will not be long," he predicted, "until we become Turks and Negroes."[1]

Kang's actions were a turning point in China's history. Liang Qichao, his most talented student, proclaimed that Kang had sparked "the beginning of the 'mass political movement' in China."[2] Kang helped to unleash the political energies of the Chinese people, a process that would come to have tremendous consequences for China—and Confucius.

China had been struggling to respond to the new challenge from belligerent foreigners for much of the 1800s. The country had fought and lost two Opium Wars with Great Britain—the first of which, in the early 1840s, had cost the Chinese the island of Hong Kong. During the second, which lasted from 1856 to 1860, British troops looted and burned the beloved imperial Summer Palace on the outskirts of Beijing. The French, Germans, and Russians had joined the British in extracting "unequal treaties" from China that gave them control of parcels of Chinese land, special trade concessions, and other rights. With its loss to Japan, China had sunk to its lowest point yet. It was bad enough that the country had been whipped by Western barbarians; it was even worse that it had fallen to another Asian nation that not long before had also been a Confucian-influenced society preyed upon by foreign powers. As the twentieth century approached, China was at risk of being carved up like a plump turkey into foreign-controlled colonies.

The embarrassing defeats spurred a painful process of soul-searching among the Chinese elite. For much of its history, China had been the mightiest and richest power in East Asia, a leader in technology, art, medicine, and—thanks to Confucius and other brilliant thinkers—philosophy. However, the one-sided victories of the European powers had exposed how badly

China had fallen behind. Even more terrifying, the rise of the West posed not merely a political, economic, and military challenge to imperial China, but an ideological one as well. Western gunboats and trade agents had brought with them dangerous new ideas about democracy and human rights as well as new doctrines such as capitalism and Christianity. European missionaries were already scouring the countryside, seeking converts and criticizing Chinese traditions. The ascent of the West was threatening China's ancient institutions and beliefs—its civilization itself. Past invaders, including the Qing's own ruling Manchus, had been absorbed and co-opted by Chinese culture once they had settled down in the country—they had all been converted into Confucians. The West presented a very different face to China: for the first time, a foreign force was claiming that it was superior not only militarily and technologically but also intellectually and culturally. Westerners believed that their political systems, religions, and cultural attributes were at the pinnacle of modernity, and their ears were deaf to Confucius's message. China had never before confronted such a threat to the philosophical foundations of its government and society.

How to contend with that challenge dominated Chinese political and social discourse for much of the nineteenth century. The debates were, to a great degree, a battle between Confucians. There was widespread consensus among those of influence in the Qing that the preservation of Confucius was vital to the survival of China and its civilization, but officials and scholars did not agree on how to protect Confucius. They argued furiously over the type and nature of the reform needed to strengthen the nation and what Confucius himself might have done to rescue a failing China. Kang Youwei was on the radical end of the Confucian spectrum. He advocated a sweeping renovation of the Chinese imperial system through the importation of Western practices. Cherished institutions that had in the past served China so well, he said, simply had to go. Kang proposed transforming the Qing Dynasty into a Western-style constitutional monarchy, complete with an elected assembly, and changing the educational system to emphasize more modern, practical learning.

Nevertheless, Kang, a devoted Confucian, still placed the Supreme Sage at the center of his reform program. He was motivated by his highly unorthodox interpretation of Confucius's teachings and an equally unusual characterization of Confucius himself. No longer, in Kang's eyes, was the sage an arch-traditionalist, borrowing his teachings from bygone antiquity, but a messiah pointing the way into an enlightened era of peace and harmony. Kang was driven by the inspiration that he was carrying on Confucius's mission.

Kang's actions would lead to a series of events that brought him close to power but also had unforeseen consequences that would reverberate for decades. Unintentionally, his ideas, and the wider debate over the role of tradition in a modernizing China, brought into question, for the first time in centuries, the primacy of Confucius in Chinese society. How to repair a broken China became a question of what to do with Confucius and his enduring influence. The future of China again became inseparable from Confucius, what role he should play in politics and society, what the proper understanding of his philosophy should be, and what should be done with his legacy. Confucius would emerge from the other side of these debates a very changed sage.

How China and the West had so dramatically changed places remains one of the great riddles of history. For much of the Common Era, China was far more advanced than the West in technology and science. As Europeans were slogging through the feudal backwardness of the Middle Ages, the Middle Kingdom was inventing gunpowder and the compass. But by the nineteenth century, the fortunes of East and West had reversed. The Industrial Revolution, the emergence of modern capitalism, and post-Enlightenment achievements in science transformed European nations into the world's most advanced, while China remained an agrarian museum of premodern industries and academies, isolated from a rapidly changing world by xenophobic regimes. The Chinese had had all of the advantages in wealth and know-how, but somehow they had squandered them. What had gone so, so wrong? Or, as British historian Joseph Needham first scribbled on a letter in 1942, "Sci. in general in China—why not develop?"[3] Finding the answer became his obsession, so much so that the conundrum came to be called the Needham Question.

Needham and others have proffered many theories to explain China's technological stagnation—and inevitably Confucius got slapped with some of the blame. The Confucians' "contribution to science was almost wholly negative," Needham charged in his seminal work, *Science and Civilization in China*. That problem started with the great sage himself. "Interest in natural phenomena is first awakened by surprising or startling departures from the natural course of things," Needham explained. "Confucius had no intention of being drawn into a discussion of such phenomena, which seemed to have no bearing on the problems of human society. And for two thousand years, his followers adopted his example."[4]

Needham used Confucius's own words against him. Citing one passage in the *Analects* that says Confucius never spoke of "extraordinary things," Needham argued that the sage lacked the kind of curiosity in the natural world necessary to spark scientific experimentation. Needham also highlighted another case when Confucius was critical of a student who expressed interest in husbandry and agriculture to prove that the master failed to grasp the importance of scientific knowledge and discouraged his students from seeking it. "A small man, indeed, is Fan Xu!" Confucius said after the disciple left the room. "If a superior man loves propriety, the people will not dare not to be reverent. If he loves righteousness, the people will not dare not to submit to his example. If he loves good faith, the people will not dare not to be sincere. Now, when these things obtain, the people from all quarters will come to him, bearing their children on their backs—what need has he of a knowledge of husbandry?"[5]

Other scholars blamed the Confucian social structure for preventing the educated from engaging in the sort of tinkering and experimenting that could generate new creations. The Confucian gentleman was first and foremost a scholar, and scholars should be found buried in their books, not wasting their efforts in workshops or laboratories. Confucian education, critics also contended, combined with the Confucians' preference for government service, stood at the root of China's problems. The best and brightest in China, eager to pass the civil service examinations, were encouraged to devote their studies to memorizing and analyzing the *Analects*, not probing mathematics or the sciences.[6]

However, in the nineteenth century, when China was searching for a way to contend with the imperialist West, few in China blamed Confucius for the country's failings or questioned the continuing relevance of Confucius to Chinese life. Some Confucians were convinced that the solution to China's woes was, in essence, *more* Confucianism. In this view, China's problems were not caused by traditional Chinese culture or governing institutions, but by the moral deficiencies of the people who governed. The solution was to intensify Confucian indoctrination and bring officialdom back to the Confucian Way. This line of argument touched on a long-standing theme in Confucian thinking—good men were more important than good institutions to achieving good government. With China's ethical core strengthened, the entire country would rise again. Importing foreign ideas, institutions, or even technologies was not only useless, but dangerous. By luring the Chinese away from Confucius, foreign know-how would cut the very heart from the nation.

Woren, the Qing court's grand secretary and a leader of the conservative faction in the mid-1800s, made this case in an 1867 memorial to the throne. "Astronomy and mathematics are of very little use," he protested. "If these subjects are going to be taught by Westerners as regular studies, the damage will be great. . . . Your servant has learned that the way to establish a nation is to lay emphasis on rites and rightness, not on power or plotting. The fundamental effort lies in the minds of people, not in techniques. . . . From ancient down to modern times, your servant has never heard of anyone who could use mathematics to raise the nation from a state of decline or to strengthen it in time of weakness." Without Confucius, Woren argued, the Chinese would become the slaves of the West: "The only thing we can rely on is that our scholars should clearly explain to the people the Confucian tenets. . . . Now if these brilliant and talented scholars . . . have to change from their regular course of study to follow the barbarians, then the correct spirit will not be developed, and accordingly the evil spirit will become stronger. After several years it will end in nothing less than driving the multitudes of the Chinese people into allegiance to the barbarians."[7]

The reform faction fought back just as hard. To them, China would be doomed if it did not learn from the West and adopt Western technology and practices. They mocked Woren's ideas as naïve. Moral exhortations alone would not defend China from the barbarians; only modern weaponry and knowledge would, they countered: "If he [Woren] has no other plan than to use loyalty and sincerity as armor, and rites and rightness as a shield, . . . and if he says that these words could accomplish diplomatic negotiations and be sufficient to control the life of our enemies, your ministers indeed do not presume to believe it."[8]

Initially, the goal of the reform movement was not, however, an overhaul of China's Confucian system, but the defense of it. The reformers saw no contradiction between using Western ideas to modernize China's schools, economy, and government and the continuation of the nation's Confucian traditions. Zhang Zhidong, an imperial official who was both an ardent Confucian and a reformer, stressed "Chinese learning for substance, Western learning for function." He warned that China should not confuse its ancient institutions with its ancient teachings; the government could be reformed with China's Confucian culture fully intact. "Law and institutions are that with which we meet changing situations; they therefore need not all be the same," Zhang wrote. "The Way is that upon which we establish the foundation; it therefore must be uniform." Zhang and other reformers believed that if Confucius had confronted the problems of their day, he would not have stubbornly insisted on maintaining old practices, but would have joined in the movement for change. Opponents of reform "do not know that the Way of the sages is valued only because it can make proper accommodations according to the times," wrote influential journalist Wang Tao around 1870. "If Confucius lived today, we may be certain that he would not cling to antiquity and oppose making changes."[9]

DESPITE THE FIERCE resistance of the conservatives, the case for reform could not be dismissed. China lay prostrate before the Western powers; if the country didn't fight fire with fire, who knew what could happen. The Qing government opened schools teaching Western science and technical skills, sent students and diplomats around the world to learn foreign ways, built a modern army and navy, and promoted new industries. China was finally joining the modern world by copying the ways of the West.

But China's defeat in the war with Japan made it all too clear that the reforms had not gone far enough, which handed more ammunition to those who called for a more radical restructuring of China's government and society, such as Kang Youwei.

Kang believed that simply buying a few modern guns or educating a handful of Chinese students in Western skills was insufficient to resurrect China. The country had to match the West, not just in the caliber of its cannons, but also in the strength of its institutions that made those cannons and other aspects of modernity effective. China's entire society—the Qing administration, education, even religious observances—had to be reformed in fundamental ways. Confucius, too, required a reformation. Strengthening the role of Confucius in Chinese society was the only way to revive and protect China.

But the Confucius of the empire was no longer the Confucius China needed. So Kang, like so many other Confucian scholars throughout Chinese history, conjured up a new Confucius to meet the demands of a new age. By Kang's reckoning, previous efforts to revitalize the country had failed because the government had merely grafted imported know-how onto the rotting imperial regime. The true solution to China's problems required much deeper change—Confucius's teachings needed to be merged with foreign ideas to form a more potent mixture capable of propelling China into the modern world. A combination of traditional Chinese culture and globalization would end China's misery and launch the nation into a brighter era.

Kang arrived at his synthesis after experiencing a personal crisis. Like other sons of prominent families, Kang immersed himself in the study of the Confucian classics as a young man, aiming to pass the civil service examinations. But Kang grew restless and began to question the purpose of cramming for the exams. "My intelligence and comprehension became confused, for every day I was buried amid piles of old papers, and I developed a revulsion for them," he remembered in his memoirs. "Thus I gave it up and in my own heart I fancied seeking a place where I might pacify my mind and decide my destiny. Suddenly, I abandoned my studies, discarded my books, shut my door, withdrew from my friends, and sat in contemplation, nurturing my mind."[10]

It was then, when deep in meditation, that Kang had a (very Neo-Confucian) revelation. "All of a sudden I perceived that Heaven, earth, and the myriad things were all of one substance with myself, and in a great release of enlightenment, I beheld myself a sage and laughed for joy; then suddenly I thought of the sufferings and hardships of all living beings, and I wept in melancholy."[11] Kang's epiphany propelled him on a (very Confucian) quest for learning. He traveled to Hong Kong and Shanghai, where he marveled at the bustling modern cities, and began devouring Western philosophical and historical texts. In the process, he devised a Confucianism that would have been unrecognizable to the great sage.

Kang saw the world progressing through stages, eventually entering the Age of Great Peace (or Unity), in which all conflicts and troubles would evaporate in universal love. This period would arise as the process of globalization continued, with modern technology tying nations together to create one unified world. All distinctions between people would vanish, and everybody would become equal. "There will be a day when everything throughout the earth, large or small, far or near, will be like one," Kang wrote. "There will no longer be any nations, no more any racial distinctions, and customs will be everywhere the same. With this uniformity will come the Age of Great Peace." Kang used this utopian vision as the rationale for the drastic reform of China. "It is therefore necessary to propagate the doctrines of self-rule and independence, and to discuss publicly the matter of constitutional government," he contended. "If the laws are not reformed, great disorder will result."[12]

Kang went to great lengths to link his theories to Confucius in order to give his agenda doctrinal legitimacy. He claimed that Confucius had predicted the coming of the Age of Great Peace in the classical texts. Kang's notion of universal love was, in his mind, a broadening of Confucius's core virtue of benevolence, which began in the family and then was meant to extend to the rest of humanity. Kang wrote that benevolence "means that the way of men is to live together. . . . It is the power of love."[13]

But Kang took Confucius's thinking in directions that knocked away the very foundations of his philosophy. Confucius had believed that a just and prosperous society was built on strong institutions—the family and the state. In Kang's vision of the Age of Great Peace, such institutions were an impediment to progress and had to be eliminated. "If we wish to attain the beauty of complete equality, independence, and the perfection of (human) nature, it can [be done] only by abolishing the state, only by abolishing the family," Kang contended. Coming out strongly against marriage, Kang said he thought it better for a man and woman to cohabitate for only a year and then switch partners than to enter into a permanent union. The results of such a process would have made the prudish Confucius blush. "As there are no husbands or wives," Kang said of his new society, "there is no quarrel over women, necessity to prevent adultery, suppression of sex desires."[14]

Kang also transformed Confucius in a way that would lend support to the cause of reform. In his 1897 book *Confucius as a Reformer*, the great sage is no longer a purist striving to reconstruct order in China on the cherished principles of antiquity, but an avid change-agent who refashioned the country. "Every founder of doctrine in the world reformed institutions and established laws," Kang wrote. "Chinese principles and institutions were all laid down by Confucius. His disciples received his teachings and transmitted them so that they were carried out in the country and used to change the old customs." That's why Confucius "was a godlike sage king," he wrote. "He is . . . the most accomplished and perfect sage in the history of mankind." Kang wished to establish Confucianism as a state religion modeled along the lines of Christianity, with Confucian "churches" and a clergy watched over by a state Ministry of Religion. Instead of reading passages from the Bible in Sunday services, Confucian priests would preach from the *Analects*. Kang, believing that Christianity was behind Europe's success, even tried to equate Confucius with Christ.[15]

Many of Kang's ideas sound very un-Confucian. How could a devotee of the sage ever conceive of Confucianism without the family at its heart? Or without filial piety or saintly kings? But Kang and his disciples, like so many Confucians before them, contended that Confucius had been badly misunderstood over the centuries, and that they had finally discovered what the great sage *really* intended. Confucius, they believed, never meant to support the imperial government—he was a democrat. He abhorred hierarchy and preached egalitarianism. Confucius was nothing at all like what he had become. "When Confucius first set forth his teachings, he discarded the ancient learning, reformed existing institutions, rejected monarchism, advocated republicanism, and transformed inequality into equality," wrote Kang's disciple Tan Sitong. Confucian scholars, Tan continued, had irresponsibly allowed the great sage to be kidnapped by the imperial establishment to justify its archaic and repressive rule. Some Confucians "forgot entirely the true meaning of Confucius's teaching but clung to its superficial form," he wrote. "They allowed the ruler supreme, unlimited powers and enabled him to make use of Confucianism in controlling the country."[16]

Kang's version of Confucianism rocked the Confucian establishment. Kang's disciple Liang Qichao declared that the impact of his works was like "a cyclone . . . a mighty volcanic eruption and huge earthquake," and compared him to Martin Luther.[17] Kang was just as controversial among the Confucian conservatives as Luther had been among Catholicism's cardinals. They vilified Kang as a threat to China's future. To them, his proposed reforms would mean replacing Confucianism as the philosophical core of Chinese government and culture. That was something they simply could not accept.

Zhu Yixin, a well-regarded Confucian scholar, accused Kang of appropriating the sage's name to forward a misguided plan to remake China with foreign ways. "By referring to Confucius as a reformer, your real intention is to facilitate the introduction of new institutions," Zhu wrote. "The accounts of Confucius as a reformer come from apocryphal texts and cannot be wholly believed. But even if the sage has spoken thus, he was only taking a simple pattern and elaborating upon it in order to return to the ancient institutions of the . . . sage-kings. How could he have intended to use 'barbarian ways to reform China?'" Foreign ideas, Zhu continued, ran counter to the basic principles of Confucius's teachings and would bring disaster to China. "Do you mean that the classics of our sages and the teachings of our philosophers are too dull and banal to follow, and that we must change them so as to have something new? . . . Barbarian institutions are based on barbarian principles. . . . Now, instead of getting at the root of it all, you talk blithely of changing institutions. If the institutions are to be changed, are not the principles going to be changed along with them?" The true solution to China's problems, these conservatives argued, could only be found in the moral repair of the country and its leaders. "The path to good government is, above all, the rectification of the people's minds-and-hearts, and the establishment of virtuous customs. The perfecting of institutions should come next."[18]

At the heart of the conservatives' argument against Kang was their insistence that Confucius's teachings remained superior to all others. "An examination of the causes of success and failure in government reveals that in general the upholding of Confucianism leads to good government while the adoption of foreignism leads to disorder," an official named Ye Dehui wrote. "The essence of Confucianism will shine brightly as it renews itself from day to day.... Only fools would say that Western religion excels Confucianism. Insofar as there is morality, there must be Confucianism."[19]

KANG'S MISHMASH OF ideas looked more and more appealing as China became increasingly desperate near the end of the nineteenth century. Although the imperial government had initially harassed Kang and his followers, the Qing emperor, Guangxu, and a handful of court officials became willing to listen to his radical ideas as the foreign powers continued to hover over a stumbling China like hungry vultures. Just as Confucians had done for centuries, Kang sent memorials to the throne, pleading with the emperor to support his ideas. "Your majesty knows that under the present circumstances reforms are imperative and old institutions must be abolished," Kang implored in early 1898. "After studying ancient and modern institutions, Chinese and foreign, I have found that the institutions of the sage-kings . . . were excellent, but that ancient times were different from today."[20] Kang proposed drafting a constitution and urged the emperor to personally spearhead rapid reform by bypassing the obstructive bureaucracy.

Kang got Emperor Guangxu's attention. On June 16, 1898, Kang was summoned to his first personal meeting with the emperor. The two talked for five hours, with Kang promising that his methods would restore China's wealth and power. "The prerequisites of reform are that all the laws and the political and social systems be changed and decided anew, before it can be called a reform," Kang told the emperor. "Now those who talk about reform only change some specific affairs and do not reform the institutions." Kang went on to attack the old-fashioned examination system as the root of China's ills. "The trouble today lies in the non-cultivation of the people's wisdom, and the cause . . . lies in the civil service examinations," he said. The candidates "do not read the books written since the Qin and the Han, nor do they investigate the facts about all the nations on the globe. . . . Today, among the numerous array of ministers none of them can adapt himself to circumstances."[21]

Impressed, the emperor granted Kang the unusual privilege of sending memorials directly to him, thereby allowing the Confucian scholar to circumvent the hostile court bureaucrats. Kang's conference with Guangxu led to a radical shift in imperial policy called the Hundred Days' Reform. Edicts, some of them probably penned by Kang, began gushing from the imperial court. The emperor's orders aimed to strengthen the military, promote industrialization, and found a new national university. The standard essays of the exam system were replaced with discourses on current affairs. In August, the emperor began abolishing certain government offices and announced his intention to further reorganize the structure of imperial state.

These measures, however, posed a direct threat to most of the vested interests within the Qing—a bureaucracy jealous of its prerogatives and control over policy; court eunuchs and officers marginalized by the emperor; and, most of all, Emperor Guangxu's imperious aunt, the empress dowager Cixi. On September 21, she led a coup against the emperor, reasserting her own control over the Qing government. Emperor Guangxu was forced into solitary seclusion. Cixi reversed most of her nephew's proposals and then exacted her revenge on the reformers, even executing some of them. Kang managed to escape to safety in British-controlled Hong Kong. In an imperial edict issued in 1901, she called Kang and his disciples "rebels" and his policies "less reform laws than lawlessness."[22]

COULD KANG YOUWEI and his unorthodox brand of Confucianism have saved the empire? That question is impossible to answer. But after Cixi's coup, the dynasty continued to falter until the abdication of the last Qing emperor in 1911. China's imperial age had come to an end 2,100 years after the First Emperor of the Qin had unified China. The collapse of the Qing Dynasty ushered in a period of war and political chaos that lasted for the next seventy years and cost tens of millions of lives.

Much like Confucius in the fifth century BC, the country's new politicians, writers, and thinkers searched for ways to repair China. Unlike Confucius, however, many found the answers not in the traditions of Chinese antiquity, but in the rejection of tradition. That meant the rejection of Confucius. No longer would reformers battle over which incarnation of Confucius could save the nation. Now they determined that the only way to rebuild China was to get rid of the great sage once and for all. Confucius became a symbol of everything that was wrong with China, the cause of the country's decay and decline. He was the man standing between the Chinese and the modern world.

The impetus for this critical shift in the biography of Confucius was a nationalist upsurge among China's youth in the wake of the collapse of the Qing Dynasty. Attempts to unify China under a republican government faltered, and the country was fractured into fiefdoms controlled by warlords. Students and other young people in China became impatient for reform and modernization. On May 4, 1919, the discontent boiled over into a massive protest in central Beijing against China's feeble response to the Treaty of Versailles (which ended World War I). They were furious that the Chinese delegates had failed to prevent the British and their allies from awarding Japan rights over Chinese territory previously held by the war's loser, Germany. But what became known as the May Fourth Movement was much more than a street march. It was an intellectual revolution.

To the young writers and activists associated with the movement, the only way to salvage a fallen China was to uproot the influence of what Hu Shi, one of May Fourth's most creative figures, called "Confucius and sons." Anti-Confucius slogans chanted by the protesting students—"Destroy the old curiosity shop of Confucius!"—became the soundtrack of the movement. "Confucius lived in a feudal age. The ethics he promoted is the ethics of the feudal age," blasted Chen Duxiu, one of the founders of the Chinese Communist Party, in 1916. "The objectives, ethics, social norms, mode of living and political institutions did not go beyond the privilege and prestige of a few rulers and aristocrats and had nothing to do with the happiness of the great masses." To Chen and others, Confucius's teachings were simply incompatible with modern political ideals. "In order to advocate Mr. Democracy, we are obliged to oppose Confucianism, the codes of rituals, the chastity of women, traditional ethics and old-fashioned politics," Chen penned in 1919. If China didn't rid itself of Confucianism, the nation would end up under the thumb of the imperialistic West. "It is plain that those races that cling to antiquated ways are declining, or disappearing," Chen wrote in 1915. "Now our country still has not awakened from its long dream, and isolates itself by going down the old rut. . . . I would much rather see the past culture of our nation disappear than see our race die out." Just because Chinese tradition had originated with its ancient sages did not mean it was worth anything in modern times, Chen argued. "That which brings no benefit to the practical life of an individual or of society is all empty formalism and the stuff of cheats," he went on. "And even though it was bequeathed to us by our ancestors, taught by the sages, advocated by the government and worshiped by society, the stuff of cheats is still not worth one cent."[23]

Another influential writer, Lu Xun, chose to assault Confucian culture through fiction. His classic short story "Diary of a Madman" from 1918 purports to be written by a man who at first appears to be insane. He believes that his neighbors, and even his older brother, are trying to eat him. However, it quickly becomes apparent that the diarist is being consumed figuratively—by oppressive Chinese traditionalism, imposed by his own family and townspeople. They look at him with hostile eyes because he questions Chinese social norms. If, he laments, others would stand up against tradition, the oppression of Chinese society would cease, but the pressure to conform is too overwhelming. "How comfortable life would be for them if they could rid themselves of such obsessions and go to work, walk, eat and sleep at ease," the narrator says. "They have only this one step to take. Yet fathers and sons, husbands and wives, brothers, friends, teachers and students, sworn enemies and even strangers, have all joined in this conspiracy, discouraging and preventing each other from taking this step." He comes to the horrible realization that "I have been living all these years in a place where for four thousand years they have been eating human flesh."

Another Lu Xun story, published in 1919, is named after the main character, Kong Yiji, an elderly Confucian scholar who failed to pass the civil service exams and descended into poverty. He is relentlessly mocked and taunted by heckling townsfolk. Kong, we're told by the narrator, "used so many archaisms in his speech, it was impossible to understand half he said"—that is, he repeats Confucius's words, which only elicits guffaws. With no other means of support, Kong is reduced to stealing, though he refuses to acknowledge his crimes, and each time he arrives in the tavern where the narrator works, he has more scars on his face from the beatings meted out to him as punishment. He is last seen crawling out of the tavern on his hands, and is later presumed dead. Kong Yiji is Lu Xun's stand-in for Confucian literati, who, in his view, were unaware of the damage they had done to the world or the fact that they had become laughingstocks.[24]

Since Kong Yiji shares the same family name as Confucius, it is easy to speculate that Lu Xun meant to be passing judgment on the old sage himself. Some of the attacks on Confucius by China's new writers were surprisingly personal. No longer the Supreme Sage possessed of supernatural powers, a paragon of moral virtue, or a fount of boundless wisdom, Confucius now became "the living, erring, struggling, inconsistent mortal," writer Lin Yutang said in a 1930 speech. Examining Confucius's life as revealed in the ancient texts, Lin remarked that "we find Confucius doing many things that shocked both decency and respectability." Furthermore, Lin added, "I think no modern girl would marry a man if she knows beforehand that he is going to be as exacting and fastidious as Confucius." So great were Confucius's sins that Lin could think of no honest justification for them. "When I see those ardent defendants of Confucius trying to invent excuses for his scandals or to disprove them against the evidence of the *Analects* itself, I always picture to myself a forty-year-old clerk trying to jump over high hurdles. It happens, however, the scandals are so many and the hurdles are so high that these Confucian clerks never had a chance."[25]

MAO ZEDONG IMBIBED this rabid anti-Confucianism, and when he defeated the US-backed Nationalists in 1949 and founded the People's Republic of China, he declared war on Confucius. To the Communists, Confucius was a dangerous counterrevolutionary, an elitist from a feudal age who oppressed the toiling classes and constructed the social order that exploited them. In Mao's eyes, China could not move forward into a glorious new age of communism with the sage's influence still so pervasive. China, Mao wrote in a famous 1940 essay called *On New Democracy*,

> has a semi-feudal culture which reflects her semi-feudal politics and economy, and whose exponents include all those who advocate the worship of Confucius, the study of the Confucian canon, the old ethical code and the old ideas in opposition to the new culture and new ideas. Imperialist culture and semi-feudal culture are devoted brothers and have formed a reactionary cultural alliance against China's new culture. This kind of reactionary culture serves the imperialists and the feudal class and must be swept away. Unless it is swept away, no new culture of any kind can be built up.[26]

Under Mao that sentiment became official state policy. He launched the most concerted assault on Confucius in Chinese history. For almost the entire second half of the twentieth century, the Chinese were deprived of the knowledge of their own philosophical heritage and history. A society once dominated by the great sage became ignorant of the man, his ideas, and his moral mission. Ceremonies venerating Confucius that had been a routine feature of Chinese life for almost two millennia were banned. The new state orthodoxy became Marxism, and Mao's *Little Red Book* replaced the *Analects* as China's must-read philosophical text. Confucian books vanished from Chinese classrooms; Confucian scholars were hunted down like criminals and tossed into work camps; Confucian temples were vandalized; relics were burned. The doctrines of Confucius "are a reactionary ideological system embodying the old thinking, old culture and old traditions," blasted a 1975 article in the *Peking Review*. "Reactionaries in the past adapted and remolded them continuously for use in ruling and corrupting the people and in maintaining the decadent economic base and reactionary political rule. . . . The doctrines of Confucius . . . which advocate hanging on to the old and restoration and retrogression must be demolished and traditional concepts of the exploiting classes must be destroyed; only then can the new ways of the proletariat be established and the communist revolutionary spirit brought into full play."[27]

THE RED GUARDS were the foot soldiers in Mao's war on Confucius. Unleashed in 1966 when Mao launched his destructive Cultural Revolution, the Red Guards, mostly students, swept across China rooting out what they saw as vestiges of the nation's corrupted, pre-Communist past, or the "four olds"—old customs, old habits, old culture, and old thinking. Their quest was often a violent one. The Red Guards beat up professors, intellectuals, and less radicalized members of the government; smashed temples; and destroyed ancient relics. Although today many Chinese regret the upheaval caused by the Cultural Revolution, at the time these youngsters believed they were on a lofty mission to help Mao destroy an old, enfeebled China and usher in a modern, enlightened age without corruption, oppression—or Confucius.

No one represented the "four olds" more than Confucius himself, and the great sage became enemy No. 1 of the Red Guards. Soon after the Cultural Revolution began, the radicalized students targeted Qufu, Confucius's hometown, which has three of the most important historical sites in Confucianism—the sage's tomb, the Temple of Confucius, and the old mansion of the Kong family. To the Red Guards, eliminating the "four olds" could not be complete without destroying these three Confucian sites. The struggle that ensued in Qufu over the second half of 1966 was representative of the attacks on Confucius taking place nationwide.[28]

The trouble in Qufu began on the night of August 23, when members of the local Communist Party leadership were awakened in the middle of the night with terrible news. Red Guards from a naval academy had smashed old stelae and defaced inscriptions on the cliffs of a nearby mountain and were headed their way, intent on obliterating the three famous sites. Qufu's leaders were gravely concerned. What the Red Guards considered the lethal "four olds," the Communists of the historic town saw as priceless national treasures and a source of local pride. The Qufu cadres sprang to action to protect the Confucian relics.

Choosing to fight the Guards with Mao's own rhetoric, local students hung banners on the temple's main gate that read, "Long live the proletarian Cultural Revolution!" and "Emergency brigades arise, prevent all destructive activities of the class enemies!" Nearby, at the Kong Family Mansion, members of a local agricultural organization began to guard the house. They wore strips of red cloth on their chests that read, "We are poor farmers," hoping to appeal to the Red Guards' class preferences. After the sun rose on the 24th, Qufu Country Committee Secretary Li Xun told an assembly of local officials that the State Council, the governing body in Beijing, had listed the Qufu sites among the country's protected cultural relics, and he vowed to uphold the law. "These sites are truly invaluable, not only in China, but in the world," Li explained. "No person may casually destroy them." At the same time, though, Li and the rest of the Communist leadership in Qufu were worried about an ugly confrontation with the Red Guards, and Li pleaded with the local residents to avoid violence. When the Red Guards arrived, he said, "we must reason with them, engage them in revolutionary dialogue, and send them safely on their way."[29]

The Red Guards, however, were fanatical, organized, and quick to resort to force, and they were unlikely to be turned back by a friendly debate. What was about to take place in Qufu was a struggle between two visions for the course of the revolution. The Red Guards believed that anything standing between China and its grand Communist future must be eradicated, even if that meant challenging the authority of the Chinese state itself. Li Xun and his colleagues believed the revolution depended on upholding that same state. Ironically, that meant that Li was willing to use Communist ideas to defend a man—Confucius—who had been deemed a counterrevolutionary by the Communists. Yet Li did not perceive his protection of the Confucian sites as a defense of Confucius or Confucianism. More than two decades later, Li told a journalist that he believed that Confucius was "a symbol of feudalism," but had felt compelled to preserve the Confucian relics in Qufu in order to protect national property and, through that, national order.[30]

Soon after Li Xun issued his instructions, events were already turning against him. The Red Guards of Qufu Normal University, who originally backed Li's efforts, switched sides. Embarrassed that Red Guards from elsewhere were coming to Qufu to eliminate the "four olds" in their own backyard, these Qufu Guards decided to take matters into their own hands. The next day, the 25th, the Qufu Red Guards marched to the Kong Family Mansion and found staff members of the Cultural Relics Management Committee there, who blocked them from entering. A county magistrate, Wang Huatian, told the Guards that the mansion was under the direct protection of the national government. "Whoever tries to destroy anything here is violating the law," he warned.[31] The Red Guards refused to back down. "Topple Old Kong's watchdog!" they yelled. Then some workers in the employ of the relics committee came to Wang's defense. Like their ancestors before them, they were responsible for caring for the Kong sites, they told the Guards. One elderly worker lectured that Chairman Mao had never said the ancient sites were part of the "four olds." The workers, with their impeccable class pedigree, were able to convince the Red Guards to withdraw.

But not for long. On the night of the 26th, the Red Guards made another attempt to enter the mansion, yelling slogans like "Topple Old Kong." This time they were confronted by the Peasant Red Guards, a revolutionary farmers' group. The contending forces debated and argued, and then a scuffle broke out. A few students got dragged onto the mansion grounds and beaten. After 1 a.m., the Red Guards staggered back to their dormitories.

The defenders' victory proved fleeting. Over the succeeding weeks, the fate of the Confucian sites morphed from a local to a national issue when the more powerful Red Guards of Beijing came to the aid of their outgunned comrades in Qufu. On November 9, one of the four main leaders of the capital's Red Guards, Tan Houlan, led two hundred members from Beijing Normal University to Qufu, determined to rid the nation of the Kong sites. Soon after her arrival, Tan and a contingent of supporters appeared at the offices of the county committee, whose officials welcomed her graciously in an attempt to defuse a potential confrontation. Tan, though, was not in a conciliatory mood. She read a statement to the assembled crowd, listing Confucius's supposed crimes, and then insisted that the historical monuments in Qufu be destroyed so that Mao's revolutionary thought could prevail. "Pull the 'Uncrowned King' off his horse and smash him to a pulp!" she demanded. "Burn the Confucian scholars, flatten the Kongs' graves, hand out the Kong sycophants and the reactionary 'authorities' who worship Confucius, and parade them through the streets!"[32] In response, the members of the committee began reciting some works of Mao. In a strange turn of events, both sides employed the Communist leader's rhetoric to support their contending positions.

The Qufu officials were quickly put on the defensive. When Tan toured the Kong Family Mansion, her industrious Guards uncovered flags of the Nationalist Party, a Nationalist manual on how to uproot Communists, and other incriminating items that exposed the Kongs, in the minds of the Guards, as enemies of communism. In the political climate of the day there was no way to explain this evidence away, and the country committee officials were thrown into a panic. Fearing a Red Guard onslaught on the Confucian sites, they tried to hide valuable relics the best they could, burying sacrificial vessels and old photographs, hiding paintings, and sinking sculptures into a well. On November 11, the committee also decided to consult the State Council to gain support in their confrontation with the Red Guards.

That hope was quickly dashed. In the wee hours of the morning of November 12, they received a message from the Communist Party Central Cultural Revolution Leadership Committee ordering that the three Kong sites be protected as mementos of the feudal past of Confucius and his family, but also recommending that the party "renovate" the Temple of Confucius. Most fatefully, the reply gave the Red Guards permission to exhume Confucius's grave. Upon hearing that news, Tan realized she had the upper hand. In the tradition of long-winded Communist rhetoric, she immediately formed the "National Red Guard Revolutionary Rebellion Contact Station for the Utter Crushing of the Kong Family Shop and the Establishment of the Absolute Authority of Mao Zedong Thought," the purpose of which was to encourage the Red Guards in Qufu and around the country to participate in the attack on Confucius. Soon after that, the position of the Qufu officials was completely undercut by their provincial superiors, who ordered them to stand down. Now there was nothing to stop the Red Guards.

On November 15, the destruction of the Confucian historical sites began. One group of Red Guards ransacked the Temple of Confucius. They slit the throat of the statue of Confucius in the main shrine, then tore into its belly and pulled out old books and coins. Other statues were knocked over and ripped open, too, and ancient copies of the *Analects* and other classics were removed and destroyed. Then the Red Guards called a county-wide, two-day ceremony in Qufu to mark the final victory over Confucius, ordering all work to stop so that everyone could attend. On November 28, the first day of the big event, the Red Guards dumped the mangled statue of Confucius into the back of a truck, its face smeared in red paint. A paper hat was placed on the statue that read: "Topple the No. 1 Hooligan Old Kong!" It was paraded through town, then brought to a small bridge not far from Confucius's gravesite. A bonfire had already been set below, and, amid chants from the

Red Guards, the statue was tossed into the flames, along with countless old books, paintings, and other relics.

Two days later came the ultimate insult to the great sage. Confucius's grave was dug up and the tomb cracked open. Workers removed the stone slabs of the grave with shovels and ropes, their mouths covered with masks in case the long-sealed coffin emitted noxious fumes. His remains were exposed, although, as he had been dead for nearly 2,500 years, the Guards found only dust. Perhaps that was the point—to prove to the Chinese people that there was nothing left of China's greatest sage.

THE SACRILEGE IN Qufu was just the start of Mao's assault on Confucius. In 1973, he personally endorsed the "Anti-Confucian Campaign," which vilified the sage more savagely than ever before. Confucius was used as a stand-in for any enemy of the Communist regime, most notably a onetime party heavyweight named Lin Biao. The former general had been considered Mao's most likely successor—until 1971, when he died in a mysterious plane crash. Mao claimed that Lin Biao had been plotting to overthrow him, and in an effort to purge Lin's supporters from the government, the deceased was tarnished as a secret disciple of Confucius. Government media revealed that one of Lin's crimes had been to hang a proverb of Confucius on a wall in his office. A deluge of state-produced booklets, posters, and other propaganda linked him with the old philosopher. Images showed the two collaborating on all sorts of evil schemes, their twisted bodies sometimes filled with weapons or snakes. But the depictions also showed them paying the price for such designs. Lin and Confucius were illustrated being decapitated by workers with axes; a cover of one booklet had their heads dripping with blood or tears. The government issued an illustrated booklet of children's songs entitled *Heavy Gunfire for Criticizing Lin Biao and Confucius: Selected Children's Songs for Shanghai Little Red Guards*. One ditty, "Target Practice," written for second-graders, tells the heartwarming tale of a little boy and girl who use straw effigies of Lin and Confucius to learn to aim and fire rifles. The two revolutionary youngsters "send Confucius flying to heaven," the last line goes.

Such violent imagery was common in the propaganda and poster art of the time. Confucius was routinely associated with death and decay. Often he was portrayed as a frail old man, or just a skeleton; sometimes he was shown with tombstones, skulls, and coffins. Propagandists twisted the honorary titles bestowed on Confucius during imperial times. One picture showed a tombstone substituting the usual "Perfect Sage and First Teacher" with "Perfect Sacrificial Victim, the First to Die."

Confucius had reached his lowest point in Chinese history since the days of the Qin Empire. In fact, Mao boasted that he did more to destroy Confucius's influence than Qin Shihuangdi, the despised First Emperor, had with his infamous "Burning of the Books" more than 2,000 years earlier. The Qin emperor "only buried alive 460 scholars, while we buried 46,000," Mao told party cadres in a 1958 speech. "In our suppression of the counter-revolutionaries, did we not kill some counter-revolutionary intellectuals? I once debated with the democratic people: You accuse us of acting like Qin Shihuang-di, but you are wrong; we surpass him 100 times."[33]

MAO'S ASSAULT, COMBINED, as we'll see, with the impact of globalization and westernization, had eroded Confucius's influence in Asia to a degree that would have been unthinkable just a few decades earlier. By the 1960s, "Confucianism was a dead subject in East Asia for all but a few scholars who could easily be written off as antiquarians," wrote the great American scholar William Theodore de Bary. "Virtually off-limits to any kind of serious study in Mao's China, Confucianism survived elsewhere, it was often said, only as a museum piece."[34]

That may have been true in academic circles and government offices. But in other ways Confucius was very much still alive. After century upon century of Confucian education and indoctrination, ridding Asian society of the great sage was not so easy. His ideas had become embedded in East Asian cultures, such a natural part of life that people adhered to them almost automatically. What emerged in the second half of the twentieth century was an international debate over Confucius, his legacy, and the role he should, or should not, play in a modern society.

Part Two

Confucius at Home,
But Not at Ease

Chapter Five

Confucius the Father

Give your father and mother no other cause for anxiety
than illness.

—Confucius

Vincent Lo is a Hong Kong tycoon, except on Sunday evenings. The scion
of a prominent business clan, he founded the real estate company Shui On
Group, which develops shopping malls, office complexes, and apartment
towers across China. The demands of his empire keep him on airplanes constantly as he looks for new opportunities to increase his $2.7 billion fortune.[1]
Yet wherever he might be, whatever deals he might be pursuing or financial affairs he must settle, Vincent always tries to make his way back home
to Hong Kong on the weekends for Sunday dinner with his ninety-three-
year-old mother, Lo To Lee-kwan. "The family is very important," Vincent
explains. "My father was very dutiful to my grandfather and grandmother.
He always preached to us that we had to respect our elders."[2]

Vincent and his eight siblings take their father's admonition very seriously. One sweltering June evening, the dining room at Vincent's mother's
house, which is perched on Victoria's Peak on Hong Kong Island, is crammed
with Vincent's brothers and sisters, grandchildren and great-grandchildren—
four generations in all. Vincent's son, Adrian, fresh from his graduation from
Trinity College in the United States, is there as well, not out with friends or
playing video games as most young people in America would be on Sundays.
"I can't think of life without Sunday family dinners," Adrian says. "With my
[American] friends in college, when they turned seventeen or eighteen, they
just wanted to move out [of their parents' house]. There wasn't so strong a
sense of belonging with the family."

The Los' dinners aren't quite as traditional as they used to be, however. Vincent's late father, Lo Ying-shek, used to dominate the proceedings. Vincent recalls how he and his siblings sat quietly staring down at their plates while their father lectured them on the importance of education and discussed their futures. Such scenes were (and still are) common throughout the region. Vincent describes his dad as "a typical Chinese father." Ying-shek continues to hector his children from the grave. Framed calligraphy from his own brush, hanging on a wall near the dining room, contains homespun advice that reads like the family's own *Analects*. One implores them to work hard and be frugal, another to always study and learn.

With their father no longer lording over the dinner table, and since nearly everyone in the family has been educated in the United States or Australia, the evenings have absorbed some less severe Western characteristics. The youngest children no longer nervously stare at their food but play and romp cheerfully, while those at the table erupt into a cacophony of competing stories, arguments, and opinions. A noisy debate breaks out over the next family vacation. Mom Lo, even at her advanced age, still takes a trip once a year, and much of the clan joins her. The next journey was supposed to be to Singapore, but Vincent suggests a change of plans, warning the family of the terrible air pollution there from forest fires in nearby Indonesia. That sparks a raucous discussion on where to go instead. Only Mom can silence the siblings. Though not as commanding as their father used to be, Vincent's mother, as the matriarch, is the foremost authority in the room, and when she speaks, the rest listen. In some other ways, too, the family remains surprisingly conservative. Three of Vincent's brothers live with their wives at their mother's house, which has been divided into four apartments. Vincent and his siblings bow to their mother to show their respect twice a year—on her birthday and Chinese New Year. "We have the best of both worlds," Vincent says. "We are quite westernized, but we still maintain the traditions."

Those traditions are pure Confucius. The sage has had his greatest impact on Asian society through his influence over the family. It is hard to imagine an American CEO worth billions scheduling dinner with Mom as a weekly priority, or even more, still living with her. But in East Asia, family responsibilities generally carry more weight than in the West. That's because no single Confucian teaching has been drummed more persistently into East Asian minds over the past 2,000 years than the sage's vision of the ideal family. Confucius created families bound tightly together by mutual responsibility. Parents are fiercely committed to supporting and educating their children, and children are expected to care for their parents in their old age. The practice of abandoning elderly parents to live alone, so common in the West, is still stigmatized as shameful. Confucius also forged a very strict pattern of hierarchical relations within families. The father, aloof and stern like Vincent Lo's, demands deference from his children but at the same time cares deeply about their futures. The mother is subservient to her husband, but still a commanding force in the household and a strong, loving figure deserving of reverence. The children, eager to please and follow their parents' wishes, often place the needs of their father and mother above their own. Such devotion doesn't even end with their parents' deaths. Children are expected to venerate the spirits of their parents through the practice of ancestor worship.

Aspects of this Confucian family might feel very familiar. Dominant fathers are common to traditional families in India, the Middle East, and even the West. Children everywhere are taught to obey their parents. The fifth of the Ten Commandments, after all, instructs "Honor thy father and mother"—words that could easily have come directly from Confucius's mouth. In more modern times, children in the West have been told that "Daddy knows best" and "Children should be seen but not heard." Teenagers who won't do their homework or who break curfews are labeled rebellious. Every culture stresses the importance of good family relations and encourages multigenerational cohesion. I have fond childhood memories of spending Sunday lunch each weekend at my grandparents' house. My grandfather, the proprietor of a small restaurant, prepared piles of pierogi and meatballs and steaming bowls of chicken soup for the table.

Still, Confucius's perfect family is one aspect of his thought that is quite foreign to the Western experience. What makes Confucianism different is the centrality of the family to the entire philosophy, the primacy that Confucius placed on loyalty to parents over every other obligation in society, and the extreme lengths to which familial relations evolved under his influence. To Confucius, the family was nothing less than the foundation of a happy and healthy world. If the family is strong, peaceful, and, as the Confucians like to say, "well regulated," then all of society will be strong and peaceful—and therefore prosperous. On the flip side, if families were in disorder, all of society would similarly tumble into chaos. While Confucius is renowned for his views on good government and spoke endlessly about sage-kings, the true Confucian society is not lorded over by a domineering state, but by paternalistic fathers, each controlling his own brood. All sorts of human behavior and institutions have been shaped by Confucian ideas about the family. "The family system is the root of Chinese society, from which all Chinese social characteristics derive," explained writer Lin Yutong in 1936. "Face, favor, privilege, gratitude, courtesy, official corruption, public institutions, the school, the guild, philanthropy, hospitality, justice and finally the whole government of China—all spring from the family and village system, all borrow from it their peculiar tenor and complexion, and all find in it enlightening explanations for their peculiar characteristics."[3]

The well-regulated Confucian family is built on the concept of filial piety, or *xiao*. It is fair to say that filial piety lies at the core of Confucius's entire philosophy. In the good Confucian family, children are always supposed to be filial, or deferential, toward their parents and put their parents' interests and needs above their own. Filial piety became the primary yardstick by which Confucians judged a person's moral qualities. In fact, Confucians came to believe that filial piety was the foundation of all other virtues and the basis of proper social behavior in all aspects of life. If you were a child who revered your parents, you would also be a loyal citizen, an honorable gentleman, and a devoted spouse.

The Confucians expended a lot of ink detailing how children were to behave toward their parents. The rules governing filial piety became minute, strict, and indelible. The power that parents commanded over their children was nearly absolute. In premodern China, children had practically no freedom of action. Parents decided who their sons and daughters would marry, what careers they would pursue, even where they would live. "There are very few choices and very few uncertainties" in the Chinese family, wrote anthropologist Francis Hsu in 1971. "All routes are, so to speak, barred except one, that which follows the footsteps of his father, his father's father, and the whole line of his more remote ancestors. Along the established path, life is agreeable; all other trails lead to misery and self-destruction."[4] There were seemingly no limits to the obligations of filial piety in Confucian society. Beginning in the Tang Dynasty (618–907), for instance, the Chinese even practiced a sort of "filial cannibalism." If a parent was suffering from an incurable disease, a reverent child would cut off a bit of flesh from his or her own body, cook it, and feed it to the sick parent.

Granted, few went to such extremes, but what makes Confucian filial piety so important to East Asia today is just how pervasive its influence has been and continues to be. Historian Keith Knapp wrote that filial piety "has shaped nearly every aspect of Chinese social life: attitudes toward authority, patterns of residence, conceptions of self, marriage practices, gender preferences, emotional life, religious worship and social relations."[5] Simply put, Confucian filial piety determines a person's place in the world and forges the very structure of East Asian society. Nearly every human relationship has taken on a familial quality—the connection between the government and the governed; the management of East Asian companies; and patterns of social interactions between just about any two people who meet, whether at the office, at a party, or on the street.

There is always a "father" nearby who deserves deference—your boss at work, a teacher, the ruler of a state, any older person who happens to be nearby. Relationships generally take on a superior-to-subordinate nature, similar to that between father and son. What has resulted is a society constructed as a hierarchy. Your status relative to the person in front of you determines how you should act toward him or her. Are you older or younger? Do you hold a loftier job title, or are you closer to the bottom of the corporate ladder? Confucius believed that all people have prescribed roles to play in society based on who they are and what they do, and that society would be peaceful if each person understands and fulfills his or her designated role. That's why Confucianism has sometimes been labeled "a religion of names." The obsession with status continues to this day. Walk into any business meeting in East Asia and you'll find that the first requirement is to exchange name cards—the title printed on them instantaneously determines your position in the meeting versus everyone else.

The pervasiveness of filial piety has made it a target of fierce criticism. Filial piety, and the confining hierarchy it created, have been lambasted for generating all sorts of abuses—stifling entrepreneurship, encouraging playground bullying, inhibiting corporate competitiveness, even laying the groundwork for authoritarian governments. "The effect of the idea of filial piety," one twentieth-century critic complained, "has been to turn China into a big factory for the production of obedient subjects."[6]

In many respects, the debate over the role of Confucian filial piety in a modern society rages on to this day. Although some families, like the Los, revel in their balanced mixture of Confucian and Western family values, traditionalists lament that Western individualism is undermining the strength of society and leading to ills like abandoned senior citizens and delinquent teenagers. Others believe the purging of Confucian filial piety hasn't gone far enough; it continues to impede the independence and initiative necessary for a twenty-first-century society. Even those who still wish to adhere to Confucian family traditions are often embarrassed to admit it, fearful of appearing old-fashioned or anti-modern. Even today, in a world awash in globalization, it's impossible to understand East Asian culture and society without understanding filial piety and the role it plays in Confucius's thinking.

CONFUCIUS DID NOT invent filial piety in Asia. Archeological evidence suggests that the Chinese were already worshipping their ancestors at the beginning of the third millennium BC. By the early period of the Zhou Dynasty, some five centuries before Confucius, the concept that serving one's parents was a moral responsibility was well established. Confucius did leave his imprint on the idea, however, and probably contributed to a fundamental reformation of its meaning. He saw filial piety as much more than simply offering material support or honoring one's parents. To him, truly fulfilling one's filial duties required being reverent, deferential, and obedient as well. Confucius makes that point crystal clear in the *Analects*. "Nowadays for a man to be filial means no more than that he is able to provide his parents with food. Even hounds and horses are, in some way, provided with food. If a man shows no reverence, where is the difference?" On another occasion, Confucius said: "Give your father and mother no other cause for anxiety than illness." Most direct of all, one time when he was asked about filial piety, Confucius simply stated: "Never fail to comply."[7]

Fulfilling one's filial duties was far more difficult than Confucius made it sound. Confucius and his later followers dreamed up all sorts of rules to follow and rituals to perform. Honoring filial responsibilities was a never-ending pursuit that lasted a person's entire life and shaped most major life decisions. One Confucian text has the sage explain that "the service which a filial son does to his parents is as follows: In his general conduct to them, he manifests the utmost reverence. In his nourishing of them, his endeavor is to give them the utmost pleasure. When they are ill, he feels the greatest anxiety. In mourning for them, he exhibits every demonstration of grief. In sacrificing to them, he displays the utmost solemnity." Filial piety was so important, Confucius believed, that it should determine where children resided and worked. "When your parents are alive, you should not go too far afield in your travels," he admonished. Dutiful sons were to make economic choices based on their filial duties as well. "They are careful of their conduct and economical in their expenditure—in order to nourish their parents," he once recommended.[8]

Children's filial obligations did not even end at their parents' deaths. The true test of devoted children was whether they continued to follow their father's wishes after he passed away. "Observe what a man has in mind to do when his father is living, and then observe what he does when his father is dead," Confucius said. "If, for three years, he makes no changes to his father's ways, he can be said to be a good son." Mourning for one's parents was among the most important Confucian rituals. Confucius prescribed a lengthy three-year mourning period. During that time, "the gentleman in mourning finds no relish in good food, no pleasure in music, and no comforts in his own home. That is why he does not eat his rice and wear his finery." When a disciple argued with Confucius that three years was too long, the sage waited until the dissenter had left the room and then he snippily explained that the mandated mourning period was the least a son could do for the parents who raised him. "A child ceases to be nursed by his parents only when he is three years old," Confucius said. "Was Yu [the disciple] not given three years' love by his parents?"[9]

Over time, the rules of filial behavior became fantastically precise. One of the five Confucian classics, *The Book of Rites*, a detailed treatise on ritual practice, likely compiled in its current form during the early years of the Han Dynasty (206 BC–AD 220), instructs that at the break of dawn, the son and his wife should wash and dress themselves appropriately, and then

> they should go to their parents and parents-in-law. . . . With bated breath and gentle voice, they should ask if their clothes are (too) warm or (too) cold, whether they are ill or pained, or uncomfortable in any part; and if they be so, they should proceed reverently to stroke and scratch the place. They should in the same way, going before or following after, help and support their parents in quitting or entering (the apartment). In bringing in the basin for them to wash, the younger will carry the stand and the elder the water; they will beg to be allowed to pour out the water, and when the washing is concluded, they will hand the towel. They will ask whether they want anything, and then respectfully bring it. All this they will do with an appearance of pleasure to make their parents feel at ease.

At meals, the son is ordered to live off only the scraps that his parents leave behind. "At their regular meals, morning and evening, the (eldest) son and his wife will encourage (their parents) to eat everything, and what is left after all, they will themselves eat."[10]

How, EXACTLY, COULD sons and daughters be compelled to scratch their parents' itches and scrounge through their leftovers, and do so with "bated breath"? Generally, religious doctrines and moral codes are aimed at getting us to do things that may run counter to our personal desires, and Confucianism in many ways excelled in that endeavor. Fathers, scholars, and government officials managed to convince the sons and daughters of China that filial piety served the interests of both parents and children. In part, sons could take heart in the knowledge that, at some point in the future—if they lived long enough—they would replace their parents at the top of the Confucian family and earn their own opportunity to be king of the household. The Confucians' campaign to promote filial piety was so extensive that it was difficult for young people to reject the concept, even if they didn't look forward to the perquisites of adulthood. The importance of filial piety was drilled into the heads of children from an early age, within the home and at school. Over time, filial piety became so ingrained in the East Asian household that its practice was unquestioned. It became almost automatic, a regular part of daily life.

One of the most effective methods of pounding filial piety into young brains was the popularization of short fables that upheld children who took their duties seriously as the ultimate paragons of righteousness. These tales began to circulate widely among the educated elite in the Later Han period, and over the centuries, they became a form of folklore, told and retold in towns, villages, and homesteads throughout China and elsewhere in Confucian-influenced East Asia. Just about anybody, educated or not, could recount a tale or two. An illustrated collection of such stories entitled *The Twenty-Four Filial Exemplars*, probably written during the Yuan Dynasty (1279–1368), was one of the most popular books in Chinese history. Most of the tales describe the amazing feats of self-sacrifice that sons were willing to endure in order to fulfill their filial responsibilities. In one story, a son fights off a tiger with his bare hands to rescue his father; in another, a son allows mosquitoes to feast on his blood so the insects don't pester his resting parents. Many of the stories uphold behavior that is extreme, even disturbing. In one of the more stomach-turning yarns, a model son tastes his father's feces to gauge the seriousness of his illness.[11]

If moral suasion wasn't sufficient to convince children to be dutiful, these tales added extra incentive by claiming that those who honored their parents would see good fortune showered upon them. One story tells of a man named Shun who honored his parents even though "his father was obstinate and his mother was boorish." So impressed was the emperor of China that "he sent nine of his sons to wait on him and two of his daughters to be his wives, and later abdicated the throne in his favor." Another tells us of poor Guo Ju, who is struggling to provide enough food for both his old mother and his three-year-old son. In a gruesome filial sacrifice, Guo Ju decides to kill his son so as not to deprive his mother. "Our son is sharing Mother's food," Ju tells his wife. "Why not bury this son?" As he is digging the grave, however, he discovers a pot of gold—a gift from heaven for his filial dedication.[12]

The power of filial piety was believed to be so great that venerating one's parents could bring about miracles. One tale recounts the magical bounty that a man named Meng Zong earns through devotion to his sick and elderly mother. She wants to eat soup cooked from bamboo shoots, but it is the middle of winter, when such shoots cannot grow, and Meng has no idea how to satisfy her needs. Meng walks into a bamboo grove and begins to weep. "His filial piety moved heaven and earth," we're told. "In a moment, the earth cracked open and many stalks of bamboo shoots appeared." He collects the magical shoots and the soup he makes with them cures his mother's illness.[13]

In another story, a man named Dong Yong wishes to give his deceased father a proper burial, but he is so poor that he has to borrow the money. To pay back the debt, he pledges to work for the moneylender. On his way, he meets a woman who asks to be his wife, and she joins him in service to his creditor, who requires them to weave three hundred bolts of silk. "His wife wove for a month and then was finished," the story goes. On the way back home, "they returned as far as the locust tree where they had met, when she bade [Dong] good-bye and vanished." Dong's filial piety had convinced heaven to award him this "fairy concubine."[14]

THE INFILTRATION OF filial piety into the core of Chinese culture tells us a lot about how Confucius became the most important philosopher in East Asian civilization. A few government edicts and the earnest admonitions of a handful of scholars could not turn China into a Confucian society. That took time—centuries, in fact—and had many causes. One was the elevation of filial piety to a place of primacy in Chinese homes. Confucius may have been critical in shaping the East Asian family, but the East Asian family was also crucial to the spread of Confucianism. Filial piety was one of the teachings that made Confucius vital to the lives of regular folk in East Asia. As Confucian family practices and rituals became common in households throughout the region, the importance of and reverence for Confucius became ingrained as well.

In fact, there is something of a chicken-and-egg problem here. Did Confucius create the typically hierarchical East Asian family, or did the hierarchical East Asian family propagate the teachings of Confucius? History suggests that there were dual forces at work. The idea of filial piety became widely accepted within Chinese society as the nature of the family transformed over the centuries straddling the turn of the Common Era. Confucius's teachings on the family were adopted because they became useful to families that had to adapt to changing political and economic conditions in China. Just as Emperor Wu found Confucian principles very helpful to consolidating Han authority, the Chinese family discovered that Confucian ideas could be extremely advantageous politically, socially, and economically as well.

We tend to assume that Asian households were always large and complex. It is still common throughout much of Asia to find numerous generations living under one roof—as is the case with Vincent Lo's family. Grandparents cohabitate with their children and grandchildren. However, this was not the norm at the time of Confucius. Families tended to look more like today's—smaller groupings of four or five persons. Government policy actually encouraged nuclear families. As the Zhou imperial order disintegrated, the leaders of the Warring States wished to break down larger families into smaller units. Soldiers were mustered based on the household; the more households there were, the more men could be drafted. The Qin Dynasty (221–206 BC) was especially aggressive in employing tax measures to diminish family size.

Over the course of the Han Dynasty (206 BC–AD 220), however, the extended, multigenerational household became the ideal. There are numerous theories as to why that happened. Technological innovations in agriculture, such as the introduction of plows pulled by oxen, made farming more productive, but also labor intensive. The need for extra farmhands may have incentivized families to pool resources and live together. Another possibility is that families grew in size as the power of the Han Dynasty declined. With the heightened political uncertainty, the Chinese economy faltered, and it became imperative for families to assemble into big households in order to marshal resources. Large families possessed more leverage with local authorities and could better maneuver relatives into official state positions. Therefore, big clans tended to dominate the local political and business affairs of the areas in which they lived. What was happening was a great shift of power from the imperial state to large, influential families—and the Han were too weakened to prevent it.

Whatever the motivation, by the second century AD, the more relatives there were under one roof, the more influential the family became. Elite clans began referring to themselves as the "one-hundred mouths"— and occasionally that was literally the case. Hundreds of people could find themselves living together in gargantuan compounds—grandparents, grandchildren, brothers and their wives, cousin upon cousin. Yet holding these giant households together was extremely difficult. Sibling rivalry erupted as pressure from wives to protect the interests of their own children caused relations between brothers to fray. Sons had a clear incentive to pry themselves out from under the thumb of their fathers to start their own, independent families—and claim part of the family fortune in the process. But the material and social benefits to be gained from maintaining an extended family were so great that doing so became a priority. How, then, could fathers keep their offspring under one roof?

Enter Confucius. Patriarchs realized that they needed to enforce a strict hierarchy in which they wielded almost unquestioned authority and sons and grandsons felt a responsibility to comply. Confucius and his ideas on filial piety thus became extremely attractive. Filial piety transformed obedience to one's father or family elder into a moral imperative, a measure of a man's worth, and a basic standard of civilized behavior. It was custom-made to convince sons to set aside their personal interests for the good of the overall clan. Therefore, the need to maintain extended families was a key factor behind the penetration of Confucianism into Chinese society. The hierarchical family was already in the process of being constructed—Confucius just provided the cement to bind it together.[15]

NOT ONLY DOMINEERING fathers found filial piety useful. Anyone in a position of authority could manipulate Confucian filial piety to good effect—all the way up to the emperor. That fact was not lost on the Chinese government and its Confucian advisers. If filial piety could create obedient sons and daughters, couldn't it also produce citizens loyal to the king? The appeal of filial piety as a tool of government was another reason the concept, and with it, Confucius, became so infused into Chinese society. The escalating importance of filial piety in China was directly linked to the role it began to play in the dynastic order.

The emperors began heavily promoting filial piety all the way back in the Han Dynasty. The government inculcated children in the idea in schools, offered tax breaks and other rewards to those who exemplified filial behavior, and named filiality as the most attractive attribute for recommending candidates for the civil service. Every Han emperor (except the dynasty's founder) had the word *xiao* added to his name after death to highlight his own filial nature. Imperial regimes continued to propagate filial piety for the next two millennia. In the late fourteenth century, for instance, the founder of the Ming Dynasty issued an edict ordering that filial piety be preached from house to house throughout the empire—literally. "A bell with a wooden clapper shall be prepared," the proclamation read. "Old persons, disabled persons unable to function normally, or blind persons shall be selected and guided by children to walk through [the neighborhoods] holding the bell. . . . Let them shout loudly so that everyone can hear, urging people to do good and not violate the law. Their message is: 'Be filial to your parents, respect elders and superiors, live in harmony with neighbors, instruct and discipline children and grandchildren. . . .' This shall be done six times each month."[16]

The goal of this imperial policy was to convince the Chinese masses that it was just as important to be deferential to the emperor as to honor their own fathers. The Confucians handed the emperors more than enough doctrinal support for this effort, most notably in a short but highly influential treatise called *The Classic of Filial Piety*, or the *Xiao Jing*. This work purports to be a transcript of a conversation between Confucius and one of his disciples in which the great sage expounds on the principle of filial piety at length. Tradition has it that the words spoken by Confucius in this question-and-answer session are his own, and at times in Chinese history the text was held in great esteem. However, modern scholars believe that *The Classic of Filial Piety* was compiled long after Confucius's death—probably during the early period of the Han Dynasty—and they debate how much of the material came directly from Confucius. Whatever its origins, the text is of great historical significance because it elevates filial piety to heights that Confucius himself may never have intended.

In the *Analects*, Confucius stressed benevolence as the foundation of virtuous behavior, but *The Classic of Filial Piety* puts very different words into his mouth. "Of all the actions of man there is none greater than filial piety," he proclaims. Filial piety became the virtue at the heart of all others: "a perfect virtue and all-embracing rule of conduct." And if that alone wasn't enough to pound home its significance, Confucians also infused the concept with cosmic gravity. The "well-regulated" family, with the father in a position of unquestioned authority, became the will of Heaven, indispensable for the prosperity of society at large and the main bulwark against chaos. Confucian scholars credited filial piety with making the land fertile and fish plentiful. Without it, disaster would strike mankind. Filial piety became the vital connection between man, Heaven, and Earth, and thus necessary to maintain order in the universe. "Filial piety is the constant of Heaven, the righteousness of Earth, and the practical duty of Man," Confucius explains in *The Classic of Filial Piety*.[17]

That text, though, didn't just stress the primacy of filial piety, but outlined in detail how it should be practiced in different walks of life in a way that made the transition from household to empire seamless. To the Confucians, filial piety was never meant to be confined to the living room. People were to learn how to behave in the wider world first and foremost inside the family home. The filial relationships developed there prepared people to interact properly on the job, at school, with friends, or in any social situation, and the morals learned within the household were easily transferable to society at large. In other words, the Confucian family was the primary training ground for virtuous people. Good sons and daughters not only made good children, but good students, good colleagues, and good citizens. "He who serves his parents, in a high situation, will be free from pride; in a low situation, will be free from insubordination; and among his equals will not be quarrelsome," Confucius tells us in *The Classic of Filial Piety*. "He who loves his parents will not dare to incur the risk of being hated by any man." If everyone observed their filial responsibilities, both inside and outside the home, from the lowliest farmer to the emperor himself, society would be put in its proper order and peace would come to the world. When filial piety was practiced, "the people were brought to live in peace and harmony," Confucius said.[18]

The Confucian secret to societal well-being, therefore, was the replication of the father-son relationship across the full spectrum of human interaction. Anyone in a position of authority, whether at work or in one's civic and personal life, was deserving of the same loyalty and reverence one showed his or her parents. In one of many examples in *The Classic of Filial Piety*, Confucius explains how junior civil servants should treat the emperor and his senior ministers as they would their own fathers. "As [junior officials] serve their fathers, so they serve their rulers, and they reverence them equally," Confucius says. "When they serve their ruler with filial piety they are loyal; when they serve their superiors with reverence they are obedient." Thus the Confucians took a critical analytical step—equating the filial duty a son shows his father to the loyalty a citizen shows to political leaders. Filial piety "commences with the service of parents; it proceeds to the service of the ruler," one passage in *The Classic of Filial Piety* asserts. The treatise also goes on to explain that "the filial piety with which the superior man serves his parents may be transferred as loyalty to the ruler. . . . His regulation of his family may be transferred as good government in any official position."[19]

In Confucian thinking, then, the state became an enlarged photocopy of the family. If the state operated the same way a family did, good government would be achieved and order maintained in society. *The Great Learning*, one of the most important Confucian treatises, states simply that "from the loving example of one family a whole state becomes loving." At the top of the family stood a commanding yet benevolent father, controlling yet caring for his children; at the top of the nation stood the emperor, enjoying unrivaled authority over the people, yet committed to serving the best interests of the common man. *The Classic of Filial Piety* highlights an ancient Chinese poem that calls the ruler "the parent of the people." And just as filial piety was supposed to cultivate well-behaved, devoted children, who would be reluctant to resist parental authority, it was supposed to generate equally loyal imperial subjects who were unwilling to rise up against the state. In the second passage of the *Analects*, one of Confucius's disciples is recorded explaining that "it is rare for a man whose character is such that he is good as a son and obedient as a young man to have the inclination to transgress against his superiors; it is unheard of for one who has no such inclination to be inclined to start a rebellion."[20]

ON THE SURFACE, the Confucian concept of filial piety allowed those in authority to wield unlimited power. The son was to be deferential to his dad, the citizen loyal to the emperor. Obedience and filial piety were the same thing. Or were they? Perhaps the single most vexing question facing Confucians has been whether there were limits to filial piety, and if so, what they were. The answer is critical. It gets at the Confucian view of authority, how it should be exercised and what recourse people have against it. Here we hit at the heart of Confucian ideas on human rights generally. If all of society is like a big family, the rights that sons may or may not possess to resist their fathers have a direct bearing on what rights, in Confucian doctrine, people have against the government. How fathers and sons interact with each other has implications for how the state treats its citizens, how people confront official abuse, and the scope for civil liberties in East Asian societies. Basically, Confucian beliefs about filial piety have a direct bearing on democratization in East Asia.

Confucius's views on filial piety are much more complicated than they at first appear. On the one hand, Confucius never expressed any clear limitations on the practice of filial piety. In most of his recorded comments, he emphasized compliance, without any qualifications. That fact alone suggests that Confucius expected sons to obey their fathers no matter what. On the other hand, he was opposed to blind devotion to parents, or to anyone in authority.

In *The Classic of Filial Piety*, his interviewer asks him point-blank if filial duty entailed unquestioned obedience. "What words are these!" Confucius exclaims in horror. It was the duty of a filial son to protest, or "remonstrate," against improper behavior committed by his father, Confucius insisted. That was the only way to correct wrongs and foster moral behavior. What was true for the son also held for anyone in a subordinate position—most of all, ministers serving the ruler. "If the Son of Heaven [the emperor] had seven ministers who would remonstrate with him, although he had not right methods of government, he would not lose his possession of the kingdom," Confucius explains. "And the father who had a son that would remonstrate with him would not sink into the gulf of unrighteous deeds. Therefore when a case of unrighteous conduct is concerned, a son must by no means keep from remonstrating with his father, nor a minister from remonstrating with his ruler. Hence, since remonstrance is required in the case of unrighteous conduct, how can obedience to the orders of a father be accounted filial piety?"[21]

How far was this "remonstrating" to go? What was a son to do if his father ignored his advice and persisted in his wicked ways? Did Confucius permit the son to rebel against his father? In other words, did doing what was moral trump the duties of filial piety? Confucius's answer here was a definite no. In his view, a son had an obligation to *attempt* to correct his father—but no more. There were boundaries to how forcefully a son or subordinate could challenge authority in Confucian thinking. In the end, a son had to fall in line no matter what evil deeds his father might commit. Confucius spelled this out in the *Analects*: "In serving your father and mother you ought to dissuade them from doing wrong in the gentlest way," the master says. "If you see your advice being ignored, you should not become disobedient but remain reverent. You should not complain even if in so doing you wear yourself out." *The Book of Rites* takes this point even further. "If a parent has a fault, (the son) should with bated breath, and bland aspect, and gentle voice, admonish him," the text instructs. If the father fails to heed the advice, "rather than allow him to commit an offence against anyone in the neighborhood or countryside, (the son) should strongly remonstrate. If the parent be angry and displeased, and beat him till the blood flows, (the son) should not presume to be angry and resentful, but be more reverential and more filial." Such constraints on protest were not slapped on sons alone. "In serving a prince, frequent remonstrances lead to disgrace," one of Confucius's disciples says in the *Analects*.[22]

Perhaps no single story in any Confucian text stresses the preeminence of filial piety in Confucius's teaching more bluntly than a conversation he had with the governor of the district of She while he was on his long journey through China, as recounted in the *Analects*. The governor tells Confucius about a local man who was highly regarded because he gave evidence to the authorities against his father, who had stolen a sheep. Surprisingly, Confucius didn't approve. "In our village those who are straight are quite different," Confucius responded. "Fathers cover up for their sons, and sons cover up for their fathers. Straightness is to be found in such behavior." The implication is that the loyalty of son to father takes precedence over the law of the land, or even basic principles of morality. This account seems to contradict much of the rest of Confucius's teachings—which put a premium on doing what is right in all circumstances, whatever the consequences. Cheng Yaotian, an eighteenth-century scholar, attempted to defend the passage by arguing that Confucius was simply conceding that it was only natural to place the interests of blood ahead of those of the state or society. If a son sacrifices his own father for the public good, he does so with his own selfish interests in mind.[23]

Critics of Confucius, however, were horrified by his preference for family over everything else. An early assault on Confucian filial piety came from Legalist philosopher Han Feizi. Confucius believed that there was no conflict between the interests of the family and of the state or community—that, in fact, they were one and the same. Han Feizi, however, believed just the opposite. There is inherently a major distinction, he argued, between the needs of the state and those of the family, and therefore, Confucian ideas on filial piety could undermine social order. By absolving one's obligations to society when it came to matters of the family, Confucius was fomenting opposition to state authority.

To prove his point, Han Feizi tells a tale about a man in Confucius's home state of Lu who "followed the ruler to war, fought three battles, and ran away thrice." When questioned by Confucius, the man replied: "I have an old father. Should I die, nobody would take care of him." According to Han Feizi, Confucius "regarded him as a man of filial piety, praised him, and exalted him." The impact on Lu was disastrous, claimed Han Feizi: "After the reward of the runaway by [Confucius], the people of Lu were apt to surrender and run away." Such an outcome, he wrote, shows that "the dutiful son of the father was a rebellious subject of the ruler." Going further, Han Feizi argued that the entire idea that families are a source of order is misguided. Fathers, he pointed out, routinely struggle to control unruly sons, even though the bond between father and son is the strongest of all. How, then, can this relationship be a model for preserving order in society at large? "It is human nature," Han Feizi wrote, "that nobody is more affectionate than parents. If both parents reveal love to their children, and yet order is not always found in a family, then how could there be no disorder in a state even though the ruler deepens his love for the ministers?"[24]

IT IS HERE, in Confucius's ideas on loyalty and authority, that his teachings begin to feel very foreign to us in the West. The extreme importance of filial piety in his thinking—and the unconditional obedience it is meant to induce—is perhaps the most fundamental way Western mores and Confucian philosophy differ. In the United States, people aren't encouraged to slavishly obey parents, teachers, bosses, or political leaders. Standing up to abusive or immoral authority is considered heroic. Children ultimately are supposed to find their own course in life, become independent from their parents, and develop their own opinions and personalities. The Confucian idea that people ought to blindly submit to anyone in a position of authority is beyond the Western mentality.

Did, however, Confucius truly intend to create a society filled with mindless, submissive lemmings dominated by overbearing overlords? Did he expect people to cower before injustice and brutality? Not at all. In Confucius's moral system, no one is free to do as he wishes, no matter what position he holds in the social order. Yes, fathers are to be revered and respected, but they also must return that loyalty with kindness, by caring for their families' well-being with the utmost sincerity and generosity. The Confucian filial relationship, in other words, is not a one-way street. Simply put, dads aren't supposed to be dictators—and, by inference, neither are government leaders. If a father has a responsibility to be benevolent and provide for his children, then a king, as "father of the nation," has the same obligation to rule his loyal citizens virtuously.

There is ample evidence for this interpretation in the *Analects*. Zigong once asked Confucius: "Is there one word which may serve as a rule of practice for all one's life?" The master answered: "Is not RECIPROCITY such a word?" Remember that Confucius preached a form of the Golden Rule: "What you do not want done to yourself, do not do to others." There were no exceptions made—not for fathers or kings, or sons and subjects. The respect that sons ought to show their fathers and elders is the basis of how everyone should be acting toward everyone else. "Let the superior man never fail reverentially to order his own conduct, and let him be respectful to others and observant of propriety—then all within the four seas will be his brothers," one disciple says in the *Analects*. No one, not even a person in a position of great power, is permitted to misuse that power. "The superior man is correctly firm, and not firm merely," Confucius stipulated. The proper gentleman should also define his own success and well-being by uplifting the people around him. "The man of perfect virtue, wishing to be established himself, seeks also to establish others," Confucius said. "Wishing to be enlarged himself, he seeks also to enlarge others." Confucius expected the emperor himself to abide by these commandments: "There is filial piety—therewith the sovereign should be served. There is fraternal submission—therewith elders and superiors should be served. There is kindness—therewith the multitude should be treated," *The Great Learning* explains. Confucius may have advocated hierarchical relationships both within the family and throughout society, but he did not intend fathers to become domineering, or emperors dictatorial, with everyone below them quaking in terror.[25]

Still, reality and philosophy sharply diverged. Confucian filial piety came to be a tool wielded by the powerful to bludgeon the weak. The partner of each relationship in the position of superiority—father, ruler—claimed all of the rights and privileges, while the subordinate member—son, subject—got stuck with the duties. Confucius may have been well intentioned, but he never understood how easily his beliefs on filial piety could be manipulated, and he did not properly account for such behavior in his discourses on morality. Perhaps the biggest crime Confucius committed was naïveté.

CONFUCIUS'S CRITICS ACCUSED him of much, much worse. As China and its neighbors began to get bombarded by Western culture, ideals, and ideologies in the nineteenth century, Confucian filial piety came under vicious attack from Asians and non-Asians alike. It was transformed from the most perfect of all virtues into a social anachronism that condemned China to backwardness. "Filial piety, and the strength of the family generally, are perhaps the weakest point in Confucian ethics, the only point where the system departs seriously from common sense," British philosopher Bertrand Russell wrote in 1922. "Family feeling has militated against public spirit, and the authority of the old has increased the tyranny of ancient custom. In the present day, when China is confronted with problems requiring a radically new outlook, these features of the Confucian system have made it a barrier to necessary reconstruction."[26]

Chinese writer Lin Yutong concurred. Sounding much like Legalist thinker Han Feizi, he argued in 1936 that the Confucians had eroded the dedication to community and nation that was so vital in the West by elevating the family too high. "The conflict is between the family mind and social mind," he wrote. "Seen in modern eyes, Confucianism omitted out of the social relationships man's social obligations towards the stranger, and great and catastrophic was the omission. Samaritan virtue was unknown and practically discouraged. . . . The family, with its friends, became a walled castle, with the greatest communistic cooperation and mutual help within, but coldly indifferent toward, and fortified against, the world without." As a result, Lin believed, filial piety unintentionally spawned endemic corruption, rotted institutions from within, and encouraged resistance to modernization. Government ministers, for instance, filled their offices with job-seeking relatives, making them fierce opponents of any sort of political change. "Sinecurism and nepotism developed, which . . . became an irresistible force, undermining, rather than being undermined by, any political reform movement," he wrote. "The force is so great that repeated efforts at reform, with the best of intentions, have proved unsuccessful." Graft, he went on, "may be a public vice, but is always a family virtue."[27]

Critics also contended that the Confucian family was stifling the independence that the Chinese needed to function in the modern world. "The family system is the negation of individualism itself, and it holds a man back, as the reins of the jockey hold back the dashing Arabian horse," Lin wrote. Modernizers looked to the West and saw that its political and economic systems were based on personal freedoms. Democracy depended on the ability of individuals to cast their votes and speak their minds; capitalism was propelled by the energy released by individuals pursuing their own profits. By placing sons under the thumbs of their fathers, Confucius, to these thinkers, was preventing the emergence of a modern China. "When people are bound by the Confucian teachings of filial piety and obedience to the point of the son not deviating from the father's way even three years after his death, . . . how can they form their own political party and make their own choice?" asked radical writer Chen Duxiu in 1916.[28]

Such criticisms can still be heard today. Korean-American writer Wesley Yang pointed to the submissiveness caused by filial piety as one reason why Asians in the United States have generally failed to grasp leadership positions within American businesses and in society more broadly. "Here is what I sometimes suspect my face signifies to other Americans: an invisible person, barely distinguishable from a mass of faces that resemble it," Yang wrote bitterly in 2011. "An icon of so much that the culture pretends to honor but that it in fact patronizes and exploits. Not just people 'who are good at math' and play the violin, but a mass of stifled, repressed, abused, conformist quasi-robots who simply do not matter, socially or culturally. . . . Let me summarize my feelings toward Asian values: Fuck filial piety."[29]

THESE ATTACKS TAINTED Confucian filial piety as anti-modern and led young people to question its value in contemporary society. Yet more than rhetoric is undermining Confucian family traditions. Tremendous social and economic forces are at work. The fears of Chinese imperial officials— like the stodgy court conservative Woren, who fought against reform in the nineteenth century—that an influx of Western ideas would threaten the stature of Confucius and his teachings have proven true. As Asian nations have adopted Western-style political systems and ideologies (democracy and communism), economic practices (capitalism), and social norms (dating, women in the workplace), the old Confucian patterns of family life have been watered down. The demands of modern society have conflicted with Confucian admonitions on filial behavior. Confucius may have told sons not to travel far from their parents, but the fierce competition for good jobs in today's globalized business and financial networks presents children with little choice but to venture across the nation, even around the globe, for school and career, splitting families apart for long periods of time. The pressures of twenty-first-century society are "putting an end to the last hope of Confucius's teaching," says Feng Wang, a sociologist at the Brookings Institution.[30]

The result is that East Asian families are functioning more and more like those in the West. Children are not nearly as frequently married off by their fathers as they once were; now they date and choose their own spouses. More and more, sons and daughters are moving out of their parents' homes at a young age to live on college campuses or independently with friends. Whatever personal freedoms young East Asians might have gained, however, the breakdown of filial piety has spawned significant social problems as well. One of the reasons Confucius was so fixated on filial piety was that without it, he feared the elderly would be abandoned by their sons, who naturally would be more concerned about their own children and wives. That worry has become reality in modern East Asia. Gone, to a great degree, are the days when four generations would cram into one Chinese household. A 2013 study of the living conditions of China's 185 million people over sixty years of age showed that only 38 percent resided in the same household with their children. Caring for the region's growing army of senior citizens has become a major headache for policymakers, who can no longer rely on families to provide the necessary support. In Singapore, the government became so concerned that it resorted to legislation to ensure that irresponsible youngsters fulfilled their ancient filial duties. The Maintenance of Parents Act, instituted in 1995, allows elderly parents to haul their wayward kids into court if they aren't providing sufficient financial support.

Walter Woon, a former lawmaker who drafted the legislation, believes the law was a response to what he sees as the decay of traditional family values. "I've seen cases where parents were left without means of support from their children. It didn't seem to me this was a good thing," Woon says. "The opposition [to the law] came from educated Chinese who said you can't legislate this kind of thing. They said you are trying to legislate Confucian ethics. It should come out of a sense of filial piety. My response was this has nothing to do with filial piety. This comes in when filial piety fails. If Confucianism applied, we would not need a law. The point is that [filial piety] is breaking down, so we do need a law."[31]

Singapore's policymakers, following in the footsteps of China's imperial functionaries, are also employing propaganda to reinforce Confucian filial piety. The government promotes the Confucian virtue through a TV marketing campaign. One short 2010 video, called simply "Filial Piety: Father and Son," tells the story of a man who is caring for his elderly mother—reverently helping her walk, fussing over her at the dinner table (to the point of insulting his wife), and watching over her in the hospital. All the while, the man's young son is watching. When he asks his father why he is so devoted to his mother, the video flashes back to the man's childhood. We witness his mother rushing through the rain to get him to a doctor when he was sick. The commercial concludes with the man singing to his mother, tears welling in his eyes, as she lies gravely ill in a hospital bed while his son looks on. "How one generation loves, the next generation learns," the video tells us.[32]

Singapore's government is not the only one in East Asia attempting to revive filial piety. Some policymakers see Confucius as a corrective to the evils they believe are caused by an infiltration of Western ideas. South Korea's Ministry of Culture, Sports, and Tourism and various municipal governments have resurrected hundreds of dormant Confucian academies and transformed them into local schools to teach Confucianism. In the days of Korea's Joseon Dynasty, the academies' classrooms were filled with students studying the Confucian classics to prepare for the civil service examinations. These newfangled schools proffer a much more simplified version of the sage's teachings, what Lee Hui Bok calls "Confucian manners."[33]

Lee runs one of these Confucian schools in Gwacheon, a suburb of Seoul, in a modern office building next to one of the old academies. In a crowded classroom one morning, two dozen women are being instructed in proper Confucian family relations. The teacher emphasizes the standard Confucian view that good behavior within the family will form the basis of a harmonious society. On other days, the school holds sessions for parents and children to teach them the value of filial piety. One booklet used in the sessions employs cute drawings and simple language to press home the importance of traditional family roles. A cartoon shows a father and son singing together to Grandmother. "Parents like children, children like parents, then you become the best type of friend," the text reads. Another re-creates the tale of one of the old Twenty-Four Filial Exemplars. The drawings show a mother holding a stick while her son weeps next to her. He says he is crying not because she hit him, but because it no longer hurt when she did—an indication that she was aging and becoming frail.

Such Confucian instruction is crucial, Lee insists, to restore morality to a corrupted Asia. "Filial piety is very important for a proper society," he explains. "Twenty years ago, people were more polite. Young people gave up their seats to older folks on the bus. No one does that anymore. Now there are a lot of social problems. In the modern family, people have lost their manners and don't associate with their grandparents. Children don't respect their fathers and mothers. Society has become very chaotic. There is a need for more order." Thus, Lee says, officials have stepped in to once again indoctrinate Korean youth in their filial duties. "The government believes we have to reintroduce Confucianism to make children more polite."

Officials in China couldn't agree more. Even the Chinese Communists, who vilified Confucius violently in the days of Mao, are reintroducing filial piety in an attempt to foster greater social cohesion. Beijing has followed Singapore's lead, introducing its own filial-piety regulations in 2013. "Family members who live apart from their parents should often visit or send regards to their parents," stipulates the Chinese Elderly Protection Law. Another article prohibits relatives from "overlooking or neglecting the elderly."[34]

The law is part of a greater government campaign to get Chinese feeling filial again. "Admittedly, feudal filial piety exerted a considerable adverse impact," an essay in the state-run *People's Daily* newspaper explained in 2012. However, "it is not a bad idea to open up our minds more and do such things as reviewing the 'filial piety' culture, getting rid of its bad parts, finding its universal values and developing its functions that meet the requirements, from the development of the socialist market economy and the construction of a harmonious society." Not surprisingly, the authoritarian Chinese state has also looked to filial piety to breed loyalty to the government, just like the mandarins of China's imperial dynasties. Echoing *The Classic of Filial Piety*, the *People's Daily* essay emphasized the connection between deference to parents and state authority. "Only those who respect their parents are loyal to their countries," it proclaimed.[35]

CHINA'S COMMUNISTS WILL have their work cut out for them if they intend to truly revive filial piety. Not only did Chinese authorities spend decades vigorously uprooting Confucian values, but they also instituted population-control policies that further undermined the traditional family. In 1979, in an effort to curtail the growth of its population, which by then had reached nearly 1 billion, the government restricted many couples to only one child. The policy, by tamping down the number of new mouths to feed and workers to employ, did aid in the country's drive for economic development, but it also hastened the aging of the population. In 2012, the workforce actually began to shrink, with potentially negative consequences for future growth. In 2013, the Communist Party finally decided to loosen the one-child policy to allow some families to have more children. But by then, the damage was done. Due to the one-child policy, each son or daughter, together with his or her spouse, is forced to care for and support four senior citizens, something many cannot afford. "The one-child policy altered the kinship and family networks and would certainly have short-term and long-term implications both on the parents and the children," says Brookings' Feng Wang. "With only one child, parents will be looking at the children as increasingly unlikely to be around them when they grow older. The challenge is that they need a manager. There are times simply when they cannot manage their own lives. It is a very lonely life. We are going to see so many Chinese elderly in the future who will have that kind of life."

Loneliness is only part of the problem. The 2013 survey of China's elderly also painted a depressing picture of their welfare. Almost 23 percent of them, or more than 42 million senior citizens, live below the poverty line, which means they exist on less than $1.50 a day. Unlike in the United States and Europe, where government social safety nets provide protection for the aged, the Chinese have not constructed welfare systems nearly as extensive. Pensions are inadequate, the quality of health care is often poor, and medical bills can be hefty. When it comes to caring for the aged, China has simply not provided an alternative to Confucian filial piety. "In Western societies, the elderly have their wealth, they are used to independent living," Wang says. "In this system in China you really wonder, [aside from] the elderly who bene-fited from this recent wealth boom, how they would manage in their old age. This is not a Confucian idea. Life should get better; the older should not just receive respect but support. There are many beauties in the Confucian teach-ings. It has figured out the essence of life. The Confucian teaching is a rea-sonable life trajectory. It is multigenerational obligations in a kinship setup. But now, by force, by many different forces, those contracts are broken."[36]

But not entirely. The 2013 survey offers some intriguing evidence to sug-gest that Confucian filial piety has not completely vanished. Nearly 89 percent of the elderly in China who require assistance to perform daily activities re-ceive that help from family members, while 47 percent not residing with their children still get financial support from them. "In contrast to Western coun-tries such as the U.S. where resources flow downward from parents to children, in China resources flow upward from children to parents," the report notes.[37]

In some cases, children are finding ways of fulfilling their filial duties with modern conveniences. Popping up around China are homes for the elderly, something new to the culture. Na Na, who comanages the Yiyangnian home for the aged in Beijing with her mother, says that centers like hers are a nat-ural response to the hectic lives that modern Chinese lead. "A lot of people don't have the time to take care of their parents, or the parents get lonely at home alone," Na explains. "Here in the past, in the traditional culture, if you had a son, he'd be responsible for you [when you aged]. Now, if you have a boy or a girl, they both have to work and earn money."[38]

Some of the 150 residents of the center seem to have accepted that. Zhang Zizhong, eighty-two, has chosen to live at Yiyangnian rather than in his own apartment or at his son's house. He realizes that his son, an engi-neer, and daughter-in-law, a journalist, don't have the time to care for him. But after his wife passed away in 2012, he didn't want to sit home by him-self. Even though he isn't living with his son, as tradition would dictate, he doesn't believe the Confucian traditions are dying. His son visits him often, and is even willing to pay for him to join a trip the center is planning for its residents to the United States. "He is very good about caring for my hap-piness," Zhang says. In fact, Zhang feels that his son is representative of a larger trend: young people in China today are more supportive of their par-ents than his own generation, he believes, which was influenced by the rad-ical anti-Confucian rhetoric so common in the days of Mao. "People didn't respect their parents," says Zhang. "Confucian ideas were crushed in peo-ple's minds." But more recently, "the Confucian idea is changing among the younger generation. There is more respect for filial piety. Children are more tolerant and supportive of their parents," he says. "You wouldn't expect anyone to follow Confucius, but that is happening."[39]

Na herself seems to be one of those newly filial. Before joining her mother at the nursing home, the twenty-six-year-old had been living in Sydney, Australia, where she had enjoyed her job managing a duty-free shop and spending her evenings playing poker and singing karaoke with friends. But her mother began pressuring her to return. In 2011 Na's mom had opened the Yiyangnian—her second old-age home—and needed Na's help running the family business. "You shouldn't be so lazy," her mom scolded.

So Na, to the bewilderment of her Australian friends, packed up, sold her new car, and moved back to Beijing. "I respect my mom and look up to her," Na says. "That made me want to be here."

HERE, IN NA'S sentiments about her mother, we can find the true essence of filial piety. Perhaps Confucius went too far in his emphasis on obedience in his redefinition of filial piety; his successors only compounded the problem by turning the virtue into a tool of imperial political and social control. What has gotten lost in the centuries of government propaganda and obsession with hierarchy is the fundamental intention of Confucius's teaching: that members of a family should respect, support, and aid each other throughout their lives, for the good of both the household and society at large. His motivation was to ensure that men and women fulfilled their moral responsibilities to both their parents and children.

Like so many of Confucius's ideas—as we'll see over the course of the rest of this book—the way to reconcile the great sage with the modern world is not by eradicating his doctrine but by stripping away the centuries of self-serving reinterpretations to dig down to the doctrine's heart—and the universal values that transcend the ages. Cynics might ask, Why expend any effort revisiting the ideals of a man who lived 2,500 years ago? The answer can be found in the dining room of Vincent Lo and his family. What, after all, is so wrong about Sunday-night dinners with Grandma, or family vacations with siblings and cousins? Where is the evil in ensuring that an elderly matriarch is cared for by her loving family?

That, after all, is why Confucian filial piety has managed to survive in the hearts and minds of so many East Asians, defying the challenges posed by globalization, economic change, and political revolution—even for those who would appear least likely to be committed to Confucian family rituals.

Wang Huifeng is one such person. Born in Ho Chi Minh City in Vietnam to immigrant parents from Shantou in China's Guangdong Province, Wang moved with his family to Germany when he was only three years old. There he grew up and assimilated—learning German and making German friends—but only to a point. The family retained its Chinese identity and the Confucian values that came with it. One day in 2011, Wang got a phone call from his father, who was visiting Shantou. He told Wang that he had met a young girl there who he thought would make a wonderful wife for him and suggested Wang call her. Wang, as most sons in the West would, initially resisted. He would prefer to find his own spouse, he told his dad. But the matter wasn't that simple. The girl happened to be the daughter of his father's friend, and the two eager dads had made an agreement that their children would not get involved in other relationships before meeting each other. Wang found himself in an awkward position. He couldn't just say no and walk away—that would embarrass his father—but he was dead set on squirming out of his dad's intrusive arrangement.

Soon afterward, Wang got on a plane for Shantou. Now that his father's reputation was on the line, he felt he couldn't ditch the girl over the phone. He'd have to let her down face-to-face. Yet when he actually met her, Wang, to his surprise, discovered his dad wasn't a bad matchmaker. The two hit it off, and after a short courtship, they married in January 2013. Wang relocated to Shanghai, where he (appropriately) works as a cross-cultural trainer for corporations.

Wang loves his wife dearly, but at the same time, he admits that in part he agreed to his father's matchmaking to make his parents happy. "One reason [I married her] is that I knew my parents would be okay with it," Wang says. "From the Chinese perspective, it's not that two people marry, but two families marry. You are not different from your family." But what about all that Western influence, which preaches independence and individualism? Wang came to realize that those values were not his own. "We all say our parents are important to us, but in the Chinese, it is inculcated into our identity," he says. "As long as they protect us, we give them respect and loyalty. Even now, it is difficult for me to make a choice outside of that bond. You know at every stage in your life where you stand. This is old-fashioned Confucian filial piety. It has been working quite well for 2,000 years."[40]

FILIAL PIETY WAS the primary Confucian ideal that shaped the East Asian family—but far from the only one. The sage has left his imprint on other aspects of familial relations beyond the bond between parent and child, and in ways that are no less controversial in today's society. One of those influences has helped to define the Western perception of the modern East Asian family and made some westerners question their own values and family traditions: the Confucian emphasis on education.

Chapter Six

Confucius the Teacher

If the gentleman studies widely and each day examines himself, his wisdom will become clear and his conduct be without fault.

—*Xunzi*

Oh Dong Jin has made the ultimate sacrifice for his daughter: he lives 7,000 miles away from her. When Ji Hae was only eleven years old, she and her mother left their home in Seoul, South Korea, to reside with Oh's sister-in-law in New York City. Ten years later, they are still there. Oh lives alone in Seoul in a small apartment and enjoys time with his wife and daughter for only a few weeks a year. Why separate a child from her father, and for so many years? Oh, a film critic, believes Ji Hae can get a better education in America. Koreans go to extreme lengths to make sure their children get the best education available—in Oh's case, that meant sending his daughter to the other side of the world and missing out on her teenage years. Scrimping and saving, Oh sends every dime he can to his wife to support Ji Hae's studies. "I never thought of it as a sacrifice," Oh says. "I think it is right for parents to put everything first for the education of their child. It is part of our DNA."[1]

Oh is no exception. So many Korean fathers are living on their own while their children study abroad, usually in the United States, that they have been given a nickname: *gireogi*, or "wild geese," because they migrate like birds back and forth from Korea to visit their far-off families. These fathers often lead lonely, stressful lives. The strain of paying the huge bills to maintain their wives and kids overseas causes them to work too hard, and the long periods spent away from their loved ones sometimes dump them into deep depression. Yet these fathers believe their personal happiness doesn't matter—only the quality of their kids' education does. "The best thing for my daughter is to get the best education. It comes from Korean culture," says Lee Bang Soo, an executive at a Korean electronics company and a member of the *gireogi* flock.[2]

The "wild geese" of Korea are only one manifestation of an obsession with education that grips all of East Asia—an obsession inherited directly from Confucius. Confucius's ideas on the importance of learning may be the only major aspect of his teachings that has survived into modern time largely unscathed by the attacks and debates that have plagued other tenets of Confucianism. That is because of the positive influence those ideas have had on the region. The generally high level of skills in East Asia attracted the investment that initially propelled the region's astronomical growth, and then, as wealth advanced, prepared the workforce for the technology industries that are so critical to today's international commerce. East Asian students now flood into the world's best universities and routinely outscore Americans in standardized tests.

East Asian governments, also influenced by Confucian thinking, have offered their citizens better and better opportunities by making universal education a priority, spending heavily to build strong school systems. The education bug infects even the children themselves. Unlike in the United States, where the smartest kids in class are often taunted as "nerds" while the cool kids smoke in the bathrooms, in Asia the top performers are the most admired. For those kids who may lack the self-motivation to study hard on their own, Asian mothers have become famously (or in some cases, infamously) known as "tiger moms" for the relentless parenting techniques they use to push their children to excel in and out of the classroom. Yale law professor Amy Chua created an international stir with her book *Battle Hymn of the Tiger Mother*, which details the grade-obsessed child-rearing practices of what she calls "Chinese parenting." "The Chinese mother believes that (1) schoolwork always comes first; (2) an A-minus is a bad grade; (3) your children must be two years ahead of their classmates in math," Chua wrote.[3]

Chua's methods are common to East Asian families throughout the world. But her comments instantaneously sparked controversy. Some critics were horrified by the pressure she inflicted on her children. But the superior academic performance of many East Asian kids, including Chua's, has convinced some envious Western parents that their own children would be better able to compete if they became tiger moms too. "There are moments when [Chua] makes you ask yourself what the Chinese are doing right and we are doing wrong," commented journalist Allison Pearson. "Amy Chua's philosophy of child-rearing may be harsh, but ask yourself this: Is it any more cruel than the laissez-faire indifference and babysitting-by-TV which too often passes for parenting these days? Millions of failing British children could use a Tiger Mother in their tank."[4]

LEARNING WAS CENTRAL to Confucius's entire program for the improvement of both self and society. A gentleman simply could not be a gentleman without being educated. "The artisan, in any of the hundred crafts, masters his trade by staying in his workshop," one of Confucius's disciples tells us in the *Analects*. "The gentleman perfects his way through learning." Knowledge was critical to anyone trying to hone his or her moral qualities. Education acted as a guide to help the gentleman judge right from wrong and gauge the best course of action. Even the pursuit of the most beloved Confucian virtues could potentially lead a man astray if not tempered by learning. "To love benevolence without loving learning is liable to lead to foolishness," Confucius instructed. "To love trustworthiness in word without loving learning is liable to lead to harmful behavior."[5]

Mencius and Xunzi may have argued over many issues, but they agreed that study was the method by which a person fosters morality and ensures good behavior. "Since man's nature is evil, it must wait for the instructions of a teacher before it can become upright," Xunzi wrote. For that reason, education for Confucius and his devotees was a never-ending process of self-improvement. You don't just dutifully put in your years at school and end your quest for knowledge with a degree. There was always more to learn, and always new ways to better oneself. "The gentleman says: Learning should never cease," Xunzi wrote. "If wood is pressed against a straightening board, it can be made straight; if metal is put to the grindstone, it can be sharpened; and if the gentleman studies widely and each day examines himself, his wisdom will become clear and his conduct be without fault."[6]

Learning was part of a larger process that Confucius thought was of utmost importance: self-cultivation. Here we find one of the most appealing aspects of Confucius's teachings. He believed that the first place to find fault was within oneself. If things go badly—if you argue with your wife, scold your kids, or fail to convince your boss of a new business proposition—you aren't supposed to point blame at others, or rage against the injustice of the world. You should look inward to uncover where you might have gone wrong, and then fix yourself so you won't make the same mistake again. "When you meet someone better than yourself," Confucius once said, "turn your thoughts to becoming his equal. When you meet someone not as good as you are, look within and examine your own self." The biggest mistake of all was to make the same mistake twice. "Not to mend one's ways when one has erred is to err indeed," he admonished.[7]

With education and self-cultivation also comes responsibility. Scholars have a duty, in Confucius's eyes, to employ their knowledge for the good of society and all those people who do not have the opportunity or ability to study. In fact, learning was the basis of good government. To be a virtu-ous, successful ruler, one had to start with the "investigation of things"—the questioning and seeking that led to true wisdom. "The ancients who wished to illustrate illustrious virtue throughout the kingdom first ordered well their own States," says *The Great Learning*. "Wishing to order well their States, they first regulated their families. Wishing to regulate their families, they first cultivated their persons. Wishing to cultivate their persons, they first rectified their hearts. Wishing to rectify their hearts, they first sought to be sincere in their thoughts. Wishing to be sincere in their thoughts, they first extended to the utmost their knowledge. Such extension of knowledge lay in the investigation of things. Things being investigated, knowledge be-came complete."[8]

The Doctrine of the Mean similarly makes clear that education is the secret to being a good leader. "He who knows these three things [knowl-edge, magnanimity, energy], knows how to cultivate his own character," the text reads. "Knowing how to cultivate his own character, he knows how to govern other men. Knowing how to govern other men, he knows how to govern the kingdom with all its States and families." Education and self-cultivation, therefore, were the foundation of a peaceful, harmonious so-ciety. "From the Son of Heaven down to the mass of the people, all must consider the cultivation of the person the root of everything besides," reads *The Great Learning*.[9]

These practical matters of government aside, education to Confucius was still a very personal mission. In some respects, we could even say that the quest for learning was a form of enlightenment to Confucius. The Buddha may have discovered the answers to life while meditating under a bodhi tree; Confucius sought his nirvana in books of poetry, history, and philosophy. "I once spent all day thinking without taking food and all night thinking without going to bed, but I found that I gained nothing from it," he once said. "It would have been better for me to have spent the time in learning." Man's ultimate goal should not be for stature or riches, but to become a good person, whatever fortune or frustration life may bring. "What the gentleman seeks, he seeks within himself; what the small man seeks, he seeks in others," he said.[10]

Confucius's view on learning helps us understand his concept of humanity itself. He believed in the perfectibility of man through knowledge. With continuous study, anyone could overcome his flaws and disadvantages and become a gentleman—even a great sage. "It is not easy to find a man who has learned for three years without coming to be good," Confucius said.[11]

CONFUCIUS PERSONALLY SET the standard for studiousness in East Asia. He took immense pride in his lifelong search for knowledge and considered his undying love of learning to be his most admirable trait. "In a hamlet of ten households, there are bound to be those who are my equal in doing their best for others and in being trustworthy in what they say," he says in the *Analects*, "but they are unlikely to be as eager to learn as I am." According to historian Sima Qian, Confucius read his copy of *The Book of Changes* so frequently that he wore out the tongs binding the bamboo-strip pages three times. To Confucius, learning, reading, and debating with his disciples were a great source of joy. "Quietly to store up knowledge in my mind, to learn without flagging, to teach without growing weary, these present me with no difficulties," he once said.[12]

Confucius had probably learned a lot more than most people of his day. In antiquity, books were rare and cherished items, even in a society so devoted to writing as China, and Confucius probably had better access to works of history and poetry than most of his contemporaries. Nor did the average person in China during his day enjoy the luxury of time to sit around and read; there were farms to be plowed and mouths to feed. As a result, Confucius became well-known during his lifetime for his almost encyclopedic store of knowledge. The old histories reveal how people would seek him out with all sorts of obscure queries, and he was able to solve their riddles. On one occasion, a falcon fell dead, shot with an arrow, at the court of the duke of Chen, who asked Confucius about the strange incident. The master instantaneously identified the source of the weapon. "This falcon has come a long way," he informed the duke. "The arrow belongs to the Jurchens," a nomadic tribe from China's northern frontier. How, exactly, did Confucius know this bit of trivia? The Jurchens, Confucius explained, had sent similar arrows—made of thorn with stone arrowheads—as tribute to an ancient king of China, Confucius recounted. The duke went into his own treasury, and sure enough, found the arrows stored there; they had been given to the court years before as a gift.[13]

Most of Confucius's knowledge, however, was far more useful. He was highly regarded for his expertise in history, court ceremony, and the culture of Chinese antiquity. This knowledge made Confucius a popular teacher who spent long periods of his life as an educator. Fung Yu-lan, a twentieth-century Confucian thinker, concluded that Confucius may have been China's first full-time teacher. He further speculated that the sage became the prototype of a class of scholars—the *ru*, or literati—who would come to play a critical role in Chinese history. "Confucius was the first man in China to make teaching his profession, and thus popularize culture and education," Fung wrote. "It was also he who inaugurated, or at least developed, that class of gentleman in ancient China who was neither farmer, artisan, merchant nor actual official, but was professional teacher and potential official."[14]

Fung may have overstated his case, but there is no denying that Confucius influenced the very structure of Chinese society through his emphasis on education. His followers, taking Confucius's example, became diehard advocates of education throughout the imperial age and elevated the role of the learned in government and society. Beginning in the Han Dynasty, Confucians popularized the idea that men were segmented into four groups of occupations, ranked in order of their virtue and perceived contributions to society. At the top, of course, were the scholars, who, because of their superior learning, had a responsibility to guide everyone else. Thereafter followed, in descending order, farmers, artisans, and merchants. The prestige awarded to the learned helps to explain why East Asians have been and still are so manic about education. There is no better way in East Asian society to raise your stature, ensure your success, or forward your family than getting a doctorate from a well-regarded university.

Most importantly, the Confucians believed that everyone was deserving of education—and the opportunities that came with it—no matter what one's background might be. Confucius was at the forefront of bringing learning to the masses. In his day, scholarship in China had been the purview of the wealthy, who could afford to fund a son's education and forgo his labor on the farm or in the workshop. Confucius, though, welcomed everyone into his lectures, whatever their class or income level. "I have never denied instruction to anyone who, of his own accord, has given me so much as a bundle of dried meat as a present," he said. Even more critically, by offering access to education to the lower classes, Confucius opened up an avenue of social mobility. His influence on education, Fung contended, "truly constituted a great step toward emancipation." The Confucians thus instilled the ideal that society ought to be a meritocracy, where people's success should be linked to their knowledge and ability, not, as was common in ancient China and elsewhere, to their family pedigree, social status, wealth, or political connections.[15]

By promoting learning, Confucius also shaped how China was governed. His emphasis on public policy as the realm of the most educated contributed to the emergence of the classic scholar-official, the man of letters who possessed the know-how and moral judgment to rule over others. These Confucian ideas became enshrined in China's famous civil service examination system. For much of imperial Chinese history—and especially since the beginning of the Song Dynasty in the tenth century—a man had to pass a series of intense exams to prove his academic qualifications in order to become a government official. We cannot overestimate the impact this system had on Chinese society. Confucian education determined who entered the Chinese governing elite. The exams also elevated the role of Confucius in East Asia. Throughout their history, the examinations were based on the Confucian classics, and that meant that anyone who desired a meaningful government job had to immerse himself in Confucian teachings.

The examination system became instrumental to the spread of Confucianism in Chinese society. Thus, the entire imperial bureaucracy was tutored in Confucian thinking, and although that doesn't mean every official was a saintly Confucian *junzi*, it does mean that Confucius's doctrine became the basic ideology of government.

The connection between Confucius and government service made knowledge of Confucianism the best route to career advancement. Confucius may have believed in learning for learning's sake, but in imperial China, the Confucian classics became equated with material betterment and social status. Families everywhere threw their sons into Confucian studies in the hopes of getting them into the imperial bureaucracy and enhancing the family's wealth and prestige. One genealogy compiled during the Ming Dynasty (1368–1644) lectured its clan members that "those youngsters who have taken Confucian scholarship as their hereditary occupation should be sincere and hard-working, and try to achieve learning naturally while studying under a teacher. Confucianism is the only thing to follow if they wish to bring glory to their family."[16]

The exam system also gave the Confucian ideal that merit should trump inherited social stature real force in society. There were almost no restrictions on who could take the exams (with one big exception—women were not admitted), and the grading was done without any regard for social position or connections. Through education, therefore, any Chinese man, no matter what sort of family or village he came from, could win prestigious and profitable employment in government. The smartest were afforded the chance to change their families' fortunes. The exam system, however, was never quite as egalitarian as its supporters asserted—a poor peasant usually did not have the financial resources to spend his days studying the classics, nor could he afford to allow a child to do so. Yet the Chinese civil service exams did provide an avenue to prosperity and status that did not exist for most of the rest of the world's destitute until more modern times. China therefore enjoyed a form of social mobility that was generally absent in feudal Europe.

Chinese folklore is rife with stories of the poor boys who made good on their brains and pluck to pass the exams and win fame and fortune. One representative tale from the Tang Dynasty (618–907) tells of two young men, Lu Zhao and Huang Po, who were from the same prefecture. Both prepared to take the examinations, and they decided to make the journey to the testing center together. The two had very different backgrounds, though—Huang Po was wealthy, while Lu Zhao was quite poor—and as a result, the local elite lavished their attention only on Huang Po. "The prefect gave a farewell dinner at the Pavilion of Departure, but Huang Po alone was invited," the story goes. "When the party was at its peak, with lots of wine and music, Lu Zhao passed by the pavilion, riding on an old, weak horse." He rode to the city's edge and waited for Huang Po to join him. We next catch up with Lu Zhao a year later. As it turned out, Lu Zhao, not the privileged Huang Po, had been awarded the "number-one" position on the exam. Now the local officials took him more seriously. But Lu Zhao didn't forget their earlier snub, and he couldn't resist a little payback. "Once when the prefect invited him to watch the dragon boat race," the yarn continues, "Lu Zhao composed a poem during the banquet."

> *"It is a dragon," I told you*
> *But you had refused to believe.*
> *Now it returns with the trophy,*
> *Much in the way I predicted.*[17]

The competition to pass the exams was fierce. During the Qing Dynasty (1644–1911), only 1 in 3,000 candidates actually succeeded in attaining the top degree. The brave souls who strove to pass the tests spent much of the early part of their lives preparing. Historian Ichisada Miyazaki quipped that the process began even before birth.[18] When she was pregnant, a mother-to-be would spend her leisure time being read poetry and the classics—in the hopes of nurturing an especially astute fetus. If a boy was born, the family sometimes scattered coins inscribed with the words "Number One Graduate" for the servants to collect as gifts. The tutoring of sons usually began in the home at around three years of age; formal schooling started at age seven and lasted eight years.

Much of that time was spent literally memorizing the Five Classics, the *Analects*, and *Mencius*. To master the classics, a young Chinese boy had to memorize a staggering 431,286 characters of text, according to Miyazaki. Needless to say, convincing teenage boys to spend almost their entire youth studying took almost as much strenuous effort as the studying itself. Teachers, parents, and writers found all sorts of ways to exhort these youngsters to remain at their desks. One Song Dynasty emperor composed a little ditty that promised those who studied hardest great wealth and attractive brides:

> *To enrich your family, no need to buy good land;*
> *Books hold a thousand measures of grain. . . .*
> *Marrying, be not vexed by lack of a good go-between;*
> *In books there are girls with faces of jade.*
> *A boy who wants to become a somebody*
> *Devotes himself to the classics, faces the window, and reads.*[19]

FOR MANY EAST ASIANS, education has been their main connection to Confucius. Considered China's supreme teacher and ultimate wise man, Confucius has been something like a patron saint of scholarship for 2,000 years. Even today, many students seek his guidance. Although the old civil service exams no longer exist, students throughout East Asia today prepare for the all-important college entrance examinations, which determine which university they will be able to attend. The exams require the same sort of relentless study required to pass the tests of imperial days, and are no less stressful an experience. So some students still look to Confucius for assistance in the same way they had during the days of the dynasties. On a sunny June afternoon in Beijing, high school students Wang Jian and Zhao Wei paid a visit to the city's historic Confucian temple for that very purpose. Zhao knelt before Confucius's spirit tablet within the temple's main hall, while Wang stood beside her. Both prayed silently and reverently. With the exams only a week away, the eighteen-year-olds were willing to sacrifice some time away from their books to ask the great sage for aid in their academic endeavors. "I came to ask Confucius to help me get into an elite university," Wang says. "He is a great teacher, accomplished in literature," adds Zhao. "He is like a god. He must be able to help." The teenagers are just two among a steady stream of students, parents, and grandparents bowing before Confucius in the hope of winning his support. "Please, grant me good luck to get into a good university," Andy Liu, also eighteen, says he asked the sage. "If you believe," insists his mother, Lin Yan, "it will come to reality."[20]

Kids like Andy Liu need all the luck they can get. The education systems around East Asia have been shaped by the Confucian-influenced examination model of yesteryear—and not with entirely positive results. Though today's Asian youths are no longer huddled over the classics, the course of their entire lives still depends on passing a series of exams. Score well and you can gain admission to a top university that opens up job opportunities in the government and at the largest, best-paying companies. Score poorly and you may find yourself forever marginalized, unable to compete in status-conscious societies. The competition on these modern exams is no less intense than on the old civil service versions. In South Korea, for example, there are only four universities considered prestigious enough to guarantee a lucrative career. Every year, roughly 700,000 teenagers take the college entrance exams, but only 10,000 of them get accepted into those four. That's a nerve-straining 1.4 percent acceptance rate, not all that different from the percentage who passed the top civil service exams in imperial China.

As a result, the drive for learning in East Asia has turned into a pressure-cooker, boiling the region's children into stressed-out, overburdened memorizing machines. Children spend their teenage years buried in books, with little free time to pursue sports or have a social life. After their regular classes, any child with hopes of passing the exams attends costly "cram" schools, called *hagwons* in Korea. In all, Korean high-schoolers usually study fifteen to sixteen hours a day. "I wake up at 6 a.m. every day, then I get ready and go to school by 8 a.m.," says eleventh-grader Kim Jong Hun. "I finish classes at 5 p.m., and then, if I have *hagwon*, I go there from 6 to 9 p.m. or 10 p.m. Afterward, I also need to study or do homework." He gets time to hang out with friends only two or three times a month. His efforts, he fears, still may not be enough to earn him admission to the best Korean schools. "I am between the top 10 percent and 20 percent and there are some universities I won't be able to go to," Kim complains. "I don't know how the other kids with worse grades live. You study to get good results on the university entrance examination, not for anything else."[21]

Kim, though, believes the current education process is so ingrained in Korean culture that it will be almost impossible to change. "It is how the

6/15/2017

BANKS ROGENIA MAE

Item Number: 31901055988044

society works," Kim says. "It is how the system is. It is not like we can revolt and say we will not study. I don't think anything can be done." The pressure, Kim admits, becomes unbearable, to the point where he sometimes feels like giving up. "It is different for every person, but for me I feel more pressure from my friends," he says. "Some are really good students, get prizes and they are always on top. There is no way I can be at their level. So I feel bad. But I get more stress from my parents, who always want me to do better and compare me with the best students. The top student becomes their standard, so I am never good enough. That makes me sad. In those moments, I think that it is not like I would die if I did not study."

The pressure on parents is equally intense. Just as Chinese mothers in the imperial age were judged by the test-taking talents of their sons, families in East Asia today are often measured by which university accepts their children. Kim's mother, Jeon Yong Eun, says that in her district in southern Seoul, neighbors and friends prod each other over their children's performance, whipping them into a competitive frenzy. "All of the moms in the neighborhood talk about the best English tutors or the cram schools you have to get your child into, or to get your child to do this or that," she says. "When it is the exam period, all of the coffee shops and restaurants are empty. Everyone is home making sure their kids are studying."[22]

Despite all of the money, effort, and sweat, today's East Asian educational process faces criticism similar to that leveled by Wang Anshi against the examination system during the Song Dynasty almost 1,000 years ago. Wang complained that "teaching has been based on the essays required for the civil service examinations, but this kind of essay cannot be learned without resorting to extensive memorization and strenuous study. . . . Such proficiency as they attain is at best of no use in the government of the empire." Critics today charge that exam-based education, with its focus on rote learning to answer test questions, isn't producing the type of creative thinkers and initiative-takers necessary for today's economy. Morris Chang, founder of Taiwan Semiconductor Manufacturing, complains of the frustration he has experienced trying to encourage innovation at his chipmaker, blaming the education system for fostering "very little independent thinking and very little creativity." Nor do schools allow enough opportunities for specialization to produce experts who can excel based on their specific talents.[23]

What has to change, says Kim Eun Sil, a consultant and author of numerous books on Korea's education system, is the Confucian-induced fixation on the superiority of scholars. Although that preference may drive Asia's quest for knowledge, it has also tarnished other careers and made it difficult for people to take different routes to success. "There are those who are not suited to pursue scholarship," she says:

> There are people with different talents—as hairdressers, or basketball players, or artists—for whom the focus on scholarship has negative consequences. Korean schools don't have alternative choices that take different personal attributes into account. They only want the kids to study, and only the tests lead to success. In order to solve the problem, the divisions between the scholars, farmers, artisans, and merchants have to disappear. It should be okay for a person to graduate high school and become a baker. But in Korea, it is not. You are seen as a loser. The perspective has to change to change the system.[24]

Ironically, today's educators in East Asia could learn a thing or two from Confucius himself. The sage never assumed that everyone was capable of the grueling study necessary to become a *junzi*. Nor did he impose strict methods of learning onto the educational process. Far from encouraging memorization, Confucius taught through lively debates and discussions, and although his students saw him as a superior master, they were not afraid to question him or argue their own views. Confucius, in fact, was critical of disciples who slavishly followed whatever he said. "When I have pointed out one corner of a square to anyone and he does not come back with the other three, I will not point it out to him a second time," he tells us in the *Analects*.[25]

Sadly, these Confucian teaching methods have been forgotten in much of East Asia. That's why fathers like Oh Dong Jin have sacrificed so much to keep their kids *out* of Asian schools. While Korea's "wild geese" dads are symbolic of the beneficial side of the Confucian imprint on East Asian education—the devotion to academic excellence—they also represent the downside of Confucius's influence. Oh simply did not want to subject his daughter to the stresses of succeeding in Korea's test-taking sweatshop. "In South Korea, the education process is very elitist," he complains. "You know there is only a single education path. You have to be part of that order to survive. You can't develop your personal characteristics. The system makes people ordinary and takes away what makes them special." And what would convince him to bring his family home? Not just a reform of education, he says, but a transformation of the entire culture that shapes it. "Korea would have to be a whole different society," he says.

WHILE CONFUCIUS MAY still hold great sway over East Asian school systems, he doesn't have much to do with what students learn while enrolled in them. The substance of the curricula in the region has completely reversed since imperial times. In the days of the emperors, education was entirely centered on the Confucian canon, with little practical training or exposure to other subjects. Now students are drilled in math, reading, and science, with only the tiniest tidbits of Confucius thrown in. Often students learn no more than a few passages from the *Analects*. Perhaps this isn't surprising. How much Plato or Aristotle does the average American read in high school? What makes the Confucian canon different from the Greek classics, however, is how teaching the former is guaranteed to generate controversy. No one would complain if an American school district made the *Iliad* required reading—at least not on philosophical grounds. But Confucius gets a much frostier reception from parents, teachers, and students in East Asia.

Taiwan's Ministry of Education found that out in 2011 when it decided to make the study of the Four Books mandatory for all high-school students. The ministry's officials thought that a strong dose of Confucian ethics would help modern teenagers deal with the pressures of modern life. The reinstatement of Confucian learning was also an attempt to enhance young people's knowledge of their own history and culture. "In Taiwan, we would like to make the renaissance of Chinese culture a very important part of our policy," explains Chen I-hsing, deputy minister of education:

> In the ministry's mind, it is important to pass on the doctrines of Confucius. We think it is important and appropriate for students to learn the Four Books and the theories of Confucianism to lay a solid foundation for their moral teaching. The younger generation has been losing its cultural roots. It is our concern that our next generation hasn't been acknowledging its own Chinese culture, let alone putting it into practice. Being that our country has gone through so many political transitions, we are concerned that the younger generation has lost touch with our own culture.[26]

The backlash, though, was instantaneous. Students complained that they were already burdened by too much work, so why add on even more? Other critics saw politics behind the move and accused the ruling Nationalist Party of attempting to indoctrinate young people with Confucianism to solidify its position, as so many imperial emperors had done throughout Chinese history. Even proponents of Confucianism unaffiliated with the government questioned the decision, fearing that ordering kids to study the Four Books would backfire. "By forcing young people to read these books, books that they will not fully appreciate under such coercive circumstances, Confucian conservatives will simply drive young readers away," contended Williams College political scientist Sam Crane. "Students will remember the classics as those dry and abstruse books they were made to read while they were brimming with adolescent angst, and the memory, for most, will not be a pleasant one."[27]

The main thrust of the opposition, however, was that Confucius's teachings conflicted with the mores and ideals of modern society and therefore were inappropriate for young people today. Confucius had become irrelevant, even dangerous. "I don't think in a modern society you have to know the Four Books," argues Peter Lai, a high-school computer science teacher who was active in a campaign against the ministry's ruling. "Some of it is out of date. When you have a lack of order in society, you don't have to go back to the old philosophies to restore it."[28]

Chen, the deputy minister of education, counters that the foundation of Confucius's teachings is still relevant to the modern world. "Confucianism is all about benevolence. It told us how people should interact with each other," he says. "The core essence of Confucianism is about doing one's duty and being empathetic. He taught one should cultivate oneself to be a better person. His philosophy still lives with us." Sensitive to the criticism, however, Chen did add that Confucius could not be taught in the same way he had been in the past. Taiwan's schools would instruct students in an updated version of Confucius, adjusted to contemporary notions of human rights and social norms. "There are some parts of Confucianism that are an ill-fit with modern society," Chen admits. To address this, the ministry devised a special curriculum and teacher-training program to scrub unwanted notions from Confucius's philosophy. "When some of the comments made by Confucius in his time are no longer appropriate in modern times, we will fix it," Chen says. "We will find a way to make it right."

Both the proponents and opponents of teaching Confucianism single out one aspect of the sage's doctrine that they believe requires the most urgent "fixing"—its attitude toward women, which Chen denounces as "very biased." Of all the attacks on Confucius, none have stung more painfully or done greater damage to his image than the accusation that he is a hopeless misogynist.

Chapter Seven

Confucius the Chauvinist

Women and servants are most difficult to nurture. If one
is close to them, they lose their reserve, while if one is
distant, they feel resentful.
—*Confucius*

When Judy Pae joined South Korean giant LG Electronics in 1996, she discovered she was something of an oddity. That wasn't because she was especially better educated than her colleagues, or got paid any more, or had any unique expertise. It was simply because she was female. Of the 30,000 employees working for the TV and appliance manufacturer in Korea at that time, fewer than 100 were college-educated, career-minded women like herself. On her own team in the technology marketing department, Pae was the sole woman. Although there were other women in the office, they were primarily administrative staff, quaintly attired in flight-attendant-style uniforms. They were expected to do little more than serve tea, make photocopies, and quit when they got married. Pae was the sort of colleague her male peers had rarely encountered—a professional woman who was there not to serve, but to work and compete as an equal—and they simply did not know how to deal with her. "They were not ready to accept women colleagues," Pae says.[1]

At first, Pae struggled to fit in. Her officemates frequently spoke to her condescendingly, as if her gender made her unable to comprehend the responsibilities of her job. "They didn't know how to communicate with me," she recalls. "They gave me a suspicious look, like 'Does she know what I'm talking about?' They treated me like a little child." She realized the only way to succeed was to act like the men—to slave in the office for long hours, engage in after-work socializing, and sacrifice personal interests for the firm. "Being a woman, I had to prove that I was not inferior to men," Pae says.

"I tried to do everything that they did. I had to prove that I was not different, that I can do what you do." She threw herself into her work, striving to out-perform her male peers to show that she belonged. "My nickname was 200 percent," she says.

Pae, however, couldn't really be one of the boys. In Korean companies, participating in dinners and drinking sessions is considered a necessary part of team building. Pae was welcome to join, but only to a point. Her male compatriots would occasionally frequent hostess bars, known as "room sa-lons" in Korea, to cavort with scantily clad and sometimes monetarily avail-able girls. Pae got left behind. Even in the office, her tactics made her stand out, not blend in. Pae's coworkers started calling her a "Gold Miss," a term used in Korea to describe an unmarried working woman who is too devoted to her job to find a husband. "People were looking at me, saying Judy is not getting married because she is a workaholic. I hated that comment," she says. Meanwhile, the number of other professional women her age in the company dwindled as many departed to get married or raise children. "They started to drop out one by one," Pae recounts. "They were saying, 'I can't imagine work-ing here anymore, I get [fewer] chances, I didn't get promoted because I am a woman.' They were feeling a glass ceiling. How long can I survive here? I was questioning myself."

Pae stuck it out. To their credit, Pae's managers supported her efforts and promoted her with regularity, and at a slightly faster pace than many of her male colleagues. Nevertheless, she eventually came to accept that she could progress no further. At more senior positions within her department, Pae would have had to contend more directly with the Korean business com-munity at large, still very much a man's world. "I also felt the glass ceiling," she says. "Going for an executive position, there are 20 or 30 other [male] managers competing with me. Would they pick me? [The next level] involves a lot of socializing and it has been dominated by men. A female executive looking after a whole team, there is no chance that a woman can do it. There were no more steps I could go." In 2010, she quit LG and took a job at the US consulting firm Accenture, where she believes her prospects for advance-ment will be better than at a Korean company.

Pae's experience is shared every day by working women across East Asia. It is not unusual to enter the offices of a major Japanese or South Korean enterprise and find hardly any women at all. The gap between the percentage of men and women who work is larger in Korea than in any other country in the Organization for Economic Cooperation and Development. (Japan comes in second.) Most working women are in secretarial or other minor posts that hold almost no chance of promotion into the higher ranks of the corporate world. Women are in many cases still expected to leave their jobs once they get married, and especially after they have children. The result is that the executive suite is practically a men's clubhouse. Only 9 percent of management positions in Japan and South Korea are held by women, compared to 43 percent in the United States, according to a 2012 study by the International Monetary Fund.[2]

For many frustrated professional women in East Asia, Confucius is holding the keys to the corner office, and he's not unlocking it for them. For more than 2,000 years, Confucianism has taught that a woman's place is in the home, while the realm of commerce and public affairs was open to men only. That worldview is dying hard today. Many women believe they will never be treated as equals in the workforce as long as Confucius remains on the job. "Confucianism has played a big role in blocking women from going out and succeeding in their career lives," Pae says. "People think that Confucianism doesn't do good for our country. I think we should abandon that old concept."

The problem, says Pae, runs deeper than the male-dominated corporate office. Prescribed Confucian roles for the two genders are so hardened after so many centuries that those women who want a career also face resistance at home. In Confucian practice, the husband is supposed to lead, and the wife follow, and that mindset has made many men in East Asia object to their wives' professional ambitions. "There is a proverb in Korea that a family goes down when the hen crows louder than the cock," Pae complains. "That is Confucianism in the family. Let's say the wife makes more money than the husband, the husband gets mad because they feel that they are behind. The wife isn't obeying her husband. That is the starting point where Confucianism has to stop."

Such stresses have led many women in the region to believe they must choose between family and career. Fiona Bae, founder of her own public-relations firm in Seoul, has decided to forgo marriage and children in order to manage her company. "Confucianism doesn't allow women to do the same work as men and defines the woman's role as being the mother and wife. It still has a strong influence," Bae explains. "I'm serious about my career, that's my first choice. It would be difficult for me to have a kid. I felt how difficult it would be if I tried to do both. The whole family expects the mom to take care of the kids. There is a clear difference when it comes to the expectation of how much time Dad should be spending to take care of the kid. If the guy is willing to help out, even on the weekend, it is such a rare thing."[3]

The criticisms these two Korean professionals level against Confucius are mild in comparison to the vitriolic invectives that other women have hurled at the great sage over the past century. Feminist philosopher Julia Kristeva denounced Confucius as an "eater of women"; a female Chinese activist labeled his teachings a "murderous learning." For many writers of both genders, the history of Confucianism is synonymous with the intensifying oppression of women over the course of East Asia's imperial age. Confucius's attitude toward the fairer sex and women's rights has done more to tarnish his reputation in modern times than any other issue. Many women, both Asian and non-Asian, believe he was utterly patriarchal and misogynistic, a relic who still prevents them from attaining their proper place in the world. In the words of philosophy professor Li-hsiang Lisa Rosenlee, Confucianism is nothing less than "the root of gender oppression in the history of Chinese women."[4]

Confucianism must bear at least some responsibility for condemning women to centuries of systematic mistreatment throughout East Asia. During the imperial age, Confucius's teachings created a society in which women were reduced to little more than household servants and human chattel often bought and sold as concubines. Almost powerless against the demands of their fathers and husbands, they were locked away in the kitchen and bedroom with little hope of participating in public life. Many women were unable to even walk, crippled by the brutal practice of foot-binding, all for the erotic pleasure of men. The arrival of a baby girl was greeted by her family not with celebration, but with grief and shame. Since only male heirs could inherit property and carry on the family name, women were considered no more than a financial burden, another mouth to feed or dowry to pay. A girl was destined to get married and serve out her productive years in her husband's household, making little contribution to the family's economic well-being. As a result, many newborn girls were simply murdered. Female infanticide has been a stain on East Asian history for centuries, and it persists today, made even easier by ultrasound equipment that can identify a child's sex in the womb. Purging the offending female can now be achieved without enduring the usual nine months of pregnancy. In China, the one-child policy has compounded the problem. So many couples have chosen not to "waste" their lone opportunity to form a family on a girl that far more boys have been born since the population-control measure was instated in 1979. That has created a major imbalance between men and women in the country. China is expected to have some 30 million more men than women in 2020, potentially creating a major social problem.

The inferior position of women in East Asian societies has been the bloodiest and most damning legacy of Confucius's enduring influence. The relentless discrimination perpetrated against women in East Asia by Confucian practice has, more than any other issue, brought into question the sage's relevance in the modern world. As the ideal of gender parity has filtered into East Asia over the past century, Confucian ideas about the place of women in society, much like filial piety, came to seem archaic and retrograde. The issue of women's rights, perhaps more than any other, shows how Confucius's confrontation with globalization has challenged his once-unquestioned stature in East Asia. If Confucius intends to maintain his influence in the region, he is somehow going to have to repair his relationship with women.

WAS CONFUCIUS TRULY a raging misogynist? It isn't as easy a question to answer as you might think. Confucius didn't give us a very detailed explanation of his views on women. In fact, he said very little about women in his recorded comments in the *Analects*, the most reliable source on his teachings. Perhaps his reticence tells us that he didn't distinguish between men and women in his thinking as much as many believe today. All people, whatever their mix of chromosomes, were to abide by the same codes of propriety, to pursue benevolence, and to follow his version of the Golden Rule ("Do not impose on others what you yourself do not desire"[5]). A less charitable interpretation, however, would be that women simply didn't merit his attention. Women rarely figure in Confucius's life story. Although he advocated universal education, none of his known disciples were female. The rulers and ministers he sought out were exclusively male. Despite the thousands upon thousands of pages devoted to Confucius over the centuries, no one bothered to record the names of his daughters. Confucius's world was a man's world.

The few comments that Confucius did make about women—at least those recorded and handed down to us—were not flattering. In his most infamous statement, the sage unambiguously takes the position that women are inferior and should be treated as such. "Women and servants are most difficult to nurture," Confucius says in the *Analects*. "If one is close to them, they lose their reserve, while if one is distant, they feel resentful."[6] This one statement has perhaps gotten Confucius into more hot water than any other. The mere fact that Confucius bunches women and servants together is enough to offend the modern sensibility. That Confucius goes on to suggest that becoming too close to women only emboldens them to overstep their proper place just adds insult to injury.

Another story in the *Analects* suggests that Confucius did not believe women were worthy of participation in important affairs of society. King Wu, one of the many rulers Confucius encountered, boasted that he had ten able ministers, a coterie surpassing even the talent surrounding an ancient sage-king. Confucius, however, responded: "With a woman amongst them, there were, in fact, only nine."[7] In Confucius's model society, the realm of government and civil service was exclusively for men.

The women who appear in the bibliographical records about Confucius are very often portrayed as temptresses who cloud the minds of men, causing them to stray from the proper path. Remember how Confucius supposedly resigned from his ministerial post in Lu because his ruler was frolicking with young beauties rather than tending to state rituals? The most prominent woman mentioned in the *Analects* is the manipulative and oversexed Nanzi, who was responsible for corrupting the ruler of Wei. Confucius seems to have believed that fascination with women was incongruous with the pursuit of virtuous behavior. "I have yet to meet the man who is as fond of virtue as he is of beauty in women," he laments in the *Analects*. To be a true gentleman, he also warns, a young man "should guard against the attraction of feminine beauty." Like alluring sirens, women, he feared, could lead men to their doom. (Of course, such a characterization of women isn't unique to Confucianism. Recall that it was Eve who convinced Adam to nosh on the forbidden fruit in the Garden of Eden.)[8]

Discrimination against women in China, however, did not originate with Confucius. On certain issues, Confucius was ahead of his time—on his promotion of meritocracy, for instance—but not on this one. His sentiments on women were simply the standard in the China of his day. China had long been a patriarchal society by the time Confucius arrived on the scene. For generations, the Chinese elite worshipped ancestors exclusively on the father's side of the family. Lineage passed from father to son to grandson, with women factoring in only as wombs to breed sons to carry on the names of their husbands' clans. The sage's goal was to strengthen families with traditional social norms as a foundation for his harmonious society, not champion revolutionary ideas or overturn the social order.

It is also important to note that at no point in the *Analects* does the sage ever specifically outline his views on the male-female or husband-wife relationship. That was left to later texts, in which the words attributed to Confucius are not considered as reliable. Even then, what he is quoted saying can be open to interpretation. "What are 'the things which men consider right?'"

Confucius asks in *The Book of Rites*. "Kindness on the part of the father, and filial duty on that of the son; gentleness on the part of the elder brother, and obedience on that of the younger; righteousness on the part of the husband, and submission on that of the wife; kindness on the part of elders, and deference on that of juniors; with benevolence on the part of the ruler, and loyalty on that of the minister."[9] Immediately the eye focuses on the word "submission" here—an indication that Confucius saw women in a subordinate position to men. But also take note of the full phrase Confucius uses. The ideal Confucian relationship may not have been entirely equal, but neither was it meant to be abusive or unjust. As with fathers and sons, the husband-wife relationship was supposed to be reciprocal and complementary. Although Confucius, in this passage, says women ought to be submissive, their husbands were also to be righteous. The responsibilities within the relationship ran in two directions.

The Confucians, furthermore, considered the position and duties they assigned to women to be of great importance. Emphasizing the separate, but equally critical, roles of husband and wife, Mencius espoused a concept that became known as the "Five Relationships." "The relations of humanity," he said, concerned "how, between father and son, there should be affection; between sovereign and minister, righteousness; between husband and wife, attention to their separate functions; between old and young, a proper order; and between friends, fidelity."[10] Mencius here was expressing his views on the wise division of labor in society, not the creation of an oppressive hierarchy. He was responding to an inquisitor who argued that a good ruler should be so humble as to till his own food. Mencius thought that was ridiculous. It is wasteful and unproductive for everyone in society to do everything themselves, he answered. People should play roles in society based on their abilities and positions. A proper king needed to run the government, not plow the fields; that should be left to farmers, who specialized in agriculture. Ditto with husband and wife. Each had a special part to play in the world. That was why the correct relationship between a married couple was based on "attention to their separate functions."

Those "special functions" defined what men and women contributed to society. In the Confucian world, men and women were meant to occupy different realms. Public affairs, statecraft, and commerce were to be handled by men; maintaining the household and bearing and raising children were the tasks of women. "The men should not speak of what belongs to the inside (of the house), nor the women of what belongs to the outside," *The Book of Rites* tells us. Another classic, *The Book of Odes*, is even blunter, proclaiming that "women should not take part in public affairs; they should devote themselves to tending silkworms and weaving."[11]

To modern ears, all of this sounds like a ploy to keep women barefoot and pregnant, and to a certain extent, it was. Someone had to tend to children, cook, clean, sew, aid elderly parents, and, in wealthier households, manage the servants. As was the case with Confucius's concepts of "rectification of names" and filial piety, a peaceful society depended on everyone fulfilling his or her responsibilities, not pursuing personal choices—women included. But within their own realm, women were to wield significant authority. As noted above, *The Book of Rites* makes clear that a man "should not speak" of what goes on inside the household—there, his wife reigned supreme. (That led twentieth-century reformer Hu Shi to comment that in China the "woman has always been the despot of the family. . . . No other country in the world can compete with China for the distinction of being the nation of hen-pecked husbands."[12]) The "well-regulated" family simply could not function without the wife/mother doing her part. Seen in that context, the good wife was no less important to the stability and prosperity of the world than a filial son, or a virtuous ruler, or a loyal minister.

LATER CONFUCIANS, HOWEVER, were only too eager to take what they wanted from Confucius's teachings to condemn women to inferior status. Confucian scholars routinely stressed that women were to yield to men and accept a secondary position in their marriages, their households, and the world at large. Even the kindly Mencius joined the chorus. "At the marrying away of a young woman, her mother admonishes her, accompanying her to the door on her leaving, and cautioning her with these words, 'You are going to your home. You must be respectful; you must be careful. Do not disobey your husband,'" Mencius said. "Thus, to look upon compliance as their correct course is the rule for women."[13]

Women were in effect relegated to the position of assistants, whose duty it was to support men in their greater endeavors in the wider world, while they themselves were barred from pursuit of those opportunities. Men could become ministers, scholars, and officials; women, with few exceptions, never could. Instead, they were to conduct the business of the household so that men could be unfettered by such mundane matters. Men could cultivate themselves into *junzi*, true gentlemen; women could never attain this ultimate Confucian goal. Women had little independence of action on any front, or, to a certain extent, even identities of their own. A woman was always someone's daughter, wife, or mother; there was always some master to obey. "In passing out from the great gate (of her father's house), he [the new husband] precedes, and she follows, and with this the right relation between husband and wife commences," *The Book of Rites* commands. "The woman follows the man: in her youth, she follows her father and elder brother; when married, she follows her husband; when her husband is dead, she follows her son."[14]

Over time, Confucians steadily pushed aside the reciprocity in Confucius's model relationships and instead gave primacy to hierarchical roles. During the Han Dynasty, Mencius's Five Relationships got boiled down into the Three Bonds (also called the Three Mainstays)—between ruler and subject, father and son, and husband and wife. This new concept was more than just a simplification—it brought about a substantive shift from Mencius's original intention. The idea of the Three Bonds was initiated by the prolific Dong Zhongshu, who stressed the "superior" to "inferior" aspect of the pairings. "Although the Confucian five human relations are established on the basis of mutual moral obligation, at the same time the thought was inherent in the Confucian system that the ruler, the father and the husband are superior to the ruled, the son and the wife," explained scholar Chan Wing-tsit in his anthology of Chinese philosophy. "This distinction is strengthened by Dong Zhongshu, for by 'bond' is meant not merely a relationship but a standard."[15]

By the Later Han Dynasty (AD 25–220), the Three Bonds had become firmly entrenched in Confucian thought; they sat at the heart of a greater social network of relations that formed a stable society, like the ties within a sprawling net. This system was outlined in *Discussions in White Tiger Pavilion*, a record of conversations at the Han court during the first century AD. In the Three Bonds, the positions of "superior and inferior are spread out and regulated, and the way of man is adjusted and ordered," the discussions made clear. "All men harbor the instinct for the Five Constant Virtues, and possess the disposition to love; they are developed by the Three Bonds . . . as a net which has small and large net-ropes spreads out its ten thousand meshes." The conversations also defined the primary duties forged through marriage. "What do 'husband' and 'wife' mean? 'Husband' means 'support'; the husband provides the support by means of the Way. 'Wife' means 'to submit.'"[16]

Dong also awarded the inequality of the Three Bonds a sort of cosmic sanction by infusing Chinese yin-yang theory into Confucianism. Yin and yang are two complementary forces, and the interaction between them is what causes change in the world—the passing of the seasons, for example, or patterns of life and death. Yang is the stronger element and is more active or positive, representing brightness and assertiveness. Yin is the weaker element and is more passive or negative, representing darkness and yielding. Dong gave these two forces their manifestations in mankind—yang is male, the dominant force, and yin is female, the subordinate force. Yang and yin are equally important—the world simply couldn't function without both of them. But by mixing yin-yang concepts into Confucian theories of human relations, Dong transformed the superiority of men and the inferiority of women into as intrinsic a distinction as that between spring and autumn or light and shadow.

The Three Bonds became so important in Chinese thought and society that the concept came to define China's self-image as a cultured civilization. These pairs of hierarchical relationships were what the Chinese believed distinguished them from the "barbarians" who surrounded them. But the concept of the Three Bonds was also a method of social control. In equating filial piety toward one's father with loyalty to the state, Confucian thinkers were trying to transfer a familial relationship to the political realm in order to construct a stable empire. By stressing the dominant-subordinate nature of marriage ties, they were attempting to promote their idea of a peaceful society. The inequality inherent in the Three Bonds, however, became a primary reason for Confucianism's reputation as misogynistic and unjust. "In the modern egalitarian and liberal perspective, the least defensible legacy of Confucian ethics is the so-called Three Bonds," commented Tu Wei-ming, one of the most important Confucian scholars of the twentieth century. "The Three Bonds have been depicted as three forms of bondage and Confucian ethics condemned as despotic, autocratic, patriarchal, gerontocratic, and male-chauvinistic."[17]

Tu blames the formation of the Three Bonds on the Confucians' assumption of political influence within the imperial system. Once ensconced in the halls of the palace, the Confucians felt it necessary to craft policies to appeal to the government's interests and bolster their own position at court. The formulation of the Three Bonds represents a persistent conflict within Confucianism that began the instant its proponents transferred themselves from their study halls to the royal court—the tension between the doctrine's idealistic roots and the political prerogatives of managing states and maintaining influence with the emperor. The result of that friction, said Tu, was an extremely altered Confucianism and Confucius. "The word 'Confucian' here has taken on a new meaning," Tu wrote. "It is no longer the teachings of Confucius and his disciples.... Rather, the Confucians who propounded the logic of the Three Bonds were prominent scholars of the Han court who, as shapers of an emerging political ideology . . . , were invited by the emperor to reach a national consensus on the vital cosmological and ethical issues confronting the state."[18]

THE CONFUCIANS WASTED no time in indoctrinating women on their proper role in society—in fact, their brainwashing began only hours after emerging from their mothers' wombs. "On the third day after a girl was born, people placed her at the base of the bed, gave her a pot shard to play with, and made a sacrifice to announce her birth," explained Han Dynasty–era scholar Ban Zhao in her treatise *Admonitions for Women*, probably the most influential Confucian text on proper female behavior. "She was put below the bed to show that she was lowly and weak and should concentrate on humbling herself before others. Playing with a shard showed that she should get accustomed to hard work and concentrate on being diligent." Boys were sent off to study the classics, while girls were kept at home and schooled in household duties from an early age. "Daughters remain behind in the women's quarters and should not be allowed to go out very often," instructs *The Analects for Women*, another important how-to guide, which is credited to Tang Dynasty scholar and court tutor Song Ruozhao. "Teach them sewing, cooking and etiquette. . . . Don't allow them to go on outings, lest some scandal spoil their good names." That training prepared girls for the hard labor they would perform for the rest of their lives. "Industriousness means going to bed late, getting up early, never shirking work morning or night, never refusing to take on domestic work, and completing everything that needs to be done neatly and carefully," Ban Zhao taught.[19]

Confucian ritual texts laid down the responsibilities and rules for a woman's daily life in excruciating specificity. *The Analects for Women* expounded at length on the "wifely way," or *fudao*, instructing women on all manner of household tasks. "To be a woman one must learn the details of women's work," the text says. "Learn how to weave with hemp and ramie; don't mix fine and rough fibers. Don't run the shuttle of the loom so quickly that you make a mess. . . . Learn how to cut out shoes and make socks. Learn how to cut fabric and sew it into garments. Learn how to embroider, mend, and darn." The proper wife started her day at dawn and immediately got to her chores. "Go to the kitchen, light the fire, and start the morning meal," the text orders. "Scrub the pots and wash the pans, boil the tea water and cook the gruel. Plan your meals according to the resources of the family and the seasons of the year, making sure that they are fragrant and tasty, served in the appropriate dishes and in the proper manner at the table. If you start early there is nothing you can't get done in a day!"[20]

Not only were the tasks of men and women made distinct, but the sexes themselves were supposed to be kept at a distance. The rules governing the separation of the genders reached amazing degrees of complexity in old ritual texts. Stuffy Confucian morality dictated that the sexes should have almost nothing to do with one another, either in the household or in public. "Male and female should not sit together (in the same apartment), nor have the same stand or rack for their clothes, nor use the same towel or comb, nor let their hands touch in giving and receiving," *The Book of Rites* mandates. "Male and female, without the intervention of the matchmaker, do not know each other's name. Unless the marriage presents have been received, there should be no communication nor affection between them." Women, in fact, were supposed to be almost entirely hidden from the eyes of anyone who was not a relative. "The inner and outer quarters are each distinct; the sexes should be segregated," insists *The Analects for Women*. "Don't peer over the outer wall or go beyond the outer courtyard. If you have to go outside, cover your face."[21]

The only relationship a woman was allowed to have with a man was the one that was selected by another man, her father. A girl rarely had any say in the choice of her husband; parents made all of the arrangements for both bride and groom. The concept of marriage in imperial China was extremely different from today's understanding in the West. It was more a pairing between families than a union of individuals; the actual intimacy of the relationship between man and wife was secondary—if it mattered at all. Once betrothed, the newlywed woman departed from her father's home and entered the household of her husband's clan. Here she became subjected to a new tyranny imposed by her parents-in-law, for whom she was effectively expected to be a personal servant. The rules dictating her behavior toward her husband's parents were numerous, strict, and overbearing. "No daughter-in-law, without being told to go to her own apartment, should venture to withdraw from that (of her parents-in-law)," *The Book of Rites* says. "Whatever she is about to do, she should ask leave from them. If any one give the wife an article of food or dress, a piece of cloth or silk, a handkerchief for her girdle, an iris or orchid, she should receive and offer it to her parents-in-law. If they accept it, she will be glad as if she were receiving it afresh. If they return it to her, she should decline it, and if they do not allow her to do so, she will take it as if it were a second gift, and lay it by to wait till they may want it." *The Analects for Women* elaborates even more restrictions. "Respectfully serve your father-in-law. Do not look at him directly (when he speaks to you) . . . and do not engage him in conversation. If he has an order for you, listen and obey. When your mother-in-law is sitting, you should stand. When she gives an order, you should carry it out right away."[22]

When a married woman was not serving her in-laws, her main responsibility was to bear and raise children. Having kids was practically a Confucian commandment; not doing so was the worst offense to the virtue of filial piety. "There are three things which are unfilial, and to have no posterity is the greatest of them," Mencius said.[23] As a result, a woman often got impregnated ten or more times over the course of her life. Having just any child would not do, however. A wife did not fulfill her duties to her husband until she bore a male heir. Daughters simply did not count.

A LIFE LOCKED away from view, at the mercy of husbands and in-laws, slaving away in the kitchen and pumping out babies might sound stifling, demeaning, and degrading. Yet it is misleading to see the Confucian ideal of womanhood through our twenty-first-century lens. Although most women found that any possibility of personal development was crushed, the Confucians nevertheless handed them a critical role in their social system—as nothing short of the guardians of morality in society. Possessed of the immense responsibility of teaching children, and even husbands, the rules of proper behavior within the home, women were the cultivators of gentlemen, the selfless mentors who instilled the morals that sons and husbands required when they set out to govern the world. Confucius believed that much of what a man needed to know about being a proper gentleman could be learned within the family home; wives and mothers were the ones who taught them.

This point becomes clear in *The Classic of Filiality for Women*. Following a format similar to the original *Classic of Filial Piety*, this text was likely compiled by Chen Miao, the wife of an official in the Tang Dynasty. The treatise purports to be a transcript of a conversation between Ban Zhao, standing in for Confucius as the font of knowledge, and some eager but inexperienced girls who are seeking advice on correct womanly behavior. Ban Zhao explains to them how women, by being virtuous themselves, can transform society as a whole. "By your guiding of him with respect and love, your gentleman [husband] will not forget his sense of filiality to his parents," she says. "By your presenting him with a model of virtuous conduct, he will improve his behavior. . . . By your demonstrating the difference between good and evil, he will understand what conduct is unallowable." Nearly plagiarizing a passage from the original, Ban Zhao recoils in horror when her charges equate womanly virtue with absolute submission. Women, like sons, were obligated to speak up to correct wrongdoing. "We dare to ask whether if we follow all our husbands' commands, we could be called virtuous?" the girls inquire. "What kind of talk is that! What kind of talk is that!" Ban Zhao exclaims. "If a husband has a remonstrating wife, then he won't fall into evil ways."[24]

In the Confucian view, then, women were almost saintly figures—submissive, yes, but with a grander purpose. They sacrificed for the good of their families and the world. "Let a woman modestly yield to others; let her respect others; let her put others first, herself last," Ban Zhao wrote. "Let a woman be composed in demeanor and upright in bearing in the service of her husband." The vast majority of women passively endured lives of housework and servitude and willingly obeyed their fathers, husbands, and in-laws to adhere to this Confucian model of womanhood. Many today would say that they had no other choice. Yet women were responding to a set of social norms that were highly esteemed in Chinese society. They were upholding a moral standard that had become unquestioned. "Mothers were . . . credited with training their daughters to be sweet, agreeable, deferential and reserved," explained Patricia Ebrey, a modern expert on the history of women in China. "Mothers did not look on cultivation of these traits as complicity in women's oppression. Rather, they took pride in rearing daughters whom others would praise as beautiful and feminine." Gu Ruopo, a poet and devoted mother, captured these sentiments in a 1632 letter to her sons. "I tasted all sufferings and experienced every tribulation," she wrote. "In fear and caution I rose early to toil and retired late to ponder the day. My only thought was to avoid any mistake so that my ancestors' law will not be violated and my parents' concerned care will not be in vain. Do you suppose that I endured all the hardship because I enjoyed it? . . . Every fiber and every grain this family owns are the fruits of my industry and hardship over several decades. Preserve and magnify them. These are the high hopes I have for my two sons."[25]

The Confucians achieved such enthusiastic compliance by building paragons of proper feminine behavior against which women judged themselves and were judged by others. One of the more effective forms of indoctrination was through folksy stories that were told and retold in living rooms and village courtyards throughout the country. Just as the tales in *The Twenty-Four Filial Exemplars* aimed at infusing loyal behavior in children, another compilation, *Biographies of Exemplary Women*, attempted the same for the fairer sex. Collected in the first century BC by Han Dynasty scholar Liu

Xiang, in part from much older material, the biographies highlight female figures whom the Confucians presented as models for all proper women to follow. The stories tell of righteous women who were devoted mothers and dutiful wives, obedient, wise, and, of course, unquestionably modest and chaste. (The uptight Confucians were as insistent on female chastity as any parochial school headmaster.)

Typical of the entries is the biography of the mother of Mencius. Mother Meng, the story goes, moved her household twice to protect her son from bad environments (a graveyard and a marketplace), eventually settling near a schoolhouse—just the right spot for an education-minded mom. When the young Mencius was slacking on his studies, Mother Meng took a knife and sliced through cloth she was hard at work weaving. "Your being remiss in your studies is like my cutting the web of my loom," she lectured. Scared straight, Mencius "studied diligently morning and evening without respite," the biographer tells us, and "consequently became the most famous scholar of the whole nation"—all thanks to his mother's timely intervention. When Mother Meng grew old, Mencius wished to seek employment in a different state, but he refrained, feeling it was his duty to remain with his beloved mother. Noticing his despondency, Mother Meng saw an opportunity to impart a lesson on the proper position of women. "It does not belong to the woman to determine anything herself," she told Mencius. "When married, she has to obey her husband; when her husband is dead, she obeys her son."[26]

As is the case with filial piety stories, these biographies sometimes praised extreme behavior. One story tells the tragic tale of Jiang, the wife of King Zhao of the state of Chu. The king had gone off on a trip, leaving Jiang on a terrace near a river. While he was away, the river began rising, becoming a flood threatening to burst its banks, and placing Jiang in mortal danger. The king dispatched an official to bring her to safety. When the official arrived, however, Jiang refused to accompany him. In his rush to save the queen, the messenger had forgotten his seal of office, and, as Jiang told him, her arrangement with her husband mandated that she only accept orders from men carrying such a seal. The official warned her that delay might end in tragedy. "Now, the river is rising very high," the anxious official said, "and if I return to get the seal, I fear that it will be too late." Still, the queen wouldn't budge. The occasion allows Jiang to educate the reader about the importance of loyalty, even when facing certain death. "I have learned that the duty of a chaste woman is not to break an agreement," she told the official. "To break an agreement and violate righteousness is not so good as to remain here and die." As the official hurried off to retrieve the seal, the raging waters washed

Jiang away. When the distraught king heard of her fate, he lauded her and gave her the honorary title of "Jiang the Chaste."[27]

CONFORMING TO THE ideal Confucian conception of womanhood took on more and more extreme forms, especially during and after the Song Dynasty (960–1279). Most barbaric of all was the practice of foot-binding. Starting when girls were as young as five years old, strips of cloth were wrapped around their feet to prevent them from growing. The small, fragile feet that resulted—often no more than four inches long—were highly prized by men as a mark of good breeding and erotic beauty. Yet the process was excruciating; the girls who endured it suffered not only physically but also emotionally. Some left heartrending tales of the desperation, depression, and revulsion they felt, and their frantic, fruitless efforts to escape the relentless pain.

"Both feet became feverish at night and hurt from the swelling," one woman, a maid, known to us only as Chang, once recounted. "Mother rebound my feet weekly, each time more tightly than the last. I became more and more afraid. I tried to avoid the binding by hiding in a neighbor's house. If I loosened the bandage, Mother would scold me for not wanting to look nice. . . . Corns began to appear and thicken. . . . Mother would remove the bindings and lance the corns with a needle. . . . I feared this, but mother grasped my legs so I couldn't move." Chang, betrothed at age nine to a neighbor's son, was sent to serve in her future husband's house, where her fate worsened:

> My mother-in-law bound my feet much more tightly than mother even had, saying that I still hadn't achieved the standard. She beat me severely if I cried; if I unloosened the binding, I was beaten until my body was covered with bruises. . . . Looking down, I saw that every toe but the big one was inflamed and deteriorated. . . . I had to be beaten with fists before I could bear to remove the bindings, which were congealed with pus and blood. To get them loose, such force had to be used that the skin often peeled off, causing further bleeding. The stench was hard to bear, while I felt the pain in my very insides. . . . Mother-in-law was not only unmoved but she placed tiles inside the binding in order to hasten the inflammation process.

In the end her feet were only three inches long.[28]

Such tales horrified later observers, both Chinese and foreign. Lin Yutang, the influential twentieth-century writer, condemned foot-binding as a "monstrous and perverse institution." Yet we should note that women often bound their feet willingly; like many fashions (plastic surgery, for instance), it improved a woman's prospects of landing a good husband. Still, it is highly improbable that Confucius would have condoned such a violent practice. More likely, he would have criticized foot-binding as a violation of filial piety. In *The Classic of Filial Piety*, he specifically states that "our bodies—to every hair and bit of skin—are received by us from our parents, and we must not presume to injure or wound them." Nor was foot-binding directly promoted or advocated by Confucians or Confucianism. Yet some scholars have argued that the Confucians were complicit in popularizing foot-binding by crafting a restrictive standard of proper female behavior and pressuring women to adhere to it. Foot-binding, in this view, was a natural consequence of Confucian influence on social practice, since it allowed a woman to flaunt her devotion to Confucian ideals by rendering herself even more dependent on men and displaying her willingness to sacrifice for her family. "Foot binding was the way women in China supported, participated in, and reflected on the Neo-Confucian way of being civilized," one modern scholar asserted.[29]

Not even the death of her husband freed a woman from her wifely responsibilities. Confucians had always frowned upon the remarriage of widows, believing it was a breach of a woman's commitment to her husband, but the Neo-Confucians touched off a near-obsession with the prohibition. Neo-Confucian philosopher Cheng Yi solidified opposition to widow remarriage by stating that death was preferable to such a dishonor. "If a widow is alone and poor with no one to depend on, is it all right for her to remarry?" Cheng Yi was asked. "This theory arose only because in later ages people fear freezing or starving to death," he responded. "But starving to death is a very minor matter; losing one's integrity is a matter of the gravest importance."[30]

Unmarried widows were treated as national heroines. During the Ming Dynasty (1368–1644), women who remained devoted to their deceased husbands were praised by local officials and held up as models of womanly virtue. A history of Fuzhou in Fujian Province from the Ming period tells of Xu Sungjie, whose husband died before she was able to bear a son. As he lay ill, he implored her to remarry after he passed away, but Xu, after weeping over his coffin, instead hanged herself. An official, "impressed with her fidelity," had a banner displayed at her door that read: "Filial Piety and Propriety." In another example among many, a woman named Huang Yijie lost her fiancé when she was merely fifteen, and a matchmaker started arranging a new husband for her, but without Huang's knowledge. When the young girl heard of it, she "took a bath, combed her hair, and changed into new clothes. Those things done, she took a knife and cut her throat." Apparently, she was not successful on her first try. "In the morning, when her family found her body, there were traces of three cuts."[31]

BY THE NINETEENTH century, both Chinese and Western reformers were beginning to see women such as Huang Yijie not as exemplars to be emulated, but as victims to be rescued. The Confucian social practices and family rituals that had been the hallmark of the Chinese self-image of superiority morphed under the gaze of missionaries, revolutionaries, and feminists into a system of abuse and a source of national embarrassment. May Fourth Movement writer Chen Duxiu, rather than praising unmarried widows as so many Ming Neo-Confucians had, blamed Confucius for their lonely fate. "These women have had no freedom," he penned. "Year after year these many promising young women have lived a physically and spiritually abnormal life. All this is the result of Confucian teachings of ritual decorum."[32]

Examined under a spotlight of Western concepts of equality and egalitarianism, the condition of Chinese women came to represent what seemed to be the backwardness of the civilization in which they lived and the doctrine that had shaped it. Feminists looked upon Chinese women as symbols of global discrimination against the "second sex," and Confucianism as representative of the outmoded doctrines that oppressed them in the name of morality and social stability. "[Chinese] women are, at best, passed over in silence," feminist philosopher Julia Kristeva said. "Cloistered in their houses, . . . they are, according to Confucianism, destined only for housework and reproduction."[33] For many, the housebound Chinese woman took on tremendous meaning, becoming a mark of the failure of East Asian civilization to adjust to the modern age and evidence of the supremacy of Western over Eastern culture.

The repression of women in East Asia, and the conviction that Confucianism was responsible for it, were important factors prompting the wider reassessment of the sage and his teachings and their value in the modern world. Many young Chinese thinkers, heavily influenced by ideas from the West, came to see Confucius and modernity as simply incompatible. They concluded that the only way for East Asian women to advance and gain their freedom was to purge Confucianism—or, more accurately, what

Confucianism had become over the centuries—from the family and society. "The learning of Confucianism has tended to be oppressive and to promote male selfishness," wrote He Zhen, a member of an anarchist movement in the early twentieth century:

> Therefore, Confucianism marks the beginning of justifications for polyg-
> amy and chastity. People of the Han Dynasty studied Confucianism and
> felt free to twist the meaning of the ancient writings as they pertained
> to women in order to extend their own views. . . . Cunning people have
> dressed up these theories to their own advantage. Stupid people believe
> in these theories with a superstitious force impregnable to skepticism. I
> don't know how many of us women have died as a result. . . . If we do not
> utterly abolish the false doctrines of the Confucian writings, the truth will
> never again be heard.[34]

Just as Chen Duxiu and others were blaming filial piety for the oppres-
siveness of Chinese society, female reformers saw the Confucian family as
the institution responsible for the sorry fate of Chinese women. "The family
is the origin of all evil," blasted Han Yi, another radical, in a 1907 essay. "Because of the family, women are increasingly controlled by men. . . . As long
as the family exists, then debauched men will imprison women in cages and
force them to become their concubines and service their lust. . . . The destruction of the family will thus lead to the creation of public-minded people in place of selfish people, and men will have no way to oppress women."[35]

IN RECENT YEARS, however, some scholars have been rethinking Confucius's
relationship with women. Rather than simply dismissing China's most important philosopher as inherently misogynistic and assuming women can
only become equals by eradicating him, they are revisiting Confucius's original teachings to try to reconcile the sage with the modern Asian woman
and her ambitions. This process is critical for the future of Confucius in East
Asian society. If Confucianism cannot adjust to the needs of women today,
its founder's influence may be destined to decline and his reputation will remain blackened.

These new scholars look at Confucianism not as a dogmatic set of beliefs
forged for a bygone age, but as a living doctrine with intrinsic worth that can
adapt to the changing needs of a changing world. One of them is University of Hawaii professor Li-hsiang Lisa Rosenlee. "I was a graduate student

attending a philosophy conference in Hawaii and one Western scholar during a panel discussion made a comment regarding the viability of Confucianism to confront the issue of gender parity," she recalls. "In his opinion, Confucianism is hopelessly misogynistic and paternalistic, and hence as far as gender is concerned, Confucianism is irrelevant. I was deeply puzzled by such a comment, since if Confucianism is unable to deal with the issue of gender, then the whole intellectual tradition itself is useless for modern life. No ethical theory should call itself such if it is unable to deal with the issue of gender."[36]

This incident inspired Rosenlee to theorize about how Confucius's teachings could be acclimated to the needs of a new age. "To find resources within the Confucian tradition to adapt to the modern discourse on gender does not mean that Confucius himself is a feminist or his teaching somehow is pro-gender parity," she explains:

> I am not primarily interested in what Confucius said in his historical time and for what audience and with what intent. As a philosopher, I am interested in what the implication of a particular Confucian concept is and how it can be applied in our own time. And philosophers do this all the time. What I am interested in is to bring in whatever is available in Confucian tradition to make contributions to contemporary feminist theories that seek solutions to gender oppression. Confucius himself might not have much to say about that, but his ideas, just like other great Western philosophers, are still useful and should be accorded with equal value as part of the great human achievement.

In her book *Confucianism and Women*, Rosenlee attempts to tease out the elements of Confucian thought that are compatible with modern feminism. Most importantly, she contends, the walls between the inner and outer worlds of Confucianism, which allowed men the freedom to pursue personal achievement in the public realm but confined women to household and familial responsibilities, must be broken down. Confucianism never permitted women to become Confucian gentlemen—*junzi*—at least not in the same fashion as men, leaving them, in her words, "forever incomplete" and "limited beings." But Confucian practice should be altered, she suggests, so that women can attain *junzi* status by applying the expectations and opportunities for self-cultivation normally reserved for men. The original reciprocal and complementary nature of Confucian relationships should also be reasserted, Rosenlee says. In making these adjustments, Confucianism can accommodate the demands of the modern woman without discarding the main tenets of the doctrine—that personal identity can only be understood in the context of a web of human relations that define who we are and how we should lead our lives. "To admit that there are elements in Confucianism that need rectification is not the same as saying that Confucianism as a whole is essentially sexist and antifeminist," Rosenlee wrote. "Confucianism as a living tradition thrives on incorporating others into its expanding self; its adaptability has been proven again and again in history."[37]

Rosenlee is attempting to do what so many other scholars have managed throughout Confucian history, from Dong Zhongshu to Zhu Xi to Kang Youwei: to reinterpret Confucius in a new way for a new age. Her philosophical exertions may not help the likes of Judy Pae—women fighting to make their way in a Confucian-created, male-dominated East Asia—at least not in the short term. But ultimately, Rosenlee's methods may offer a long-term solution—a reassessment and reinvigoration of Confucian traditions and ethics that keep them at the heart of East Asian culture while adapting them to modern preferences for gender equality and personal freedoms. Confucius has shown such flexibility many times before, and that is why he has enjoyed such a long life through so many twists and turns in history. Whether it was Dong Zhongshu's syncretism or Zhu Xi's reformation, Confucianism has shown again and again that it can morph to fit the needs of changing times. Perhaps Rosenlee's philosophical experiments will eventually come to have a real effect in the world by reshaping what it means to be Confucian in today's society.

The challenge facing Rosenlee is convincing Pae and many others that re-creating Confucius is worth the effort. But Rosenlee is not alone. Since the 1980s, officials, scholars, and businessmen have been revisiting his philosophy and, like Rosenlee, crafting a reformed Confucius for the modern world. Like Emperor Wu of the Han Dynasty, or the great rulers of the early Song, people of influence are finding Confucius useful once again. Some of the self-proclaimed new Confucians are not helping their cause by their often self-serving motivations. However, what is happening today, despite intensifying globalization and decades of rabid criticism, is not Confucius's funeral, but the emergence of a new chapter in his life.

Part Three

The Comeback of Confucius

Chapter Eight

Confucius the Businessman

Virtue is the root; wealth is the result.
—*The Great Learning*

Jin Zhanyong was at the end of his rope. The founder of Tianxia Huibao Culture and Communication, a small company in the Chinese industrial city of Taiyuan that organizes exhibitions and media events, was helplessly watching his business suffer while his workers slacked off and squabbled. Conflicts among the staff became so severe that fistfights broke out. The disorder took a toll as revenues stagnated. Jin simply didn't know what to do.

Then he hired Confucius as a human resources consultant.

For most of his life, Jin knew almost nothing about the sage. That changed in 2011, when the entrepreneur was introduced to Confucianism by other businessmen in Taiyuan who had turned to the master to help them manage their companies. As he perused the *Analects* and participated in the regular discussion sessions the businessmen held, he became inspired. "I was impressed with Confucianism," he says. "It teaches people to be kind to others, to help others, to treat others like members of your own family." Such spirit was exactly what his company needed, Jin determined. If Confucius was acting as a guide in his own life, maybe the sage could do the same for his dispirited workers.[1]

So one day in late 2012, Jin deviated from the usual agenda of the daily morning staff meeting to show a video that introduced passages from the *Analects*. He continued the presentations at subsequent morning meetings. Then he began urging his employees to read Confucian texts on their own—sweetening the request by offering cash bonuses to those who displayed the most knowledge of the sage's teachings. "The main reason I adopted Confucianism was because I thought it would be an efficient way to manage and improve the productivity of the employees," Jin says. "I was hoping it would work, but I wasn't sure. I was just giving it a shot."

The results, Jin says, were immediate and spectacular. Suddenly, the disagreements among the staff ceased. The employees began working harder and more diligently. "The workers really unified," Jin explains. They began to "take independent initiative and proactively contribute to the firm." Within three months of the first *Analects* video, his company's revenues had doubled.

Confucius performed similar wonders for Lu Mingyu, the cofounder of a Taiyuan-based construction and landscaping firm called Ruhai Industrial Group. Lu, who says he has taken interest in traditional Chinese culture since boyhood, began teaching Confucianism to his staff in 2005 by discussing the doctrine in morning meetings and inviting experts to conduct weekly lectures. "The Confucian thought went into their minds and changed their behavior," he says. "Before I introduced Confucianism, the employees would come in to work at 8:30 a.m. and leave at 5:30 p.m. exactly. They didn't want to spend one extra minute in the office. Now they voluntarily work more time. Sometimes I have to force them out of the office." Lu ascribes near-mystical powers to Confucius's mere words. In 2010, Lu confronted hundreds of angry workers who had gone on strike at a construction site. He stood before them and led them in a recitation of some phrases from the *Analects*. Within short order, he says, they all picked up their tools and returned to work.[2]

Confucian learning has also improved his own management practices, Lu says. "I used to just care about how my employees could make money for me," he explains. "Now I want to provide good jobs for my employees. I see them as my family and I want to take care of them. I focus not on moneymaking but on improving myself and my employees on a spiritual level. I tell my employees to study Confucianism and improve themselves and the profits will come." And so they have. Lu says Confucius has fostered not only a healthier workplace, but also a heftier bottom line.

Businesspeople in East Asia routinely look to Confucius for management advice. Tadashi Yanai, CEO of Japan's Fast Retailing, which operates the Uniqlo chain of casual clothing shops around the world, says that Confucianism influences the way he hires and promotes employees. Rather than simply focusing on a person's academic qualifications and skills, he also considers their moral qualities. "In our company no matter how smart you are, unless you are respectful as a human being, unless you are really trusted, you will no longer have a career opportunity," Yanai says. "Unless the candidate understands our culture, no matter how smart they are, they wouldn't be hired." The business acumen of Confucius has not gone unnoticed in the

West, either. Dale Carnegie, in his classic *How to Win Friends and Influence People*, a virtual bible for salesmen originally published in 1936, quotes the sage in his opening pages. "Do you know someone you would like to change and regulate and improve? Good!" Carnegie wrote. "But why not begin on yourself? . . . 'Don't complain about the snow on your neighbor's roof,' said Confucius, 'when your own doorstep is unclean.'"[3]

For many Asia watchers, the impact of Confucius on economics and business has gone far beyond a few happy employees. In recent decades, as one East Asian nation after another—China, Japan, South Korea, Singapore—became an industrial powerhouse, some economists credited Confucius for the region's spectacular success. Confucius, they contended, laid the cultural foundation within East Asian societies that made rapid development possible. There is great irony here. For much of the previous 150 years, Confucius's critics, both in the East and West, had pointed to Confucius as the source of Asia's weakness, identifying him as a major impediment to modernization. But as East Asia transformed itself from economic laggard to leader, Confucius's stature rose with East Asia's exports, growth rates, and incomes. The very same cultural tradition that had been so vilified as the cause of Asia's downfall began to be heralded as the cause of its resurrection. Even by the standards of centuries of shifting attitudes toward Confucius, this reversal of fortune could have given the old sage a bad case of whiplash.

The economic ascent of East Asia tipped off a wider phenomenon that continues to this day—a reexamination of Confucius's role in modern society that breathed new life into the sage's deteriorating corpse. No longer did Confucius seem a hopelessly antiquated leftover of a bygone era whose influence had to be purged to allow Asia to progress politically, economically, and socially. In light of East Asia's economic rise, some Confucian ideas seemed to hold real value once again. They could, it appeared, be a catalyst to modernity, pointing the way to a new golden age of restored Asian prosperity and international influence. After decades during which Asians and non-Asians alike assumed the region had to become fully westernized to be modern and competitive, the developments in Japan, China, South Korea, Singapore, and elsewhere showed that Asia could be Asian as well as rich, powerful, and advanced. Within the region, the burgeoning wealth offered what academic Kishore Mahbubani at the beginning of this book called "cultural confidence"—the self-assurance necessary for Asians to revisit their own traditions with fresh eyes.

The Confucius being resurrected, however, is not the same Confucius of East Asia's imperial past. Left behind was the Confucius of court ceremonies and monarchal memorials, the fundamentalist Confucius obsessed with the imagined wonders of antiquity. The Confucius who has emerged instead is dressed in a business suit, tapping on an iPhone while sipping a Starbucks cappuccino. He is still, at heart, the same old Confucius, espousing his enduring beliefs on the well-regulated family, the power of benevolence, and methods of good leadership. But he is a revitalized Confucius who fits more easily into a new and globalized culture. It is here, some have contended, in this merging of the best of East and West, that the magic behind the region's spectacular economic ascent can be found.

Even more, this new Confucius seemed to have a thing or two to teach the West. The enviable economic performance of East Asia led economists and businessmen to dissect the policies, societal patterns, and management practices of the region's CEOs, government leaders, and workers in a quest for wisdom to employ in their own countries and companies. Out of this investigation arose the idea that Confucius and free enterprise had coagulated into a new type of economic system—"Confucian Capitalism"—that in some ways was superior to the form practiced in the West. That meant that East Asia presented a "Confucian challenge" to both Western dominance in the global economy and the ideological primacy of Adam Smith–style, free-market orthodoxy. If the United States and Europe were to compete with a rising Asia, the argument continued, the West would have to adopt Confucian Capitalism. This, too, was an amazing analytical turnaround. Since the mid-nineteenth century, the East had found it imperative to replace Confucius with ideas from the West; now, some said, it was equally imperative for the West to borrow some Confucius from the East.

ANOTHER IRONY BEHIND the supposed role of Confucius in East Asia's success is that the sage did not outline a fully developed manual on economic policy or business practices. As with many other crucial issues, he left only scraps of commentary and general notions on the subject. Yet he said enough to allow us to piece together something of a model Confucian economy. In fact, some tidbits he did leave behind mesh quite nicely with the modern economic policies and cultural attributes that some argue sparked East Asia's rapid development.

Confucius, as quoted in classical texts, was in certain respects surprisingly laissez-faire in his approach to economics. To him, good government equaled small government. A state that was too big or overbearing crowded out private enterprise, extracted too much from the populace, suppressed the incentive to be productive, and, in the end, impoverished the nation. Officials would cause disaster if they tried to control markets or dominate industries; that would suck wealth into state coffers that was best left to the common man. The government should not impose burdensome taxes on the people, or waste resources in extravagant ceremonies, unnecessary military expeditions, or other self-aggrandizing schemes. Nor should the ruler demand an unfair amount of labor from the citizens—either as soldiers or workers on public projects. Such demands would only disrupt their ability to care for their farms and families.

Confucius's views were an outgrowth of his belief that government should be humane. Imposing heavy taxes on the masses was, to Confucians, a form of cruelty. People should be free to pursue the well-being of their families, and that meant allowing them to benefit properly from the fruits of their labors. The underlying philosophy of the Confucians on economic management was a version of Confucius's Golden Rule: the ruler should benefit if the people benefit; the ruler should not benefit at the people's expense. "Let the producers be many and the consumers few," *The Great Learning* advises the ruler. "Let there be activity in the production, and economy in the expenditure. Then the wealth will always be sufficient."[4]

The sage made these points clear in one of the first passages in the *Analects*. "To rule a country of a thousand chariots," Confucius said, "there must be reverent attention to business, and sincerity; economy in expenditure, and love for men; and the employment of the people at the proper seasons." He expanded on these precepts in another conversation with one of his more inquisitive disciples. "In what way should a person in authority act in order that he may conduct government properly?" Zizhang asked Confucius. "When the person in authority is beneficent without great expenditure," the master responded. "When he lays tasks on the people without their repining; when he pursues what he desires without being covetous; when he maintains a dignified ease without being proud; when he is majestic without being fierce." The master then warned Zizhang what a good civil servant should never do. "To require from them [the common man], suddenly, the full tale of work, without having given them warning;—this is called oppression," Confucius said. "And, generally, in the giving pay or rewards to men, to do it in a stingy way;—this is called acting the part of a mere official."[5]

Confucius believed that ensuring prosperity was one of the primary tasks of any good government. "The requisites of government are that there be sufficiency of food, sufficiency of military equipment, and the confidence of the people in their ruler," he said. In another case, while he was traveling in Wei, Confucius noted how populous the region was "Since they are thus numerous, what more shall be done for them?" one of his disciples queried. "Enrich them," Confucius replied. Thus it was the responsibility of the state to pursue economic development for the greater good of the nation.

Building a strong economy was good politics, too. The Confucians believed that well-fed and lightly taxed citizens would be loyal citizens, and that the king who pursued such policies would be able to expand his power and solidify his rule. "The accumulation of wealth is the way to scatter the people, and the letting it be scattered among them is the way to collect the people," *The Great Learning* instructs.[6]

Most importantly, the Confucians believed that economic prosperity was a critical prerequisite to the moral development of society. By ensuring that the common man had enough to eat, proper shelter, and economic opportunity, the ruler would be creating the necessary conditions for his citizens to pursue the Way. How exactly could a person remain ethical if he was starving and impoverished? "As to the people, if they have not a certain livelihood, it follows that they will not have a fixed heart," Mencius told one king:

> And if they have not a fixed heart, there is nothing which they will not do, in the way of self-abandonment, of moral deflection, of depravity, and of wild license. . . . Now, the livelihood of the people is so regulated, that, above, they have not sufficient wherewith to serve their parents, and, below, they have not sufficient wherewith to support their wives and children. Notwithstanding good years, their lives are continually embittered, and, in bad years, they do not escape perishing. In such circumstances they only try to save themselves from death, and are afraid they will not succeed. What leisure have they to cultivate propriety and righteousness?[7]

For centuries, Confucius's followers pressed China's rulers to infuse their economic policies with these principles. The effort began in Confucius's own day. The *Analects*, for example, shares a conversation between Duke Ai of Lu and one of the sage's disciples, You Ruo. Amid a poor harvest, the duke was concerned that his revenues would fall short of his expenditures, and he asked You Ruo for advice. He told Duke Ai to tax the people a tenth of their income. "With two tenths," said the duke, "I find it not enough—how could I do with that system of one tenth?" You Ruo answered: "If the people have plenty, their prince will not be left to want alone. If the people are in want, their prince cannot enjoy plenty alone."[8]

Mencius, too, lectured China's rulers at length on the merits of frugal and unobtrusive economic policy. "If the seasons of husbandry be not interfered with, the grain will be more than can be eaten," he told King Hui. "If close nets are not allowed to enter the pools and ponds, the fishes and turtles will be more than can be consumed. If the axes and bills enter the hills and forests only at the proper time, the wood will be more than can be used. When the grain and fish and turtles are more than can be eaten, and there is more wood than can be used, this enables the people to nourish their living and mourn for their dead, without any feeling against any. This condition . . . is the first step of royal government." By sitting back while his people struggled and starved, Mencius said, the ruler was no better than a murderer. "There are people dying from famine on the roads, and you do not issue the stores of your granaries for them. When people die, you say, 'It is not owing to me; it is owing to the year.'" Mencius, continuing to scold the king, asked him, "In what does this differ from stabbing a man and killing him, and then saying—'It was not I; it was the weapon?'"[9]

China's leaders usually failed to heed the advice of Confucius and his later followers. During the Han Dynasty, Emperor Wu's military conquests ran up larger and larger bills, and thus increased his government's thirst for revenue. He instituted state monopolies on salt, iron, and liquor, goods that had been highly profitable for private businessmen, in the hopes of funneling those profits into his treasury. The emperor also turned the state into a major trader of necessary commodities through a scheme euphemistically called the "system of equitable marketing." State officers bought up large quantities of grain and other goods cheaply, then sold them in other parts of the empire at higher prices, reaping huge profits for the government in the process.

The Confucians protested. Dong Zhongshu, the great early Han Confucian thinker, condemned Emperor Wu's policies, which, he claimed, were impoverishing the people, and he recommended ending the salt and iron monopolies and reducing the burden of taxes and labor imposed by the government. "In ancient times the people were not taxed over one-tenth of their produce, a demand they could easily meet," Dong wrote to the throne. "The people had wealth enough to take care of the aged and look after their parents, serve their superiors and pay their taxes, and support their wives and loved ones. Therefore they took delight in obeying their rulers."[10]

This time, Dong failed to sway the emperor, and the hated policies stayed in place. But the stubborn Confucians didn't give up. In 81 BC, after

Emperor Wu's death, they engaged imperial officials in a heated debate over the throne's economic policies. The discussion reads much like a modern argument over the proper role of the state in an economy. The Confucians, prefiguring the free-market devotees of today, argued that government intervention distorted prices, scared off private enterprise, and undercut prosperity. They reiterated Dong's calls for an end to state monopolies and the "equitable marketing" system. "Nowadays the government disregards what people have and requires of them what they have not, so that they are forced to sell their goods at a cheap price in order to meet the demands from above," the Confucian scholars complained. "We have not seen that this kind of marketing is 'equitable.' . . . With slick merchants and corrupt officials buying cheap and selling dear, we have not seen that your level is 'balanced.'" The state, the Confucians contended, had no place in running businesses anyway. "We have heard that the way to govern men is to prevent evil and error at their source, to broaden the beginnings of morality . . . and open the way for the exercise of humaneness and rightness," they said. "Never should material profit appear as a motive of government."[11]

The court officials fought back by portraying the Confucians as unrealistic idealists incapable of understanding the demands of managing a state. Dismantling the monopolies and reducing taxes, they said, would make it impossible for the Han to defend the empire's borders from marauding barbarians, and state involvement in trading protected the people from the vicissitudes of the market. One imperial official mocked the Confucians, pointing to their humble clothes as proof that they were unfit to guide government policy. "See them now present us with nothingness and consider it substance, with emptiness and call it plenty!" he said. "In their coarse gowns and worn shoes they walk gravely along, sunk in meditation as though they had lost something. These are not men who can do great deeds and win fame."[12]

THE TATTERED CONDITION of the Confucians' footwear reflected the limitations of Confucius's enthusiasm for free enterprise. The great sage may have preferred a small, efficient state, but that doesn't mean he was in favor of unfettered private commerce. Confucius had an inherent distrust of the pursuit of wealth, and this attitude became infused into later Confucians and their views of business and businessmen. Although Confucius did not preach asceticism (like his Hindu counterparts in India), he did see nobility in poverty, or at least the stoic acceptance of poverty. The true gentleman, in Confucius's eyes, did not desire riches. "The gentleman seeks neither a full belly nor a comfortable home," he said. Even those men who sincerely tried to act in a benevolent fashion could not be trusted if they also coveted luxury. "There is no point in seeking the views of a gentleman who, though he sets his heart on the Way, is ashamed of poor food and poor clothes," the sage said.[13]

That suspicion stemmed from his belief that the profit motive ran counter to morality. By seeking riches, man was drawn away from virtue. "The gentleman understands what is moral," Confucius said. "The small man understands what is profitable." This isn't to say that Confucius was against financial success entirely. He implied that amassing great wealth is fine—as long as one attains it while engaged in strictly virtuous behavior. "Wealth and high station are what men desire but unless I got them in the right way I would not remain in them," he said. "Poverty and low station are what men dislike, but even if I did not get them in the right way, I would not try to escape from them." In Confucian thought, wealth would come to those who were virtuous and wise. A good king could bring prosperity to himself and his entire kingdom if he followed the Way. "Virtue is the root; wealth is the result," *The Great Learning* asserts. In economics as well as politics, Confucius believed that moral power was stronger than physical force.[14]

For the most part, though, Confucians thought that China's elite did not earn their riches honorably. The Confucians tended to disapprove of commerce in general, seeing finance and trading, which they considered "secondary" economic activities, as inherently corrupting and ultimately dangerous for a country's overall well-being. Rather than actually adding to production, merchants, they believed, merely bought and sold what others made through sweat and toil, skimming off unwarranted profits in the process. Confucians preferred economic policies that favored the farmers, whom they portrayed as honest laborers engaged in the "primary" activity of producing real goods. "When the secondary is practiced, the people grow decadent, but when the primary is practiced they are simple and sincere," the Confucians told the state's officials in their 81 BC debate. "When the people are sincere then there will be sufficient wealth and goods, but when they become extravagant then famine and cold will follow."[15]

The Confucian bias against commerce became enshrined in the concept of the "four occupations." Merchants, parasitic and profit-crazed, rested on the bottom of the hierarchy, below scholar-officials, who were at the top; farmers, those paragons of honest labor, took the second rung; and artisans, the third group, supported themselves with their own skills. Those who sought wealth were seen as enemies of the greater good; by the Confucians' reckoning, the super-rich won their fortunes on the backs of the common folk. That led to a belief among Confucians that the state had a responsibility to promote economic equality and to regulate free enterprise to prevent abuses.

In his critical memorial to Emperor Wu, Dong Zhongshu blamed the economic ills of the day on the concentration of wealth in the hands of a powerful and greedy few. "The rich bought up great connecting tracts of ground, and the poor were left without enough land to stick the point of an awl into," he complained. "How could the common people escape oppression?"[16] That's why he, and many other Confucians after him, pressed for measures to improve income equality. Dong preferred a landownership system that equalized the size of plots across the populace, in that way ensuring that each farming family could sustain itself and would not be exploited by large landlords. He did not get heard on this point, and Confucians reiterated this recommendation for centuries to come.

The Confucians may not have won every argument, but they still held great sway over Chinese economic policy. For centuries, the civil servants who managed the economy had been indoctrinated with the sage's ideas through the examination system, and inevitably, these ideas filtered into government decision making. The result was what Columbia University professor Madeleine Zelin calls "a Confucian political economy." Despite their inability to break Emperor Wu's monopolies, the Confucian preference for a free economy generally prevailed throughout most of China's history. In the imperial age, China was a predominantly private market economy. Land was bought and sold freely, and traders and artisans usually were allowed to go about their business. Confucius's hand was felt most heavily in the government's tax and expenditure practices. The bureaucracy, for the most part, shied away from imposing heavy duties on the people. That created its own problems—a perpetually underfunded yet expansive state—but the Confucian principle remained preeminent.[17]

WHATEVER IMPACT CONFUCIUS had on the Chinese economy, for long periods of history China was the richest country in the world. Economist Angus Maddison figured that China and India were the two largest economies in the world for most of the Common Era. But China's position began deteriorating rapidly in the nineteenth century. In 1820, China accounted for 33 percent of world output, according to Maddison, and Western Europe and the United States a combined 25 percent. But by 1950, China held a measly 4.6 percent, while the West commanded nearly 57 percent.[18] Not only had China failed to keep pace with the West in science and technology, but it had also fallen far behind in economic innovation. The Industrial Revolution, which propelled the West to its new wealth and power, had left China almost untouched, and the country entered the twentieth century by and large an agrarian society. Nor did China develop the types of institutions that had allowed industrialists, investors, and entrepreneurs in the West to mobilize capital on a massive scale—such as stock markets and modern corporations and banks. The bottom line was that the West developed capitalism and China didn't.

That fact was a puzzle. As was true in regard to the sciences, China was far more advanced economically than Western Europe for most of history, yet the country wasn't able to develop a relatively modern capitalist-style economy until the final two decades of the twentieth century. Why, scholars began to ask, did the Industrial Revolution occur in the West and not the East? And once the wonders of Western capitalism became apparent to the world, why was China unable to effectively adopt it? In the search for answers, Confucius took it on the chin once again. Confucian culture and social systems, the thinking went, were resistant to capitalism and lay at the heart of China's economic weakness.

This argument was put forward most insistently by German sociologist Max Weber in his treatise *The Religions of China*, originally published in German (under a different title) in 1915. Weber had already made the case in his most famous work that capitalism had emerged in Western Europe because the Protestant religion possessed the necessary "spirit" to make it happen. After examining Chinese society, Weber concluded that Confucianism lacked a similar character, and that was why capitalism didn't develop in China. Confucianism, Weber contended, placed too much emphasis on tradition and was too content with the status quo for capitalism to thrive in the societies dominated by it. Rather than encouraging the Chinese to alter the world for the greater good, engage in impartial business relationships, and amass practical, specialized knowledge, Confucianism wrapped the Chinese up in stodgy social conventions and old-fashioned economic practices, preventing modern capitalism from bubbling up in the East.

The reason Confucianism was anti-capitalist, Weber argued, could be found in its view of man's place in the world. Confucianism, he noted, believed that man had a duty to conform to the prevailing social order by adhering to traditions and a code of behavior handed down from antiquity.

The Confucians' focus on harmony and tranquility led them to accept the existing state of things. As a result, the proper Confucian gentleman was incentivized to uphold tradition instead of seeking and advocating for change. Protestantism pushed Western Europeans to do just the opposite—that is, to alter the imperfect world in accordance with God's will, which in turn spurred innovation and the capitalist spirit. "Confucian rationalism meant rational adjustment to the world; Puritan rationalism meant rational mastery of the world," Weber wrote.[19]

What Confucianism lacked, Weber determined, was a vision of the afterlife that compelled the Chinese to break free of tradition and fix a wicked world. Absolved of the fear of sinning against God or eternal damnation, Confucians were concerned merely with the rules of propriety of everyday life. Being a good person had nothing to do with true moral conduct; one could reach perfection simply by abiding by customary patterns of social behavior. "'I have sinned' corresponded to our 'I beg your pardon,'" Weber quipped. With no grander calling from God, the Confucians became obsessed with mundane matters—including (seemingly paradoxically) the acquisition of wealth. "In no other civilized country has material welfare ever been so exalted as the supreme good," Weber wrote, because Confucians perceived the "value of wealth as a universal means of moral perfection."[20]

The problem, according to Weber, was that petty penny-seeking destroyed the trust necessary to conduct proper capitalist business transactions. "This distrust handicapped all credit and business operations and contrasted with the Puritan's trust, especially his economic trust in the absolutely unshakable and religiously determined righteousness of his brother in faith," Weber wrote. "The Confucian's word was a beautiful and polite gesture as an end in itself; the Puritan's word was an impersonal and businesslike communication, short and absolutely reliable."[21] Making that problem even worse was the Confucian obsession with filial piety. Since Confucians were to favor family and others close to them over everybody else, the fair and impersonal economic transactions necessary for the functioning of modern capitalism were unable to develop.

Weber's analysis has to be taken with a rather large grain of salt. Perusing Weber, one gets the sense that he examined Confucian traditions with a predetermined derision rather than the open mind fitting for a proper scholar. His notion that Confucianism encouraged greed and moral laxity is only the most obvious misrepresentation of Confucius's teachings. Nevertheless, the idea that Confucianism and capitalism didn't mix entered the standard explanation for China's economic failings. Confucianism was blamed for squelching the personal independence necessary for capitalist entrepreneur-ship and fostering a disdain for merchants—who, after all, were dumped at the bottom of the Confucian occupational order. "The different economic growth of Europe and China is symptomatic of the total cultural difference between them," historian John King Fairbank and his colleagues wrote.[22] The implications for Confucius were clear. Just as Chinese revolutionaries and feminists believed that Confucius was preventing Chinese society from reforming politically and socially, scholars and historians thought Confucianism was stopping China from progressing economically. Confucius was again accused of being incompatible with the modern world.

CHANGE, THOUGH, WAS stirring in the bombed-out cities of post–World War II Japan, which would spark a reassessment of Confucius's relationship with capitalism. To rebuild its industries and national wealth, Japan em-barked on a quest for rapid economic development, the astounding success of which took the world by surprise. The economy began posting growth rates that seemed mathematically impossible—averaging over 10 percent a year during the 1960s—and by 1967, the nation had become the world's second-largest economy, behind only the United States. Japanese compa-nies—exporting cars, steel, televisions, ships, and later, fax machines and microchips—were gobbling up market share around the world and test-ing Western industrial supremacy for the first time in centuries. By the late 1970s the West was panicking as experts began to predict that Japan could overtake America as the world's No. 1 economy.

Moreover, Japan was not alone in its ascent. All across East Asia, econ-omies that had been poverty-stricken and war-torn were becoming rich. South Korea, Taiwan, Hong Kong, and Singapore, known as the Four Lit-tle Dragons, experienced growth similar to Japan's, propelled by expanding manufacturing and exports. Economists were baffled. At the end of the colo-nial period in Asia in the mid-twentieth century, they had practically written off the economic viability of these tiny, fragile East Asian societies, which possessed few natural resources and little industry or infrastructure. Other developing nations, especially in Africa and Latin America, seemed to have far better prospects. Yet the Four Little Dragons outperformed the rest of the emerging world by just about every economic measure. The development community was so startled that even the staid World Bank declared the phenomenon a "miracle." Some analysts insisted that the Dragons' success could not possibly be understood by simple economic theory alone. Why, they asked, did these East Asian societies take the correct path to prosperity, while so many other emerging nations did not? So scholars went in search of other factors to explain East Asia's unexplainable success. Some concluded that there had to be something unique and special about these Asian societies that made them more fertile ground for rapid economic development than other parts of the developing world. Looking at Japan and the Four Little Dragons, Asia experts noticed they all had an important—perhaps even critical—element in common: Confucius.

The teachings of the great sage, some experts contended, were the defining difference between East Asia and the rest of the emerging world, the key ingredient that explained its outsized economic performance compared to the slothful pace of advancement elsewhere. These new Confucian proponents acknowledged that Japan and the Four Dragons were no longer Confucian in the way they had been during the days of the dynasties, which promoted Confucianism as a national orthodoxy, but they made the case that the sage's ideas were very much alive and well, deeply embedded in the social practices of East Asians. A term arose to describe these societies: "post-Confucian." By the reckoning of these observers, the teachings of the great sage had shaped the behavioral patterns and attitudes of the people of East Asia in ways that laid the groundwork for the region's economic progress. The evidence that Confucianism propelled economies only mounted when China, too, burst onto the world stage in the 1980s as yet another Confucian-tinged economic powerhouse. What had been the accepted mantra—that Confucianism was bad for capitalism—had been, with dizzying speed, completely reversed. British politician Roderick MacFarquhar, in a direct swipe at Weber, asserted in 1980 that Confucianism "is as important to the rise of the East Asian hyper-growth economies as the conjunction of Protestantism and the rise of capitalism in the west."[23]

Much of this counterargument rested on a renewed appreciation of the economic power of the Confucian family. No longer a deathtrap for intelligent business and entrepreneurship, the Confucian family was transformed into an engine of East Asia's capitalist ascent, providing the incentives, connections, and financing necessary for successful private enterprise. The intense, Confucian-inspired love of learning created a skilled workforce custom-made for modern industry. The thriftiness ingrained in Confucian families helped them to amass a ready pool of savings available for investment. A filial commitment to advance their families' welfare prompted East Asians to work hard and motivated them to succeed. Instead of squelching individual initiative, filial piety unleashed it. Rather than distorting business behavior in irrational ways, as Weber had insisted, the clannishness of Confucian cultures, in this altered view, actually encouraged efficient capitalist activity. Networks of family members and close friends allowed entrepreneurial ventures to thrive by providing ready sources of money, information, and trustworthy partnerships.

Moreover, the social indoctrination that the proper Confucian received inside the family also made him a model capitalist. Unlike in the self-centered, individualistic West, Confucian values inspired businessmen and workers in the East to exert their ample entrepreneurial energies not just for their own success, but also for the success of their family and community. This gave East Asian societies an edge in achieving overall economic well-being. Accustomed to deferring to parental authority, Confucian employees were similarly compliant with their bosses, an attitude that fostered peaceful labor relations. Taught to be respectful of government, they were also receptive to state policies, which allowed for the smooth implementation of critical reforms. The twentieth-century Confucian, therefore, fit all the roles necessary to achieve supercharged growth—the stoic factory worker with his chin firmly at the grindstone, the hard-driving entrepreneur, and the devoted citizen, who was willing to forgo immediate gain for the long-term greater good of the nation. "Post-Confucian economic man," wrote MacFarquhar, "works hard and plays hard, buys much, but saves more. He accepts a society stratified by age as well as by ability. . . . He perceives that his prosperity is inseparable from the good of the community and he accepts guidance as to where that lies."[24]

The desire for tranquility and deference to authority that were instilled in Confucians made them loyal, dedicated employees, and thus a better match for life and work in the modern corporation than more individualistic westerners, these thinkers argued. Confucius's influence, therefore, gave the Asian company a leg up in its competition with the West. Confucianism encouraged a collegiality between management and workers that was missing from the contentious West, and strong ties among employees made them solid team players. "If Western individualism was appropriate for the pioneering period of industrialization, perhaps post-Confucian 'collectivism' is better suited to the age of mass industrialization," MacFarquhar postulated. "In the West the 'organization man' is a somewhat repellent figure. In Japan, the company man is the ideal."[25]

Confucianism also inspired a capitalist spirit within East Asian governments. No longer were East Asian bureaucrats stuffy classicists; now they became practitioners of new forms of highly effective capitalist policymaking.

Confucius's exhortation to the best and brightest to enter public service, once criticized for holding the region back, now encouraged elite university graduates in Japan and South Korea to enter into government ministries that guided economic policy. Unlike in the West, where elected politicians drafted policies for civil servants to follow, control of the economy in Japan and elsewhere in East Asia was in the hands of the professional civil service. That allowed these super-smart bureaucrats to expertly craft policy free from the intrusions of politics.

East Asian civil servants were perceived as a modernized *junzi* who were motivated to pursue economic development and refashion policy by the same spirit that had propelled Wang Anshi of the Song Dynasty nine hundred years earlier. A long tradition of bureaucrats-know-best Confucian government made it easier for these newfangled *junzi* to intervene in free markets in order to advance growth in ways that would be unacceptable in the more laissez-faire West. Policymakers in Japan, for instance, targeted certain industries for special support, protected budding sectors from outside competition, directed banks to lend to favored firms, and organized cartels. Contrary to the wariness that exists between government and the private sector in the United States, these *junzi* forged tight ties to Japan's finance and business communities, developing a triumvirate that cooperated closely on industrial investment.

The powerful *junzi*, experts asserted, gave Japan, South Korea, Singapore, and other East Asian economies an advantage in global competition. If the United States was to keep pace with Japan, Asia expert Ezra Vogel claimed, Washington would have to develop its own elite team of *junzi*. "It is disquieting to admit that the Japanese have beaten us in economic competition because of their superior planning, organization, and effort," Vogel wrote in 1979. "Japan, with its greater sense of group orientation . . . and government-led modernization, has developed solutions . . . that America, with its more individualistic and legalistic history, might never have invented."[26]

Many of these Confucian-inspired practices and policies contradicted the West's standard assumptions about how capitalism should ideally function. To Western economists, bureaucrats were dangerous meddlers in free enterprise, not catalysts, and business dealings had to be impartial, not based on personal connections, to be rational. But the undeniably spectacular performance of East Asia caused many experts to question and reassess capitalist orthodoxy. What was emerging in East Asia, some believed, was an alternative, Confucian form of capitalism that was superior to the Western version. This great mixing of Adam Smith and Confucius, it was thought, produced a sort of super-capitalism, featuring a combination of free-market principles and government intervention. The general view had always been that capitalism depended on rugged individualism: the shopping housewife, the risk-taking entrepreneur, and the gutsy CEO would produce prosperity for all by making decisions based on their own interests. Confucian Capitalism, on the other hand, was based on the idea that a more collective, coordinated form of decision making and resource allocation could generate strong growth and competitive industries. Unlike in the West, where economic actions were scrutinized by lawyers, enshrined in contracts, and disciplined by the market, Confucian Capitalism emphasized relationships—the bonds between the *junzi*, bankers, and managers; networks of family businesses; close teamwork within corporations—and this made Asian economies more adaptable than Western ones to the demands of the moment. "The Confucian ethic cultivates a different kind of capitalism emphasizing the self as a center of relationships, the sense of personal discipline, personal cultivation, and consensus formation and cooperation," wrote business professor Min Chen. "This collective strength is the comparative advantage of an East Asian society in competing with the West."[27]

ONE OF THE most vocal proponents of this cultural explanation for East Asia's economic achievements has been Lee Kuan Yew, the former prime minister of Singapore, who has greatly influenced the politics of the region over the past half-century. In his eyes, the Asian economic miracle was very much a triumph of Confucian values over those of other societies. "If you have a culture that doesn't place much value in learning and scholarship and hard work and thrift and deferment of present enjoyment for future gain, the going will be much slower" for economic development, Lee said in a 1994 interview. Purely economic assessments of East Asia's economic ascent, Lee asserted, are based upon "the hopeful assumption that all men are equal, that people all over the world are the same. They are not." Instead, he said, "groups of people develop different characteristics when they have evolved for thousands of years separately. Now if you gloss over these kinds of issues because it is politically incorrect to study them, then you have laid a land mine for yourself."[28]

There is some irony in the fact that Lee became the chief spokesman of what became known as the "Asian values" proposition. Born to a shopkeeper in 1923, he was a proud product of the British Empire. Going by the name of "Harry," he studied law at Cambridge, where he was heavily influenced by European social democratic movements. He became Singapore's first prime minister in 1959, and for the three decades he held that post the hallmark of his policymaking was a clinical pragmatism. Yet Lee directly credited Confucian values with Singapore's stunning success. "Over the last 30 years, one of the driving forces that made Singapore succeed was that the majority of the people placed the importance of the welfare of society above the individual, which is a basic Confucianist concept," he said in 1987.[29]

Lee also infused his economic policy in Singapore with Confucian ideas. In fact, Singapore's economic model was built upon Confucianism. As the great sage would have advocated, Lee relied on the Confucian family when designing his development agenda. The care of the elderly, impoverished, unemployed, and other less fortunate members of society was left to a great degree to families, not the state. That kept welfare spending to a bare minimum, freeing up scarce resources for investment in education, infrastructure, and other projects that laid the foundation for rapid growth. Without the pressure on government budgets caused by European-style welfare programs, Lee was able to follow Confucius's policy prescription to maintain low tax rates. Economist Habibullah Khan argued in a 2001 World Bank study that Singapore had discovered a "Confucian model" for government welfare policies, one that could help politicians around the world sidestep the increasingly burdensome costs of social services.[30]

Instead of handouts, Lee offered opportunity. His government became what's known among political economists as a "development state." His priority was to create jobs and elevate incomes as quickly as possible, thus fulfilling one of Confucius's main responsibilities of good government—ensuring the welfare of the people. To do that, Lee relied more heavily on the tools of state than any American politician would dare. A state agency, the Economic Development Board, was formed to actively pursue investment from overseas. In some cases, Lee and his team played entrepreneur and started state-run companies. "This typical Confucian attitude of dependence on the government has been very prevalent in the context of Singapore's economic development," wrote business professor Tan Chwee Huat in 1989. "Singapore would not have achieved the remarkable growth if it did not have a strong, clean and far-sighted government to provide a clear sense of direction, to choose the right options and priorities and to enforce such policies relentlessly."[31]

Policy was managed mainly by a version of a *junzi*. Talent was groomed and scrupulously tested within both Lee's ruling People's Action Party and the civil bureaucracy, resulting in the creation of a highly competent, technocratic leadership. Also in typical Confucian fashion, Lee believed that he, as the prime minister, had to establish the standard of proper behavior for all to follow. "First, we had to set the example," Lee once said. "Not only in being uncorrupt, but also in being thrifty and economical, and not traveling in grand style. . . . We wanted to trim the cost of government, so we ran a very spartan government. No wastage, no lavish entertainment, no big offices. We set the tone, the example, they [the civil servants] followed."[32]

THE ADVOCATES OF Confucian Capitalism, however, were in essence making the same mistake as Max Weber. The social scientist, looking at the success of northern Europe and the stagnation of Asia, believed that Western values were superior to Asian values. Now Lee and others had reversed the argument: zeroing in on the success of East Asia, they came to the conclusion that Asian values were better than Western values. Max Weber, Roderick MacFarquhar, and everyone else who has tried to understand the ups and downs of Asia's standing in the world over the past two hundred years have, in their quest for answers, awarded Confucius a role based on what they saw happening around them. What is interesting for our story is how Confucius has been perceived across time. His influence has been seen as so dominant, so much a part of daily life in East Asia, that he has received either the credit or the blame for whatever was taking place at any given moment. Confucius the hard-charging capitalist was every bit as symbolic of the 1970s as Confucius the archaic feudalist was of the 1910s. Like a great method actor, the sage can take on whatever role he is hired to perform, depending on the script. So much stage makeup has been caked upon him that he has become barely recognizable.

It will come as no surprise, then, that when the fortunes of East Asia took an unexpected tumble in the 1990s, so did the reputation of Confucius as an economic wizard. First, Japan's ascent was stopped in its tracks when a gargantuan bubble in its property and stock markets burst. Then, in 1997, a financial crisis rocked South Korea, forcing the proud Little Dragon to accept an embarrassing International Monetary Fund bailout. The whole idea that Confucian values had created a superior form of economic model was discredited, and economists again began to question the value of Confucius to modern capitalism.

To many critics, the very aspects of Confucian Capitalism that had seemed to give East Asia its insurmountable edge became the cause of its troubles. The relationships at the heart of Confucian Capitalism—within family networks, between the *junzi* and businessmen—were now identified as the source of its downfall. In Japan and South Korea, those chummy ties between bureaucrats, financiers, and CEOs led banks to funnel money to friendly companies based on long-standing personal relationships rather than sound credit-risk analysis. In the Confucian hierarchical system, the decisions of the minister or boss went unchallenged by compliant staffers, board members, and shareholders, leading to faulty, and even megalomaniacal, choices and investments. Confucian capitalism had deteriorated into "crony capitalism," a corrupt cabal in which personal connections undercut economic rationality. "Asian values have become Asian liabilities," *U.S. News & World Report* editor Mortimer Zuckerman wrote, with obvious glee, in 1998.[33] Max Weber had had his revenge.

Such criticisms continued long after the crises abated. Confucianism has been knocked for creating the intense family bonds that can undermine sound corporate management at East Asian firms. Family managers at large South Korean companies have routinely favored promoting their sons over professionals into positions of power. Job seekers rely on connections, instead of talent, to get ahead. In a poll conducted by a state-run Chinese newspaper in 2013, 84 percent of young Chinese workers who responded said they preferred to rely on "powerful daddies" for good jobs, compared to a mere 10 percent who valued diligence as a route to success.[34] Strict hierarchy within companies, which often makes it impossible for junior staffers to speak up with ideas or disagree with management, has been blamed for stifling innovation and the open exchanges of information that could produce cutting-edge products and aid smart decision making at the top.

Confucius was even targeted for causing plane crashes. Both Asian and non-Asian experts deemed the hierarchy within the cockpits of Korean airliners a factor behind their weak safety records. Intimidated junior pilots, the argument went, were too fearful of correcting or questioning the captain—a crucial aspect of the teamwork necessary for safe flying. The problem was exposed most dramatically by the crash of a Korean Air passenger jet in Guam in 1997, which killed 228 people. Korean Air had to bring in foreign trainers and executives to break down Confucian culture and force cockpit crews to share responsibility and communicate.[35]

STILL, WITH POLICYMAKERS and executives all around the world looking for new methods of boosting competitiveness and creating jobs, dismissing

Confucian Capitalism out of hand could prove a mistake. One way in which Western, and especially American, companies differ from their East Asian counterparts is in management's attitude toward employees. Generally, the US corporate system is based on a simple work-for-pay equation: an employee gets a paycheck in return for fulfilling a specified responsibility. Companies tend to see the right to hire and fire at will as a key factor that maintains profitability and competitiveness. In East Asian firms, Confucian doctrine has seeped into management-labor relations. The intense focus on filial piety has spilled out of the family into other institutions and organizations—the modern corporation included. Management tends to be more paternalistic than in Western companies—the boss is like the father, stern perhaps, but caring for workers the way he would care for his children. In return, employees usually exhibit a higher degree of devotion to the company than Western workers do, preferring to spend much, if not all, of their careers at one firm.

Of course, this is a generalization. Not all East Asian companies treat their workers well—the regular exposure of scandalous labor practices in China attests to that. Yet East Asian executives and workers share much different expectations about the responsibilities they have toward each other than their American counterparts. For much of the second half of the twentieth century, big companies in Japan and South Korea offered their full-time workers lifetime employment, and although that commitment has broken down under the strain of global competition, the sentiment that was behind that practice remains in place. In Japan, big corporations that the public perceives as treating workers unfairly—overworking them or not caring for their welfare—are tarnished as "black" companies. Mass layoffs of the type common in the United States are considered socially inappropriate, even unseemly, in Japan and South Korea.

That is true even in times of crisis. Amid the recession caused by the 2008 financial collapse on Wall Street, American companies laid off workers en masse. Halfway around the world, Yoo Myoung Ho, founder of lock manufacturer Unilock Corporation in Incheon, South Korea, watched nervously as the meltdown in the United States spread around the world. He knew full well that his sales would take a serious hit. Nevertheless, he took a very different course of action with his two hundred employees. "We thought that even though things would be difficult, we decided not to reduce the staff," Yoo says. Instead, he eliminated night shifts on his assembly lines and spread the remaining working hours among the employees at reduced pay. Others got assigned to a team to develop new products or shifted into training programs. It would have been a dereliction of his duty, Yoo believes, to toss his employees onto the street in a time of economic distress. His employees, he says, are like members of a family, and as the "head of the family," as he calls himself, Yoo felt it was his responsibility to protect them. "We think about workers as family," he says. "It's not just that they come here and get paid and that's it. They have families, too, and you can't just let them suffer. You have to make them feel that the company is like their own. You have to make them feel like family. That's how you create economic success."[36]

Yoo stuck to his decision even as his business tanked. Sales in 2009 shrunk by a gut-wrenching two-thirds, Unilock fell into the red, and Yoo borrowed money to stay afloat. When he heard that shrinking paychecks were putting some workers under severe financial strain, he paid them bonuses out of his own pocket. "If a crisis comes, if you are the chairman, you take your salary and give it to the people," he says.

Few American CEOs would make that same sacrifice. But Yoo insists that there's good business, not merely good-heartedness, behind his generosity. During the 1997 Asian financial crisis, when Yoo's business also shrank drastically, he laid off staff to cut costs, but then discovered that when the economy recovered, many of his remaining employees, disgruntled over their treatment, bolted for other jobs. That burdened Yoo with the cost of recruiting and training new workers. By retaining his employees during the post-2008 recession, he hoped for a better outcome—and he was rewarded. This time, none of his workers departed for other jobs. With his staff fully intact, and a catalog of new products they had developed ready for market, his business recovered quickly once the crisis abated. "In traditional Confucian culture, the collective mentality is society's asset," Yoo says.

LIU CHUANZHI BELIEVES that Chinese business practices aren't just for small shops like Yoo's, but for giant multinationals as well, and he can prove it from his own personal experience. Liu is the founder of China's PC maker Lenovo Group. In 2005, he stepped out of the Beijing firm's day-to-day management after he completed the acquisition of IBM's PC unit, one of the most prominent overseas purchases to date by any Chinese firm. The deal turned Lenovo into China's first truly multinational enterprise, with employees of all races, creeds, and backgrounds sprawled across the world. Already sixty-one years old at the time, Liu believed the job of managing this new enterprise was best left to younger managers—and more importantly, not Chinese managers alone. He realized that his own team at Lenovo, though highly successful within China, lacked the global experience to guide a company of such multicultural and geographic scope, and he handed the CEO job first to an IBM executive, then to an American PC professional, William Amelio.

Four years later, however, Liu was forced out of semi-retirement and back into active service. He reclaimed Lenovo's chairmanship and filled the CEO job with a Chinese colleague. Liu's return was prompted by a steady deterioration in Lenovo's market share and profitability. "Lenovo is all of my life," Liu says. "When it looked like my life was threatened, I had to come out to defend it."[37]

There was no secret to why Lenovo was floundering. With much of its international business focused on selling PCs to corporations, the company was missing out on faster-growing consumer sales. Amelio and his managers had devised a plan to reform the business to capitalize on this other market, but they seemed incapable of executing it. Liu diagnosed the difficulty as a culture clash within Lenovo's senior management team. Amelio, Liu explains, had imported the "classic MBA way" of managing, in which a dominant CEO makes decisions and then works with the chiefs of different business units to implement them. Such a style, Liu determined, was a poor fit with a Chinese firm. "Bill was facing a very complicated situation where there [were] different teams from different cultures and nations" in Lenovo's management, Liu explains. "Using the classic approach, it was very hard to really mobilize or motivate these teams to achieve goals."

Upon his return, Liu reformed the management system by bringing back what he called "the Lenovo Way." Rather than using Amelio's method, Liu instituted a system based on collective decision making. The CEO designs a strategy through extensive discussion among a small, tight-knit group of executives, who then meet regularly to implement the plans and check on progress. The Lenovo way "is more prudent and more thorough" than standard management techniques, Liu says.

Liu might as well call "the Lenovo Way" simply "the Way." Although he professes to know little about Confucianism, the sage's fingerprints can be found all over his management style, especially in its emphasis on harmony and the importance of community. "The ultimate purposes of building a strong team of leadership are, firstly, to develop and study the strategy with collective wisdom and efforts, and secondly, to guarantee a real execution of the strategy," Liu explains. "If, and maybe only if, the strategy is developed with the consensus of all leaders, its execution will be guaranteed." The CEO, Liu continues, must be commanding, but also ready to listen to the "remonstrating" of his top executives. "A team of leadership can check and balance the power of the top leader," Liu says. "A top leader is usually strong and aggressive. But he needs to be truly open to different opinions, and to be honestly willing to accept checks and balances. Therefore, all members in the company will have a feeling of ownership." To implement his ideas, Liu established the Lenovo Executive Committee, consisting of eight senior managers—some Chinese, some not. This step was "the very first and most important move we made," Liu says. "Members discussed the company's overall situation and long-term vision. With deep discussions, or even hard debates, the members finally reached consensus and collectively worked out a strategy that best fit the company's long-term benefits."[38]

The results suggest that Liu's ideas have merit. Within several quarters, Lenovo's finances began to improve, and its market share rose. By 2013, Lenovo had not just turned around, but had become No. 1 in the world PC market.

THE REEVALUATION OF Confucius in the late twentieth century was not limited to the realms of economic policy and corporate strategy. East Asian statesmen, emboldened by their success, began to reintroduce Confucianism into the region's politics. Although Confucius has not yet become the "Uncrowned King" of East Asia, as he was during China's imperial age, East Asian governments are looking to the great sage for legitimacy in a similar way as the emperors of old. But if the role of Confucian values in economics and business has generated heated debates, how they have influenced—or should influence—politics in Asia is a topic of even greater controversy.

Chapter Nine

Confucius the Politician

A ruler who carries the oppression of his people to the highest pitch, will himself be slain, and his kingdom will perish.

—*Mencius*

Lee Hsien Loong is a sensitive man. The Harvard graduate has been prime minister of Singapore since 2004, and there is little question that he has been a successful one. Under his watch, the city-state has risen to new heights of wealth, ensuring its continued influence in an Asia bursting with rising competitors. Yet whatever his record or personal achievements, Lee cannot escape whisperings, both at home and abroad, that he is in his job for the wrong reasons.

That's because Lee is also the son of Lee Kuan Yew. The younger Lee has been dogged by insinuations that this family pedigree, rather than his own talent, is the real reason he became his nation's prime minister. The charge is lent weight by the controlled nature of Singapore's political system. Though officially a parliamentary democracy with regular elections, Singapore is in effect a one-party state, ruled since the country's independence in 1965 by the People's Action Party, or PAP, which was cofounded by Lee Sr. The Lees and their colleagues at the PAP have proven highly adept at utilizing the tools of state to suppress opposition. Although the elder Lee resigned from the prime minister post in 1990, he retains great sway over the nation's government.

Understandably, Lee the younger defends his right to rule with bitter determination. During a 2010 interview, American broadcaster Charlie Rose poked Lee on the nepotism issue, and the prime minister offered up an unusual defense: he invoked Confucius. "The whole of our system is founded on the basic concept of meritocracy," Lee explained to Rose. "If anybody doubts that I as Prime Minister am here not because I am the best man for the job but because my father fixed it, then my entire credibility and moral authority is destroyed. First you must have the moral right, then you can make the right decisions. It is a basic Confucian precept." Lee went on to say, in effect, that he would forfeit the Mandate of Heaven if his advancement was a result of his connections rather than his resumé. If people believe that "the whole system really is just a make believe, then the system will come down. It is not tenable."[1]

The statement is remarkable. After more than a century of abuse and criticism, few East Asian leaders in modern times have been bold enough to enlist Confucius in the cause of building legitimacy for their governments or policies. Yet here is a sitting prime minister claiming that he is a *junzi*, a Confucian gentleman, who has earned his position through his superiority in experience, knowledge, and virtue. Lee was suggesting that Singapore is a country ruled by *junzi*—that its government is a vigorous Confucian meritocracy in which only the most learned and capable can rise to the top—and that the current regime therefore possesses the moral right to govern. Lee's view isn't merely his own opinion. All the way back in 1982, Goh Keng Swee, then deputy prime minister and one of the architects of Singaporean economic policy, said that "Confucius believed that unless the government is in the hands of upright men, disaster will befall the country. By the way, in this respect, the PAP believes the same thing."[2]

The idea that Singapore is governed by *junzi* is part of the state's ideology. In 1991, a parliamentary White Paper outlining the tenets of an official Singaporean national identity declared that "many Confucian ideals are relevant to Singapore," more relevant than political ideologies borrowed from the West. "The concept of government by honorable men (*junzi*), who have a duty to do right for the people, and who have the trust and respect of the population, fits us better than the Western idea that a government should be given as limited powers as possible," the White Paper reads.[3]

The self-image of Singapore's governing elite represents another historical turning point in the career of the Supreme Sage. Confucius is again a player in East Asian politics, and that fact will have major consequences for the future of the region and its relationship with the rest of the world.

Lee Kuan Yew and his "Asian values" argument stood at the forefront of this Confucian resurrection. He has crafted a Confucian alternative to Western concepts of representative government. By stressing that Asian societies are a product of an entirely different philosophical and cultural tradition from those of the West—a Confucian tradition—Lee countered the Western belief that liberal democracy based on one-man, one-vote individualism is the highest form of human civilization and thus universal, to be applied to all societies, whatever their history, culture, or outlook. Lee's contention is that Confucius and Western democracy don't automatically go together—and even more, that Confucian principles of government are superior. Simply put, Lee has presented a modern Confucian challenge to the fundamental political ideology of the West.

His position has generated a tremendous amount of acrimony among democracy advocates in both East and West. Some have argued that Lee's Confucianism is self-serving, a finely embroidered cloak to cover up his authoritarian rule and give him justification for stripping his citizens of civil liberties. Critics have contended that the two Lees, with their brutal penal code, heavy-handed regulations, and ruthlessness in stifling dissent, are more akin to the hated Qin emperor and his harsh Legalist advisers than to Confucian *junzi*. "The Singaporean political elite are not Confucian gentlemen," scholar Sam Crane wrote on his Chinese philosophy blog, *The Useless Tree*. "They are Legalist tyrants, concerned only with what will keep them in power. So the next time a PAP politician trots out the tired old 'Confucian gentleman' line, just tell him to go to Legalist hell."[4]

Controversy aside, Lee has made an important point. Even the most die-hard proponents of Western liberal democracy must admit that East Asian societies have had an entirely different political history based on an entirely different philosophical foundation—a Confucian foundation. The question facing Confucius today is: What did the old sage truly intend that foundation to be? Confucius has been intimately associated with top-down imperial rule for millennia. Over the past 150 years, those forms of Confucian government have been besieged by the introduction of Western concepts of human rights and democracy. To a great degree, Confucius has lost this battle—the Confucian dynasties of East Asia have all been wiped from the map in an onslaught of revolution, protest, and democratization. Some proponents of democracy in Asia have cheered the toppling of Confucius from his throne. They have seen Confucius as an incorrigible autocrat, and have contended that the only way for Asians to claim their political rights is to uproot him from government. To them, the attempts by Singapore's Lees and other East Asian politicians to revive Confucius in politics pose a threat to freedom and the future of open political systems in the region.

However, that is not the only way Asians have interpreted Confucius's political philosophy in the age of globalization. Other pro-democracy advocates have seen in Confucius's words the seeds of democracy and argued that Confucian teachings form the basis of republican, not authoritarian, government. This view directly contradicts Lee's "Asian values" proposition by claiming that Confucius and democracy are perfectly compatible—in fact, that Confucians developed concepts of popular government before the West.

This is no academic debate. Will Confucius become a force propelling democratization, human rights, and political openness? Or will he again be used as a tool of autocrats, a justification for new forms of imperial rule?

To BEGIN TO answer these questions, we have to delve back into ancient scripture and examine Confucius's statements on good government. Much of what we find does not reveal Confucius as a democrat. Nowhere in the *Analects* or any other writings directly linked to Confucius does he advocate representative government in the modern Western sense. He never pressed for elections or assemblies, and although he lamented the pitiful behavior of China's dukes and kings, he never questioned the legitimacy or validity of monarchy as a form of government. His ideal state is organized as a hierarchy, with a king placed above all. Power flows from the top down, not the bottom up.

Beyond the actual structure of government, Confucius also contested the very spirit underpinning democracy. Representative government is based on the idea that all people are created equal and society is best served when these individuals choose their own leadership—in other words, that the average Joe is capable of self-government. Confucius expressed no such faith. He feared that the masses lacked the education and moral fortitude to make decisions for themselves or the greater community. "The common people can be made to follow a path but not to understand it," Confucius once said. In his worldview, not everyone is created equal, and therefore not everyone has an equal right to govern. Government is the preserve of the learned and wise, the *junzi*, who possess the knowledge and virtue to rule with impartiality and benevolence, and they have a responsibility to care for those unable to govern themselves. The proper government officer serves selflessly, sacrificing wealth and comfort for the people. Confucius said he could "find no fault" with a man who "lived in lowly dwellings while devoting all his energy to the building of irrigation canals." Here can be found the source of the paternalistic Confucian state, in which the ruler is meant to treat the general public as members of his own family. One of the key responsibilities of the ruler, Confucius is recorded to have said in *The Doctrine of the Mean*, was "dealing with the mass of the people as children."[5]

The entire structure of a Confucian society is, arguably, anti-democratic. Since every relationship has a dominant and a subordinate member, not everyone in society has free will. A son should obey his father; the wife, her husband. That constrains their ability to make independent political choices. The result is a society in which certain people, because of who they are and the position they occupy, have more power and influence in public affairs than others. That's why the writer-activists of the May Fourth Movement generally believed that Confucianism and democracy were simply incompatible. "Confucianism is the system which upholds these distinctions between superior and inferior and defines who is high and who is low," Chen Duxiu wrote in 1916. "The polar opposites of the class system are the doctrines of freedom, equality and independence, which are the source of the political morality of the modern West. . . . Republican constitutionalism is based on the principles of independence, equality and freedom and absolutely cannot co-exist with the system of bonds and classes."[6]

In such a hierarchical system, people do not necessarily have the same rights as conceived in the democratic West. Society is not seen as benefiting from the individual pursuit of self-interest. Instead, each person has a predetermined role to play in society, with duties to fulfill in that role. That's why when on one occasion Confucius was asked about government, he responded: "Let the ruler be a ruler, the subject a subject, the father a father, the son a son."[7] In a society based on such relationships, individuals, like the son, cannot do or say whatever they wish. In that way, some scholars make the claim that Confucius wasn't in favor of free speech or association—civil liberties considered fundamental to Western democracy. In Confucius's world, people do not have "inalienable rights," as Thomas Jefferson believed, but "inalienable responsibilities." If Confucian duties to parents, husbands, and rulers are not met, then society descends into chaos.

In short, Confucius placed the good of the greater community over the freedom of the individual. As the political scientist Samuel Huntington wrote, Confucianism is inherently "undemocratic or antidemocratic" because it "emphasizes the group over the individual, authority over liberty, and responsibilities over rights." Moreover, "Confucian societies lacked a tradition of rights against the state; to the extent that individual rights did exist, they were created by the state."[8] In the Gettysburg Address, Abraham Lincoln famously called for "government of the people, by the people, for the people." Confucius's perfect government was meant to be for the people, but not by the people.

It would be too hasty, however, to declare that Confucius was inherently authoritarian. He may not have advocated for democracy, at least not by the modern Western definition, but he wasn't in favor of autocracy, either. Confucius, remember, preferred moral power over physical force. Rulers in a Confucian system may have been awarded ultimate authority, but they did not possess absolute power. Their behavior could be neither arbitrary nor self-serving. Confucian thinking on government is all about the limitation of power. Even kings are constrained by the rules of propriety and the dictates of virtue—the code of the *junzi*. Everyone—from the king down to the ordinary farmer—is similarly bound by the Way handed down by Heaven. The average commoner may not have the freedom to say or act as he wishes, but neither do the king and his ministers. If the ruler does not follow the Way, his actions must be brought back onto the correct path—otherwise, he forfeits his authority. Recall how Confucius believed ministers had a duty to "remonstrate" against actions by the ruler that were improper or oppressive; if the minister did not protest, he was abrogating his duty and condemning his ruler, and the state, to disaster. A duke once asked Confucius if there was a single sentence that could lead a state to ruin. "There is a saying amongst men: 'I do not at all enjoy being a ruler, except for the fact that no one goes against what I say,'" Confucius answered. "If what he says is good and no one goes against him, good. But if what he says is not good and no one goes against him, then is this not almost a case of a saying leading the state to ruin?"[9] Confucians have a long history of protesting against bad policy and "remonstrating" greedy and overbearing sovereigns—starting with Confucius himself, who spent much of his life lecturing the kings and dukes of his day on their selfish and self-defeating ways. This notion—that authority must be challenged in order to avoid the abuse of power, protect the people, and produce the best policies for the nation—is one of the foundations of democracy.

Confucius, furthermore, believed that rulers couldn't expect their citizens to obey the law and act properly unless they did so themselves. "If a man is correct in his own person, then there will be obedience without orders being given," he said. "But if he is not correct in his own person, there will not be obedience even though orders are given." Rulers should also hold their ministers and officials to the highest standards. When Duke Ai, the ruler of Lu, asked Confucius how he could earn the respect of the citizenry, the sage answered: "Raise the straight and set them over the crooked and the common people will look up to you. Raise the crooked and set them over the straight and the common people will not look up to you."[10]

Confucius went so far as to suggest that a government has no need for laws and jails if a ruler is truly benevolent. The people, Confucius believed, would respond in kind and behave properly without the threat of jail terms, fines, or other penalties. "Guide them by edicts, keep them in line with punishments, and the common people will stay out of trouble but will have no sense of shame," Confucius said. "Guide them by virtue, keep them in line with the rites, and they will, besides having a sense of shame, reform themselves." Nothing more than virtue is required to rule a state, in Confucian eyes. *The Doctrine of the Mean* says that "the superior man does not use rewards, and the people are stimulated to virtue. He does not show anger, and the people are awed more than by hatchets and battle-axes." Mencius made a very similar argument. "When one by force subdues men, they do not submit to him in heart. They submit, because their strength is not adequate to resist," he said. But "when one subdues men by virtue, in their hearts' core they are pleased, and sincerely submit." If a ruler resorts to force to control his people, it is a sign of his own failings. One official asked Confucius if he should kill all those who didn't follow the Way. Confucius made perfectly clear that such drastic action would be entirely unnecessary if the ruler himself followed the Way. "In administering your government, what need is there for you to kill?" Confucius responded. "Just desire the good yourself and the common people will be good." The *Analects* records Confucius coming out firmly against capital punishment. "To impose the death penalty without first attempting to reform," he said, "is to be cruel."[11]

There is a greater message in Confucius's words as well: authority was earned through good deeds and moral acts, not simply inherited with a title or rank. Nor, more importantly, was it imposed by force. Authoritarian regimes by their very definition are coercive—maintained by riot police, kangaroo courts, arbitrary rules, and severe punishments. Confucius, however, believed that true authority was achieved by the absence of coercion. People should give their obedience willingly to an authority that abides by defined standards of virtuous behavior.

Nor did Confucius believe that the state should always be the dominant authority in society. Recall the tale of the young man who ratted out his thieving father in She. Confucius in that case believed that family commitments trumped national law—a clear indication that the sage frowned on blind deference to government. That's why Legalists like Han Feizi thought Confucius's teachings would lead to the deterioration of state power, not the enhancement of it. To Confucius, the foundation of a stable, prosperous society was not the government, but the family. Scholar Francis Fukuyama commented that "Confucianism builds a well-ordered society from the ground up rather than the top down."[12]

MODERN ADVOCATES OF Confucius have taken this argument a step further. In their eyes, Confucius was a fully committed democrat. Over the past century, as Western political ideals seeped into China, Korea, and elsewhere in the region, some Asian thinkers and politicians have insisted that the philosophy preached by Confucius and his followers laid the foundation for democracy in East Asia.

One of the most influential was Sun Yat-sen, who is heralded by both the Communists and their enemies as the father of modern China. After the collapse of the imperial system in 1911, Sun played a role in the birth of the first Chinese republic, of which he served as president. He cofounded the Nationalist Party, or Kuomintang, which is still a powerful political force today in Taiwan. Sun firmly believed that the seeds of modern democracy were sown not in Western Europe, but by the ancient sages of China. "I find China making progress long before Europe and America and engaging in discussion of democracy thousands of years in the past," he insisted. "While democracy was discoursed upon in China two thousand years ago, it has become an accomplished fact for only one hundred fifty years in the West." Sun specifically said Confucius and Mencius "two thousand years ago spoke for people's rights."[13]

Contemporary advocates see in Confucianism the basis for the idea that sovereignty rests with the people. This might seem an odd inference to draw from a philosophy that preaches elitism and hierarchy. Yet Confucian writings contain statements implying that the ruler governs only with the consent of the people, and that it is ultimately the ordinary man who retains the right to choose his own government. In the *Analects*, Confucius suggests that the role of the common people is to keep government in check and ensure that it follows sound policies. "These common people are the touchstone by which the Three Dynasties were kept to the straight path," he said. Other writings are much more direct in their link between the legitimacy of the government and the approval of the populace. "By gaining the people, the kingdom is gained, and, by losing the people, the kingdom is lost," *The Great Learning* admonishes.[14]

The strongest evidence comes from Mencius, who spoke in much greater detail about the relationship between the ruler and the ruled. Mencius spelled out that winning the support of the common man is the only route to power. "The people are the most important element in a nation; the spirits of the land and grain are the next; the sovereign is the lightest," he said. "Therefore to gain the peasantry is the way to become sovereign." On another occasion, when asked how a king could unify the country, Mencius said that "all the people of the nation will unanimously give it to him" if he governs virtuously.[15]

Mencius also suggested that a ruler did not have the right to choose his own successor—Heaven appointed the sovereign, and Heaven would anoint the person who commanded the support of the masses. "The sovereign can present a man to Heaven, but he cannot make Heaven give that man the throne," Mencius said. Referring to a transfer of power in ancient times, Mencius explained that "affairs were well administered, so that the people reposed under [the ruler]; thus the people accepted him. Heaven gave the throne to him. The people gave it to him." A sovereign who mistreated the people, Mencius argued, would fail to retain the assent to rule and would be replaced. "A ruler who carries the oppression of his people to the highest pitch, will himself be slain, and his kingdom will perish," Mencius warned.[16]

Though Mencius implied that the people had the right to choose their own government, the classical texts were unfortunately vague on how the people exercised this right. Is the people's role passive—Heaven does the appointing, based on the sentiment of the masses—or more active? In other words, can the people install or overthrow their rulers? Confucius shied away from opportunities to join rebellions against the established political order, which suggests he believed that people could only try to improve the existing leadership or form of government, and support good rulers over bad ones, but not engage in proactive attempts to replace them. Mencius, however, took a harder line. In his eyes, a malevolent ruler lost the status of a ruler. Tossing him out of office—even killing him—was therefore not rebellion, but ridding the world of a criminal. When King Xuan of Qi asked Mencius if a minister has the right to put his ruler to death, his reply was sharp: "He who outrages the benevolence proper to his nature is called a robber; he who outrages righteousness is called a ruffian," Mencius said. "The robber and ruffian we call a mere fellow [not a sovereign]. I have heard of the cutting off of the fellow Zhou, but I have not heard of the putting a sovereign to death, in his case."[17]

Sun Yat-sen interpreted Mencius's arguments to mean that Confucians believed the people had the right to topple unjust governments and depose brutal rulers—a concept, he contended, that predated the development of similar notions in the West. Mencius "already saw that kings were not absolutely necessary and would not last forever, so he called those who brought happiness to the people holy monarchs, but those who were cruel and unprincipled he called individualist whom all should oppose," he wrote. "Thus China more than two milleniums ago had already considered the idea of democracy but at that time she could not put it into operation." South Korean pro-democracy fighter and president Kim Dae Jung concurred. "Almost two millennia before [John] Locke, Chinese philosopher Meng-tzu [Mencius] preached similar ideas," Kim wrote in 1994. "The king is the 'Son of Heaven,' and heaven bestowed on its son a mandate to provide good government, that is, to provide good for the people. If he did not govern righteously, the people had the right to rise up and overthrow his government in the name of heaven."[18]

IF ANYTHING DEFINITIVE emerges from these debates, it is that making a definitive statement about Confucius's views on democracy is bordering on impossible. Yet by the nineteenth century, Confucianism was viewed almost universally as an authoritarian doctrine and considered inseparable from despotic imperial rule. What democracy advocates cannot ignore is that throughout history Confucians not only became willing participants in the formation of the autocratic Chinese state, but also crafted the ideology and wrote the texts that legitimized it. Beginning all the way back with Dong Zhongshu and Emperor Wu in the second century BC, and intensifying in the Song and later dynasties in the second millennium AD, mainstream Confucian scholars voluntarily became tools of state, actively participating in the management of government, even as the royal courts became more centralized and repressive. Although not all Confucians were mindless bureaucrats or court sycophants—many, taking Confucius's example, capitalized on their influence at court to "remonstrate" with the emperor, often paying dearly for it—they generally did not advocate for radical political change, either. The Confucians continued to collaborate with the imperial system that revered Confucius as its greatest sage, but in reality flouted many of his precepts.

There is a temptation here to absolve Confucius of any blame for what his later followers did in his name. Yet in certain respects, Confucius's own teachings and personal example compelled his many followers to cooperate with those in power. Engaging in public service was the moral duty of the educated Confucian *junzi*. That imperative placed them in a perpetual balancing act between staying in the emperor's good graces and abiding by Confucius's ethical principles. Copying Confucius's own choices, the Confucians generally preferred trying to reform the system from within. There was a key difference, however, between Confucius and later Confucians. While it is true that Confucius sought political influence at court throughout his life, he refused to compromise his principles to gain employment; Confucians in later centuries, however, did not possess such fortitude and adapted their sage's teachings to appeal to the emperors. Once they attained clout at court, they were eager to maintain it.

The Confucians were, year after year, confronted with a stark choice: serve the state even if it deviated from Confucian ideals, in order to preserve their political power, or withdraw out of moral indignation, and lose their jobs, their incomes, and possibly their lives. This dilemma was encapsulated in a letter written in 1613 by Hayashi Razan, who served the early Tokugawa shoguns in Japan. Hayashi knew that the influence he had won with the shoguns and the life of privilege that gave him should have made him happy, yet in his heart, he was not. "I am urged to conform to people who have no understanding of my skills and aspirations; what is worse, I do conform," he wrote revealingly. "I want to follow the Confucian sages. But that course implies an obligation to act according to my convictions, and that I find myself unable to do. The drain caused by this conflict is showing in me." Confucius, he knew, would have advised him to heed his conscience over his commitment to public service, but that, Hayashi confessed, was unrealistic. "I have read the books by the sages and worthies. I know that such is their intent; it is something I cannot endure. My ambition, however, to provide for my parents, and the obligations I have to my friends and brothers, do not leave me any choice. To this state things have come."[19] It is not hard to imagine other devoted Confucians sitting in government offices in China, Korea, and Japan struggling with the same inner conflict. The more the Confucians filed into the government bureaucracy, the more Confucianism became a career, and the more difficult it became for them to choose between their livelihoods and Confucius's ethical admonishments.

The Confucians, though, were not merely morally conflicted government servants. They contributed to their own predicament by consistently revising their doctrine over time in ways that further supported authoritarian practices, and claiming that these interpretations were Confucius's own. The Confucian revival during the Song Dynasty, best known for Zhu Xi's grand synthesis, also introduced new political ideas that helped to shape the dynasties of China until the end of the imperial age in the early twentieth century. In their political theorizing, the Neo-Confucians were motivated by the same goals as Confucius himself—to ensure order and stability in a society and bring about good government through moral reformation. However, their revised doctrines also provided philosophical cover for emperors who wished to centralize political authority. In their reading of history, the Neo-Confucians equated periods of order and prosperity with strong emperors and times of decay and distress with a breakdown of central authority. They believed those breakdowns occurred not because the emperor lacked the tangible power and laws to execute it, but because of moral laxity on the part of the ruler; therefore, restoring stability entailed moral regeneration. In making this calculation, though, the Neo-Confucians elevated the emperor, awarding him a special role, not only in bringing about peace, but also in the workings of the universe.

With that enhanced position came tremendous responsibility. The Neo-Confucian emperor became the one man who could determine the course of human history. Through his virtue, he could usher in an age of peace and goodness, or, through his greed and ambition, sink the world into disaster. "All affairs in the world have their basis in one man, and the person of that one man has its master in one mind," Zhu Xi explained. "Thus once the mind of the ruler of men is correct, then all affairs in the world will be correct; but once the mind of the ruler is deviant, then all affairs in the world will be deviant." According to Zhu Xi, a battle ensues within everybody—the ruler included—between the selfish "mind of the body" and the selfless "mind of the spirit." How one acts depends on which "mind" wins. That struggle takes on universal significance when it is inside the emperor. The outcome determines "the entire world's good or disordered government, peace or peril," Zhu wrote another scholar in a letter.[20]

In making these grand claims, the Neo-Confucians also urged the common people to honor and obey this incredibly important emperor. Doing so was a critical element of ensuring a peaceful world. Neo-Confucian great Cheng Yi proclaimed that "the ruler is the sun" and that "the way of preserving the people lay in putting the principle of 'revering the emperor' first." One of Cheng Yi's students went even further. "The ruler and heaven have the same virtue; in their actions they share the same Way," he wrote.

"If you wish to protect the state, you have to respect heaven; if you wish to respect heaven, you have to exalt the ruler." Confucian scholar Hu Anguo, in his highly influential commentary on the *Spring and Autumn Annals*, wrote that the "unifying theme" of that classic text on government was that people should "revere the mandate of the king and deplore the division of authority among officials." Although Confucius, too, placed his faith in sage-kings, he never placed the ruler on so high a pedestal.[21]

Later scholars went even further. Liu Ji, a Confucian thinker in the early years of the Ming Dynasty (1368–1644), wrote that it was his goal to devise a "world-saving government" and to "develop the laws and regulations and rites and music in anticipation of the rise of a true king." Such a king would lead a total reformation of Chinese society to usher in a new golden age. "The Sage establishes moral doctrine in such a way that the people's latent goodness is drawn forth and extended," Liu Ji wrote. "His sympathy moves people and fosters them. . . . Heaven, Earth and parents give birth to the people, and the ruler-teacher completes them." Unlike other Confucians, who frowned on coercion, Liu Ji believed it was unrealistic to think that China's ancient sage-kings employed only wisdom and virtue to control the country. If the ruler wished to destroy evil and uplift the people, the use of force was inevitable. The masses were so corrupt, stupid, and self-centered that there was no other way to make them see the light. Song Lian, a like-minded Confucian scholar, believed that men suffered from "dark and heedless unintelligence" that had to be purged using any means necessary. He railed against official corruption and profit-seeking of any type. Song Lian approvingly included one story in his writings that tells of court officers who feigned austerity to please their sovereign; when the ruler later stumbled onto them feasting, he had them executed.[22]

Such thinking permanently tarnished the Confucians as supporters of political absolutism. In Song Neo-Confucianism, "the subordination of the subjects to the ruler must be absolute and unqualified," contended modern political historian Fu Zhengyuan, and as a result, "the enhanced autocracy since the Song Dynasty was to a large extent inseparable from Neo Confucianism." The writings of Liu Ji and Song Lian, meanwhile, "show clearly that by the Ming period Confucianism and autocracy were inexorably entwined." Not all scholars agree with that assessment. Historian A. T. Wood has argued that although the Neo-Confucians favored the greater centralization of political power, they never intended the Chinese imperial system to become autocratic. The idea was to contain the power of the emperor by imposing moral constraints upon him, even as they implored the masses to obey him.[23]

Whatever they thought they were doing, the Neo-Confucians were dangerously naïve in their understanding of the uses and abuses of power. Once they had entrusted such prestige and responsibility to the emperor, and then ordered the people to defer to him, they in reality had no way to control him or hold him accountable to Confucian moral principles. The flaw in the Neo-Confucians' thinking, which they directly inherited from Confucius himself, is the misplaced faith that the ruler will possess the intelligence, ability, will, and uprightness to wield the great authority the Confucians handed to him for the good of the people. Far too often, the rulers of China proved unworthy of the Confucians' faith. Far too often, they abused Confucian principles to justify their own megalomania.

The Confucians found that out after the formation of the Ming Dynasty in 1368. The dynasty's founder, Zhu Yuanzhang, also known as Ming Taizu, was among the most brutal, tyrannical leaders ever to rule over China—every bit as repressive as the First Emperor of the Qin Dynasty or Mao Zedong. Taizu executed, mutilated, or imprisoned countless Chinese. Those deemed criminals had their hands, feet, or noses cut off, or their sons and grandsons killed. The Confucians were among his victims. Even senior officials who fell out of favor found themselves on the wrong end of the whip or their heads on the chopping block. Punishments were often arbitrary. Taizu ordered two palace eunuchs flogged for not covering their shoes in the rain, a sign, the emperor thought, of a frivolous display of wealth. An official who penned a memorial to the throne that Taizu believed was too long met with the same fate. Amid all of this savagery, Taizu presented himself as the prototypical Confucian sage-king, doing his Heaven-mandated duty of fostering the morality of the people and bringing security to the land. "The way of centrality and uprightness is wholly contained in Confucianism," Taizu proclaimed in 1382. That same year, in an address to university students, he assured them that "my hope is to nurture gentlemen to tread in Confucius's path."[24]

Obviously, the followers of Confucius had gone horribly wrong. A tyrant was using the sage to justify a despotic rampage against the Chinese people. Liu Ji and Song Lian were close advisers to Taizu both before and after he formed the dynasty, and although it is difficult to know with certainty how much influence they wielded with the Ming emperor, his actions and statements follow their notion that the task of the Confucian sage-king was to use whatever means necessary to uproot evil and propagate morality. In fact, historian John Dardess, in his study of Confucianism during the Ming, claimed that Taizu's tyranny "can surely be understood to have emerged from the emperor's sincere efforts to put Confucian theory as he understood it into concrete effect."[25]

Many of Taizu's statements can sound extremely Neo-Confucian. He started life as an illiterate orphan and won the empire as a ruthless rebel commander, but by the time he became emperor he had educated himself, to a certain degree, in the Confucian classics. He produced a large corpus of essays and proclamations that reveal the way he saw himself—not as a bloody despot, but a king entrusted with the responsibility to save the world and teach the people the proper Way, or the Way as he envisioned it. "The ruler controls the empire and his discrimination between the correct and the specious, his investigations into right and wrong, all proceed from his mind," Taizu once explained, sounding eerily like Zhu Xi. "If his mind isn't correct, then all measures go awry. So the work of mind rectification cannot be slighted." If the ruler shirks this responsibility, the nation will be lost. "The people could never have survived had Heaven not produced rulers to foster them," Taizu wrote in one essay. "If the ruler does not hold the lines and cords and so give security to the good, then the good will become disquieted and disoriented. The people cannot be fostered unless the evil are punished. . . . So the Son of Heaven regulates with punishments and brings men to submit through the hierarchical distinctions." In return for providing this invaluable service, Taizu expected his subjects to submit to his "teaching." "The way of the subject lies in exhausting loyalty," he proclaimed.[26]

What the later Confucians were most guilty of was selectively choosing which elements of Confucius's advice to follow. It is difficult to imagine the great sage participating in the kind of wanton slaughter Ming Taizu perpetrated. In his own life, remember, Confucius chose poverty over employment in governments that he did not believe were following the Way. Most Confucians in the Ming, worried about feeding their families and maintaining their status, made the opposite choice. If Confucius had time-warped to the late fourteenth century, he probably would have looked upon these Confucian collaborators with dismay and reminded them of what he had taught his first disciples: "Show yourself when the Way prevails in the Empire, but hide yourself when it does not."[27]

LET'S RETURN TO modern Singapore. Are Lee Kuan Yew and his compatriots in Singapore's ruling elite Confucian *junzi*, governing with an "Asian values" ideology rooted in Confucian teachings? In some respects, Lee does uphold Confucian principles. To a great degree he has adhered to the Confucian admonition to care for the economic welfare of his people, and he firmly believes in the Confucian precept to lead by example. He has designed and managed a hardworking, corruption-free administration committed to the public good, in part by exemplifying those qualities himself.

But Confucius called for government leaders to be more than just efficient. The great sage was not focused merely on the ends of policy, but also on the means—how a state is governed is as important as what it achieves. Recall that Confucius believed that a good government is built on virtue, and a true Confucian leader rules with benevolence, not coercion. To see if Singapore's governing elite has met this much more stringent Confucian test, we need to dig deeper, into the inner workings of Singaporean governance, the ideology that has underpinned Lee's rule, and how that compares with Confucius's ideas on statecraft and human rights.

After Lee's return home from Cambridge, he formed the PAP with like-minded educated Singaporeans who feared the expanding Communist inroads into the city-state's Chinese community. In 1959, the new party took over the government in the hotly contested elections held after the British granted Singapore a degree of self-rule, and Lee was named prime minister. Singapore became a fully independent country in 1965, and by the late 1960s, Lee had more or less eradicated his opposition. Although elections continue to be held regularly, the PAP goes effectively unchallenged, usually winning nearly all the seats in parliament. Lee and his PAP colleagues have utilized their control of the state's machinery to stifle any organized opposition to their dominance. Opponents are restricted in their ability to criticize Lee and his party through controls on the press, assembly, and speech, making it practically impossible for them to campaign and contest parliamentary seats. Reporters without Borders, an organization that defends journalists' rights, ranked Singapore an embarrassing 149th out of 179 countries on its 2013 Press Freedom Index, behind Vladimir Putin's Russia and Robert Mugabe's Zimbabwe. Backing up the PAP's control is arguably the harshest penal code in the developed world. Caning is a routine punishment for even minor offenses, and the country is one of the world's most active proponents of the death penalty. A 2009 United Nations report estimated that Singapore ranked fifth in the world in executions per capita, squeezing the city-state uncomfortably between North Korea and China.[28]

Lee Kuan Yew has faced a steady drumbeat of criticism for these policies. Kim Dae Jung, the former South Korean president, once criticized Singapore as "a near-totalitarian police state" that "stringently regulates individuals' actions . . . to an Orwellian extreme of social engineering." Lee, however, has remained unapologetic. In his eyes, there have been good-hearted purposes behind his tough tactics. Without his iron fist, he believes, Singapore would never have achieved the great gains in public welfare that it witnessed under his guidance. Open democracies, he has contended, are unable to provide the direction and implement the policies necessary for rapid growth. "With a few exceptions, democracy has not brought good government to new developing countries," Lee proclaimed in a 1992 speech. "Democracy has not led to development because the governments did not establish the stability and discipline necessary for development." Lee went on to criticize the fundamental underpinnings of Western democracy as misguided. "It is assumed that all men and women are equal or should be equal," Lee said. "But is equality realistic? If it is not, to insist on equality must lead to regression. . . . The weakness of democracy is that the assumption that all men are equal and capable of equal contribution to the common good is flawed." Lee has gone so far as to insist that the basic tenet of American democracy—that all people have inalienable rights—is dangerous. He believes that when the rights of the individual are put above all, the greater community suffers. The individualistic pursuit of life, liberty, and happiness has degenerated into moral decadence and selfishness, and is the root cause of the ills of American society. "I find parts of [American society] totally unacceptable: guns, drugs, violent crime, vagrancy, unbecoming behavior in public, in sum the breakdown of civil society," Lee said in 1994. "The expansion of the right of the individual to behave or misbehave as he pleases has come at the expense of orderly society."[29]

Instead, Lee believes, a government achieves better results if it is in the hands of a *junzi*, a group of elite, educated people (such as himself) who possess the knowledge and wisdom to properly manage national affairs. The success of a government, in his opinion, depends not on the process or structure of government, but on the individuals running it. "Can you have a good government without good men in charge of government?" Lee asked rhetorically in a 1994 speech to Singapore's parliament. "American liberals believe you can, that you can have a good system of government with proper separation of powers . . . and there will be good government even if weak or not so good men win elections and take charge. . . . My experience in Asia has led me to a different conclusion. To get good government, you must have good men in charge of government." Those good men, in Lee's view, should decide what is best for everyone else in order to promote the greater good of society. "I say without the slightest remorse," Lee once said, "that we wouldn't be here, we would not have made economic progress, if we had not intervened on very personal matters—who your neighbor is, how you live, the noise you make, how you spit, or what language you use. We decide what is right. Never mind what the people think."[30]

Taking his argument even further, Lee has made the case that because of Confucianism, East Asians *prefer* such an illiberal form of governance to the multiparty democracy propagated by the West. Because of Asian cultural values, he contends, East Asians place the interests of the community over those of individuals, and thus see the overall peace and order within a nation as more important than the rights of any single person. "In the East the main object is to have a well-ordered society so that everybody can have maximum enjoyment of his freedoms," Lee said. "This freedom can only exist in an ordered state and not in a natural state of contention and anarchy," he added, as created by liberal democracy. Western styles of democratic government, Lee asserts, are thus a poor fit with Confucian societies. "Simply modeling a system on the American, British or West European constitution is not how Asian countries will or can go about [creating political systems]," he explained in a 1991 speech. "The peoples of Asia want higher standards of living in an orderly society. They want to have as much individual choice in lifestyle, political liberties and freedoms as is compatible with the interests of the community. . . . No Singaporean leader can afford to put political theory above the practical need of stability and orderly progress. On this I believe I speak for most, if not all of Asia, at present." If Asia attempted to ape Western political models and social systems, he contended, it would lead to the decay and destruction of its societies. "If we are not conscious of what is happening and we allow this process [of westernization] to go on unchecked, and it seeps down, then I believe we have a bigger problem to deal with," he said in 1988.[31]

LEE'S PHILOSOPHY HAS had great influence in the politics of East Asia and beyond. Here was one of Asia's most distinguished leaders advocating a Confucian alternative to Western representative democracy as a superior form of governance and social organization for the region. Backing up his position was the tremendous economic success of Singapore, proof that Lee's Confucian system was able to produce real improvements in human welfare within an environment of political and social stability. Lee's arguments still resonate today, most notably in China. Some supporters of the Chinese regime have copied Lee's ideas to make the case that China is better served by its one-party totalitarian state than it would be by democracy. Venture capitalist Eric

Li recently argued that, "in the Chinese tradition, an enduring definition of the end of political governance was articulated by Confucius. . . . In contemporary terms it can be described as a society of general peace and prosperity with a just legal order and built upon a righteous moral foundation. . . . Measured by the 'end' as articulated by Confucius . . . , the current one-party state model has so far served China well."[32]

In the eyes of his critics, Lee, like so many Chinese rulers and officials since the days of Emperor Wu, was abusing Confucius to disguise his autocratic rule with a false veneer of Confucian benevolence. Asian values "were increasingly summoned in aid in recent years as a sort of all-purpose justification for whatever Asian governments were doing or wished to do," wrote Chris Patten, the last British governor of Hong Kong. "Old men who wanted to stay in power, . . . old regimes that feared the verdict of the ballot box—all could pull down the curtain between East and West and claim that whatever they were doing was blessed by an ancient culture and legitimized by the inscrutable riddles of the East." Francis Fukuyama was just as damning in his assessment. "Confucianism by no means mandates an authoritarian political system," he commented in 1995. "In Singapore, the current political authorities are appealing to Confucian traditions somewhat dishonestly to justify an intrusive and unnecessarily paternalistic political system."[33]

Who's right? There are echoes of Confucius in Lee's "Asian values" proposition—most notably, in his distrust of the masses to govern themselves and his emphasis on the idea that the good of the community trumps the freedoms of the individual. In his arguments that good government requires good men to run government, his words sound remarkably like the Song Dynasty's Wang Anshi. But Lee, like so many other self-proclaimed Confucians before him, has taken the bits of Confucius that serve his interests while discarding what does not. Recall Confucius's belief that moral power was greater than physical force, and that a true sage-king would not require strict laws and punishments to govern. In Confucian eyes, Lee should not have to use the death penalty or other forms of coercion to maintain his authority. Nor should the Confucian ruler be fearful of dissent—"remonstrating" was a crucial part of good government. Confucius would probably look at Lee's regime, with its executions and canings, its crushing of opposing voices and throttling of the press, and shake his head in disapproval. If the Singaporean patriarch was truly a Confucian *junzi*, none of that would be necessary. The fact that Lee has maintained his control of Singapore by coercion proves that he has deviated from the Way.

LEE'S CRITICS ALSO question just how Confucian the Singaporeans actually are. By asserting that Confucian values make his people culturally opposed to Western-style democracy, Lee is claiming that his populace still adheres to Confucian values (or his interpretation of those values). Yet Lee's own policies show that he does not think Singaporeans are thoroughly Confucian. Beginning in earnest in 1982, the government undertook a campaign to indoctrinate its citizens with Confucianism. No government had so doggedly propagated Confucianism since the long-gone days of imperial China.

Lee had several reasons for launching the campaign. After Singapore's growth spurt, the old rallying cry that had brought unity and purpose to Singaporean society—the desperate quest to escape poverty—had become out-of-date with the wealthier times, and Lee realized he required new principles to legitimize his government and provide direction to the nation. He had also grown concerned that something potentially sinister was accompanying the foreign money and technology that were flowing into his tiny city-state—foreign ideas. Much like the conservative Confucians of the Qing Dynasty, Lee feared that the rapid westernization of Singapore would erode the saintly Confucian virtues of filial piety and commitment to community. Making Singapore more Confucian would act as a bulwark against the perceived downside of globalization.

Lee thought the best defense against such evils was strengthening the Confucian family. In a speech in February 1982, he linked the need for "moral education"—in other words, Confucian education—to combat what he saw as a deterioration of tradition—in other words, Confucian family values. The question facing Singapore, he said, was "how to prevent the erosion of these values by the all-pervasive impact of American and British television programs, which purvey a totally different way of life." The impact of this cultural invasion was already having a detrimental effect on Singaporean society, he lamented. "Anyone brought up in the Confucianist tradition will be ashamed to let his or her old parents live by themselves in loneliness and desolation," Lee said. But young Singaporeans "see on television, and some through travel, that this is the norm" in the West. "Our task is to implant these traditional values into our children when their minds are young and receptive," Lee implored, "so that when they grow out of their teenage years, these attitudes harden and are forged for a lifetime."[34]

The main thrust of the Confucian campaign took place in Singapore's schools. In 1979, Goh Keng Swee, who was then the minister of education, issued a proposal to launch a mandatory "moral education" program in public schools. Confucianism was not originally part of the curriculum, but in 1982, Goh included a course on Confucian ethics in response to a suggestion from Lee. Goh said that Lee's request caused him several sleepless nights as he mulled over what to do, but he finally decided that a class on Confucianism was a necessary addition to the project. "It is a hard nut to crack," he said at the time, "but we'll have a try at it." In a nod to Singapore's multicultural populace (with its Indian and Malay minorities), children and their parents could choose to study several other traditions to fulfill Goh's moral education requirement—courses on Buddhism, Islam, and Christianity were also available—but Lee clearly had a preference. "For most Chinese students," he said, "Confucianism and not Buddhism will be what parents would prefer their children to study."[35]

The government also decided it needed an organization to market Confucianism to the nation. "An academy could be established to reinterpret Confucianism in line with changing times, with Singapore even developing into a center for the study of Confucianism," recommended Goh, sounding surprisingly like the Han Dynasty's Dong Zhongshu in his memorial to Emperor Wu.[36] That proposal led to the 1983 establishment of the Institute of East Asian Philosophies, which was tasked with propagating Confucianism through seminars, conferences, and reports.

The institute's efforts were only part of a wide-ranging publicity campaign aimed at "Confucianizing" Singaporeans. "Confucianism in Singapore will not be merely for the classroom," Goh said. "It will be reinterpreted as a code of personal conduct for modern Singapore." The public was bombarded by an onslaught of press stories and TV shows lauding the virtues of Confucianism and its benefits for Singapore. One typical article in the *Straits Times*, Singapore's main newspaper, under the headline "Is Confucian Ethics Relevant to Singapore?" preached that Western education may be fine for science and economics, "but it would be an irreplaceable loss for us to be cut off from most of the Confucian moral values. . . . Universal values in Confucian ethics are conducive to the molding of the 'ideal educated Singaporean.'"[37]

Lee's Confucian campaign took Singaporeans by surprise. "Many observers are puzzled by the renaissance of Confucianism," confessed Singaporean academic Tan Chwee Huat. "They include the average Singaporeans themselves, many of whom are English-educated."[38] What quickly became apparent was that Singaporeans knew almost nothing about Confucianism. Ironically, government officials had to rely on academics from the supposedly culturally inferior West to devise a curriculum for the new Confucian education program. Several US-based scholars were invited to Singapore to give lectures and write articles educating the populace about Confucian doctrine.

In the end, despite the resources and high-level promotion lavished on the Confucian campaign, it was a flop. The Confucian onslaught alienated the city's Indian and Malay minorities but failed to lure many Chinese Singaporeans. More students chose Buddhism and Bible study than Confucian ethics in Goh's moral education program. In October 1989, the government changed course. No longer would Confucian ethics or other religious studies be mandatory for Singaporean students. The Institute of East Asian Philosophies got a makeover, with its research mandate broadened to include modern Asian economic and political studies; its name was changed to the Institute of East Asian Political Economy. (Today, it is the East Asian Institute at the National University of Singapore.)

Lee and his ministers, however, weren't prepared to concede defeat. They shifted to a new agenda—forging a "national identity" for Singapore. President Wee Kim Wee raised the idea in a 1989 speech to parliament. "If we are not to lose our bearings, we should preserve the cultural heritage of each of our communities, and uphold certain common values which capture the essence of being a Singaporean," he recommended. What were those values? The government obligingly provided a formal list of five two years later in a "White Paper on Shared Values." The paper explicitly proclaimed that these values were not specifically Confucian. The government "cannot force Confucianism on the non-Chinese," the paper said. Yet at least some of the five values sound very Confucian indeed. One, in particular—"Family as the basic unit of society"—seemed practically plagiarized from the *Analects*. Another—"Nation before community and society above self"—could easily be understood as Confucian.[39]

What is also apparent in the White Paper is that Lee was using the "Shared Values" proposition as a way of reinforcing his "Asian values" argument by crafting a manufactured Singaporean "national identity" that was supposedly incompatible with Western-style concepts of civil liberties. "A major difference between Asian and Western values is the balance each strikes between the individual and the community," the report said. "On the whole, Asian societies emphasize the interests of the community, while Western societies stress the rights of the individual." Singapore's future rested on ensuring that that emphasis continued. "Singapore is an Asian society. It has always weighted group interests more heavily than individual ones," the report stated. "We should preserve and strengthen it." Since "Asian values" were supposedly superior to Western ones, losing them would undermine Singapore's ability to compete globally. "No Asian society has successfully modeled itself on a Western prototype," said the report. "Singaporeans are not Americans or Anglo-Saxons, though we may speak English and wear Western dress. If over the longer term Singaporeans become indistinguishable from Americans, British, or Australians, or worse, become a poor imitation of them, we will lose our edge over these Western societies which enables us to hold our own internationally."[40]

PERHAPS THE MOST conclusive counterargument to Lee's "Asian values" thinking can be found in the region's recent history. Since the 1980s, East Asia has become a far more democratic place than it was previously. In earlier decades of the twentieth century, much of "Confucian" Asia was ruled either by dictatorships (South Korea, Taiwan, and China) or by de facto one-party states (Japan and Singapore). That is no longer the case. South Korea and Taiwan have been transformed into vibrant, healthy democracies. Japan's one-party dominance has come to an end as politics have become more contested and opposition parties have gained more power. Citizens in Hong Kong have regularly taken to the streets to defend their civil liberties ever since the British handed the territory back to China in 1997; many wish their political system will become fully democratic. The Confucian influences in these societies are arguably much stronger than in multicultural Singapore. Yet these Confucian East Asians have taken to democracy with great fervor and devotion, and in some cases, took great risks to win their democratic rights. In Korea, Kim Dae Jung encouraged what became a "righteous rebellion" against authoritarian rule. In 1987, massive street protests forced the military dictatorship to agree to free elections. Just as Confucius has not been a hindrance in Asia's pursuit of capitalist wealth, as many had predicted, he is also not an obstacle to democratization.

Contrary to Lee's arguments, Confucius and democracy do go together quite nicely. Confucius believed that a government's primary purpose was to serve the people. The exact form such a government takes is secondary. Confucianism, rather than offering an alternative to democracy, as Lee has contended, instead points to an alternative route to democracy, one based on an Asian philosophical and cultural foundation instead of ideas borrowed from the West. In that way, Confucius's interaction with globalization shows that democracy is truly universal, not confined to set historical conditions or geographical limitations.

Yet Lee's arguments are far from dead. They have taken hold in the most powerful of all East Asian nations—China.

Chapter Ten

Confucius the Communist

Confucius can guide China into the future.
—*Hotel manager Zheng Wanlong*

"Bai!" commands the master of ceremonies. "Bow!" Richard Kong obeys. The businessman is a descendant of Confucius—the 78th generation—and he has come to the Beijing Confucian Temple on a warm September morning in 2011 to honor the birthday of the Supreme Sage—his 2,562nd. Kong bows deeply before a spirit tablet inscribed with Confucius's title inside the temple's main hall, then lifts a carefully folded parcel of yellow silk above his head and lays it in front of the shrine, an offering to satisfy the spirit of his illustrious ancestor.

For thousands of years, millions upon millions of Chinese had performed such rites at Confucian temples across the nation. Yet this ceremony held special meaning—simply because it was taking place at all. Only a few years earlier, Kong could never have honored Confucius in China, at least not so publicly. When Mao Zedong was ferociously attacking Confucius, such a display would probably have landed Richard Kong in prison—or worse. The Beijing temple, where the emperors once venerated Confucius, was locked up tightly during the Cultural Revolution. Now, however, Kong was not only able to perform this ancient ritual right in the heart of the national capital, but was also doing so at the (rather insistent) invitation of Beijing's Communist cadres. That tells us something extremely important about the future of China.

Confucius is back.

In perhaps the most unexpected chapter in Confucius's long and winding biography, the Uncrowned King of imperial times has once again been restored to his Chinese throne. After a century of ridicule and abuse, the ageless sage is being embraced by the Chinese government in much the same way that the imperial courts had since the days of Emperor Wu. Children in Chinese schools recite proverbs from the *Analects* along with the sayings of Mao. Confucian temples have been repaired, and the state-controlled Chinese press regularly reports on the ceremonies that again take place within them. The annual birthday rites that Richard Kong performed were resumed at Beijing's temple in 2008. The government even promoted a 2010 feature film based on Confucius's life starring Hong Kong action hero Chow Yun-fat. State officials restricted the number of theaters showing American megahit *Avatar* in an effort—some movie fans in China suspected—to draw crowds to *Confucius*.

Rather than vilifying Confucius, Communist cadres now strive to be associated with him. In 2013, China's president, Xi Jinping, like the old emperors of the Song Dynasty a thousand years ago, made a pilgrimage to Confucius's hometown of Qufu, where he visited the Kong family mansion, which was ransacked by Red Guards in the 1960s. He promised to read Confucian texts and praised Confucius's moral principles. "Our nation will be full of hope as long as the Chinese pursuit of a beautiful and lofty moral realm continues from generation to generation," the state media dutifully reported Xi as saying.[1] Confucius's birthday celebration in Beijing was far from a family affair for Richard Kong. Officials from the local government and other dignitaries performed the same rituals as Kong, each bowing in turn before the sage's shrine.

The procession made for a surreal sight. Here were members of a political movement that was supposed to despise traditional mores and bow only to the radical ideology of Marx now venerating a figure from a hated past like a bunch of imperial eunuchs. The party's change of heart is in reality a mark of its desperation. Having replaced Marxism with capitalism—or what they prefer to call "socialism with Chinese characteristics"—the leaders of modern China have been left scrambling for an alternative governing ideology to legitimize their rule. Fearing the influence of Western liberalism and its democratic ideals—which, the cadres believe, could pose a threat to Communist dominance—they have instead retreated backward in time, reintroducing the Confucianism they once sought to destroy as a true native doctrine capable of fending off imported ideologies considered dangerous to the state.

Still, the government's representatives appeared to be profoundly uncomfortable observing the Confucian rites with Richard Kong. Tightly bound in dark, Western-style business suits, they were visibly confused by the proceedings, uncertain how to act or what to do, and they obeyed the orders of the master of ceremonies nervously. That ambivalence is apparent in national policy as well. In 2011, a huge statue of Confucius was unveiled with great fanfare near Beijing's Tiananmen Square; just over three months later, it suddenly vanished, spirited away in the middle of the night. The odd movements of the statue were symbolic. Now that the Communists are bringing Confucius back, they're not quite sure where to place him within their ruling system. Their hope is that Confucius can help them preserve the status quo—and thus keep them firmly in power. In that way, they are no different from Emperor Wu or Ming Taizu: they are hiring Confucius as a public relations officer, and attempting to use (or, some would say, abuse) his image of wisdom and virtue to paint their own regime as benevolent and themselves as worthy, caring rulers.

But by upholding Confucius, they are at the same time inviting comparisons between their own practices, policies, and behavior and his high moral standards for governance. Although many Confucians throughout history allowed themselves to become servants of authoritarian emperors, others showed a tendency to resist an authority that failed to abide by their cherished principles. There are uncomfortable questions facing China's Communists as they attempt to reemploy the sage as an emblem of the state. Will a resurrected Confucius again become a toady of an authoritarian government, with a role merely to hide its barbaric ways with a few pithy slogans? Or will Confucius prove a threat to the Communist regime, a symbol of opposition to a repressive political system?

Whether modern Chinese rulers will place Confucius firmly at the center of Chinese politics and society once again is an open question. How it is answered will help to determine China's future and its position in the world.

RICHARD KONG HAS lived through the twists and turns of Confucius's modern history. Even within the Kong family itself, their heritage was a point of controversy. As a child, Richard's parents hid his illustrious lineage from him. That's because being a Kong was a life-threatening condition in Communist China. Ever since the imperial court granted the descendants of Confucius noble rank 2,000 years ago, one emperor after another had showered favors onto the Kongs. Thanks in part to land grants from the government, the Kongs controlled 246 square miles of territory by the middle of the Qing Dynasty (1644–1911). The mansion in Qufu was built at the state's expense. No wonder the Kongs called themselves "the first family of China."[2] However, landlords became the chief targets for Mao's peasant revolution, and they came no bigger than the Kongs. After Mao's Communists conquered the Qufu area, they stripped the Kongs of their landholdings. The family scattered. Some of the Kongs fled to Taiwan with the defeated Nationalist forces. Others, like Richard's family, had to make a new life in a new China.

At first, Richard's immediate family survived well enough. His father, Kong Deyong, had left the family's Qufu fiefdom and was studying music in Beijing during the civil war between the Communists and Nationalists. After Mao formed the People's Republic, Kong Deyong got a post in a music research institute under the Ministry of Culture. But with the radicalization of the Cultural Revolution of the 1960s, his Kong heritage caught up with him. "When the Red Guards said 'down with the biggest landlord in China,' that was my father," Richard says. In 1968, Richard's own aunt tipped off the Red Guards that the family still had a stash of secret wealth, and the Guards descended on Richard's Beijing home and ransacked it. Richard's mother had frantically crammed the family's jewelry into a cloth sack and hidden it between the springs in the cushions of a soft chair. But she had sealed the cushion poorly, the bag dropped out, and the Guards confiscated everything.[3]

The family got split apart. Richard's father was sent to a work camp in Hubei Province, while Richard and his mother and two sisters were shipped south to Jiangxi, where they lived from 1969 to 1971. The camps, where the Communist Party sent intellectuals, urbanites, and other perceived "counterrevolutionaries" to be "reeducated" through hard labor, were a common feature of the Cultural Revolution. Richard's mother worked long hours in the camp's rice paddies. He was left mainly on his own in a small hut with his sisters. "I was six years old," Richard recalls. "When we went to the countryside, no adults looked after you. Mom went to work early in the morning and came back late. There was no school. I didn't go to school for a while." The government eventually allowed the family to reunite in Beijing, but they had had enough of Communist China. In 1979, Richard's parents emigrated to Hong Kong, and he and his sisters joined them a few months later.

It was only then that Richard learned about his true ancestry. In 1982, his father returned to Beijing, where he met the mayor as well as Singapore's Lee Kuan Yew. His trip was a sign that the attitude toward Confucius was beginning to change. "He was very excited when he came back," Richard recalls. Then he let Richard in on the family secret. "He told us little by little," Richard says. "At first, he didn't want to tell us much. People were so scared to speak out. He felt uncomfortable at the time. Even today, my father has never been proud [of his connection to Confucius]. We still have that dark shadow." Richard, who had been brainwashed by Cultural Revolution rhetoric, wasn't happy to hear the news that he was related to Confucius, either. "People say I must have been so proud. I say, no, I was ashamed," he says. "I thought Confucius was a representative of the feudal system."

Many years passed before Richard took any real interest in Confucius. Growing up in Hong Kong, which was still a British colony at the time, he found it easy to become immersed in Western culture. He felt detached from Chinese history and society and learned little about them. That changed when the family business brought him back to China. In 2001 he settled in Shanghai, where he now runs a pharmaceutical business, and his attitude toward his homeland started to shift. "I began to hang out with local Chinese and gradually I became very much influenced by Chinese culture," Richard recounts. "It was something decent I could learn. I met a lot of people in the arts and education. Those people brought me into the cultural field."

His interest piqued, he sought out knowledge of China's past. Richard scheduled meetings with professors who specialized in Chinese history and philosophy, signed up for a class on traditional culture at Peking University, and got together with other Kong relatives in Shanghai on Saturday afternoons for study sessions about Confucian texts. Richard says he has been transformed by the discovery of his family's legacy. "I was [once] aggressive in business. I always wanted to achieve more. You are just like a soldier on the battleground," he says. But now, "I'm not so selfish anymore. If you have so many sofas, so what? You can only sit in one place. I am less greedy. I don't care what people think of me. I am happy with what I have today. Now I understand the value of life."

Richard, like his famous ancestor and the many advocates of Confucianism who followed—from Mencius to Dong Zhongshu to Zhu Xi—hopes that China's current leadership will heed the wisdom of Confucius and promote it widely to the common people. "It seems to be a very critical moment" in Chinese history, he says. "The question today is: How can we understand about Confucianism in the correct way? This is important. There are so many explanations. The Chinese government really has to consider how important it is for the younger generation to understand our own culture and history—the *real* history." Without Confucius, he believes, China may head down the wrong path. "The whole country is materialistic. That's why China has become the second-largest productive country," he says. "People want to improve the quality of their lives. There is nothing wrong with it. But if you only go in that direction, and you don't have anything spiritual, you have lost yourself."

THE CHINESE GOVERNMENT readily agrees with that observation. The Communist Party's attitude toward Confucius began to change with surprising speed after Mao's 1976 death and the close of his turbulent Cultural Revolution. One of his former protégés, Deng Xiaoping, emerged as the country's paramount leader after a power struggle among the party's top cadres, and he was more pragmatic and less ideological than Mao. As a result, Deng had suffered along with Confucius during the Cultural Revolution. He was humiliated in his Beijing home by Red Guards, then later exiled to a remote village with his wife, where they spent their days repairing tractors. But Deng, who had long been one of the most respected of China's Communist leaders, was too charismatic a figure to be kept sidelined. He was restored to the party's inner circle in 1973, and over the next five years he was able to solidify his authority over the country through a series of deft political alliances.

Deng inherited a China in desperate decay. Impoverished and weary from the tumult of the Cultural Revolution, Deng realized that a drastic new course was necessary if the Communist Party was to avoid falling victim to a new revolution. He discarded Mao's rhetoric and replaced it with fundamental reform, of both the party and, more importantly, the economy. Deng sparked China's remarkable economic miracle by cracking open the country to the outside world and encouraging free enterprise. Out went the usual Marxist bombast of the Mao era; in came very practical policies aimed at building a modern economy and getting rich.

Deng's reform movement transformed Mao's poor, isolated China into a rising superpower. But the economic success also left Deng and his reformers with a major political problem. Mao had just spent decades trying to implant Marxist ideology as a new orthodoxy for a new China. With the capitalist reform of the Deng period, however, Marxism was quickly becoming the outdated dogma of a bygone era that many Chinese wished to forget. Critically, the Chinese government lost the ideological justification for its existence. Its rule was becoming entirely dependent on the country's economic performance—its ability to deliver jobs and higher incomes. But the leaders in Beijing understood that economic success alone was not sufficient to ensure the future of party rule. The Communists were confronted with a thorny question: What could replace Marxism as the regime's philosophical foundation?

Deng and his successors found the answer in Confucius. The same sage who had been blamed for everything wrong with China became, miraculously, the guide to lead China into a glorious future. Much like Emperor Wu of the Han Dynasty more than two millennia before, China's Communists found Confucius to be a useful tool to build a new state—entrenched and domineering but draped in the benign garb of China's most venerated sage.

Confucius's rehabilitation began just as Deng was instituting his economic reforms. The effort was probably launched in 1978 when Shandong University, located in the same province as Qufu, sponsored a program to reevaluate Confucian thought. Two years later, a Confucian research institute opened in Qufu. Then, in 1984, the government established the China Confucius Foundation to promote Confucianism at home and abroad. Communist theorists began to soften their formerly hostile attitude toward Confucius in order to smooth the reintroduction of his teachings into Chinese society. In the early 1980s, Li Zehou, a professor at the state-run Chinese Academy of Social Sciences, for instance, reassessed the role of Confucius in Chinese history and determined that the sage wasn't that bad after all. By his reckoning, Confucius wasn't an evil elitist who helped repress the peasantry, as the Communists had previously asserted, but an advocate of the little guy. Confucius "was against ruthless oppression and exploitation and championed the cause of ancient clan rule with its comparative moderation, showing the democratic and plebeian side of his thinking," Li wrote in 1980. Some of Confucius's teachings, Li continued, were so worthy that they could no longer be suppressed. "In Confucianism, we find an active and positive attitude toward living, a conformity with rationalism, a preference for practicality over polemics," Li wrote. "Confucianism harmonizes human groups, allows for a reasonable and moderate satisfaction of the desires and passions, avoids fanaticism and blind submission. Confucianism is almost synonymous with Chinese culture."[4]

By the late 1980s, high-ranking Communist dignitaries were singing Confucius's praises. In a speech at a 1989 conference in Beijing celebrating the sage's 2,540th birthday, Gu Mu, a close ally of Deng and a leading reformer, made the Communists' new policy toward Confucius clear. No longer was Confucius, or traditional Chinese culture in general, to be criticized as the source of China's weakness. Gu Mu boasted that "for a long period of time in human history, Chinese culture, with the Confucian school of thought as the main stream, glittered with colorful splendor." Modern China, he said, could learn from the country's Confucian past to help it achieve greatness in the future. Confucian teachings "not only made positive contributions to the prosperity of ancient Chinese society, but also have profound practical significance for the survival and development of mankind today," Gu Mu asserted. The goal, he pointed out, was to integrate elements of Confucian thought into modern Chinese society to aid in the nation's development. "The Chinese people are working hard to build socialist modernization and a prosperous and strong socialist country," Gu Mu explained. "In order to reach this goal, we must develop and improve our new culture. This calls for inheriting and reforming the traditional culture of our nation."[5]

The Communists' promotion of Confucius has greatly accelerated since the turn of the twenty-first century. No longer confined to academic conferences and state foundations, Confucius and his teachings are now regularly pressed upon the Chinese public. Confucian phrases and references appear in state-run press reports as well as in the speeches of China's most senior leaders. Confucian ceremonies have been revived around the nation. Simply put, Confucius has become an integral part of Beijing's propaganda machine.

THE BIG QUESTION, though, is: Which of the many Confuciuses China has conjured up over the centuries does the Communist government now wish to resurrect? Gu Mu offered a glimpse of the answer in his 1989 speech. A wholesale reintroduction of Confucius was not the way forward, he made clear. "It is inadvisable either to be complacent about the past or to discard the past and tradition," he said. "The correct attitude is to inherit the essence and discard the dross." And which parts of Confucianism might be valuable for today's China? "As is known to all, the idea of harmony is an important component of the Chinese traditional culture," Gu Mu continued. "As early as in the last years of the West Zhou Dynasty three thousand years ago, ancient scholars elucidated the brilliant idea of 'harmony making prosperity.' Later, Confucius and the Confucian school put forward the proposition of 'harmony above all.'"[6]

The idea of Confucian "harmony" has become a recurring theme for China's leadership, reinforced again and again in press reports and other propaganda. "Confucius said, 'Harmony is something to be cherished,'" President Hu Jintao told party comrades in a 2005 speech.[7] On the surface, the idea of "harmony" holds out the promise of a Chinese society united in its new prosperity and playing a peaceful role in world affairs. But critics of the Chinese regime fear that the word "harmony"—in Communist-speak—is not as salutary as it sounds. To them, it is a code word for the preservation of the current political system. The "harmony" the Communists seek is a country free from challenges to its authoritarian rule, a "harmony" imposed by the state.

In that way, China's leaders are attracted to Confucianism for reasons similar to those of Singapore's Lee Kuan Yew and his successors. The Singaporean statesman has had great influence on how Beijing views Confucius, and the Chinese Communists seem intent on re-creating in China what Lee has accomplished in Singapore—meld together a modern, liberal economy with an illiberal political system, supported by the idea that Confucian thought is an alternative to Western notions of freedom and human rights. "The government has permitted, and even encouraged, this revival of Confucianism in order to provide a justification for a modern, authoritarian China that does not depend on western theories of history," wrote scholar Francis Fukuyama. These new Confucians "argue that China is not a democracy manqué, but rather a separate civilization founded on different but equally valid principles from the West."[8] History, then, has come full circle. The Communists used to deplore Confucius as a tool abused by landlords and imperial mandarins to suppress the masses; now they are using Confucius for that exact purpose.

SOME ARGUE THAT the adoption of Confucius by China's leadership is more than a mere propaganda device. These advocates believe that the government sincerely wishes to infuse its system with Confucian practices that lend the regime an element of legitimacy. Confucian scholar Daniel Bell and businessman Eric Li, writing in 2012, contended that China has again become a Confucian-style "meritocracy," in which only the best and brightest move up the ranks. "Over the past three decades or so, the CPC [Communist Party of China] has gradually transformed itself from a revolutionary party to a meritocratic organization," they wrote. Only the nation's top students, emerging out of the education system's grueling examinations, are able to gain access to civil service posts (just as in the old days of the dynasties), and once in the party and bureaucracy, they go through further testing before being promoted. The testing system, they said, has made China's authoritarian state more effective than Western democracies in crafting and implementing wise policies. While in a democracy, voters make choices based only on their own selfish interests, in China well-educated bureaucrats, modern versions of the *junzi* of imperial times, manage the country for the good of all. "The advantages of Chinese-style meritocracy are clear," Bell and Li concluded. "The Chinese regime has developed the right formula for choosing political rulers that is consistent with China's culture and history and suitable to modern circumstances. It should be improved on the basis of this formula, not Western-style democracy."[9]

Scholar Zhang Weiwei has gone even further, arguing that Beijing's adoption of Confucian harmony as a guiding tenet is proving a better method of governing the country than open democracy. "Beijing has revived this old Confucian ideal for a large and complex society," Zhang wrote, adding:

> Rejecting Western-style adversary politics, Beijing has worked hard to emphasize commonality of different group interests, to defuse social tensions associated with rapid change. . . . China is likely to continue to evolve on the basis of these ideas, rather than by embracing Western liberal democracy, because these ideas have apparently worked and have blended reasonably well with common sense and China's unique political culture, the product of several millennia—including 20 or so dynasties, seven of which lasted longer than the whole of U.S. history.[10]

Bell, Li, and Zhang, however, are ignoring the reality of modern China. The government's attempts to promote Confucian harmony have not soothed a restive population. Farmers, workers, ethnic minorities, and others who find themselves victims of the regime are in a constant state of unrest. They have vented their frustration in protests and riots, some of which turn violent. The Chinese government itself is aware that its bureaucrats and party cadres are far from the impartial, principled *junzi* that Bell and Li envision. Corruption has become an endemic feature of Chinese life and a source of anger among a disgruntled public. The widespread graft existing in today's China is symbolic of the moral decay prevalent in society. Materialism has become the new supreme sage of China. The result is a never-ending litany of scams and scandals. In an attempt to evade regulations, dairy farmers knowingly poured a toxic chemical into milk, sickening babies across the country in 2008. Willfully negligent construction companies built substandard schools that crumbled during the disastrous 2008 Sichuan earthquake, killing scores of children. The nation was especially horrified in 2011 when a two-year-old girl got run over on a street in the southern city of Foshan—by two separate drivers—while eighteen people walked by and did nothing to help the mangled child.

Blame Mao's attack on Confucius. By undermining the master and his teachings, the Communist Party under Mao weakened society's ethical foundation. For 2,000 years, Confucius had been the standard for moral behavior, his teachings the ultimate code for the proper gentleman. As the Communist Party whittled away at Confucian influence, it simultaneously eradicated society's paradigm for correct social behavior.

This point gets at another reason why the Communists are bringing Confucius back. The government hopes that by reinserting Confucius into society, he can once again act as moral guide for the nation. Beijing's top leaders believe that some renewed Confucian indoctrination can help stamp out rampant official corruption and abuses. "In traditional Confucianism, the cultivation of personal moral integrity is considered the most basic quality for an honest official," the state's *China Daily* newspaper lectured in 2007. "The qualities of uprightness, modesty, hard work, frugality and honesty that President Hu encourages officials to incorporate into their work and lifestyle are exactly the same as the moral integrity of a decent person in traditional culture." Similar exhortations are directed at the business community. As the *China Daily* preached in 2006:

> No society can afford to build an economy without a moral foundation.... It should also be pointed out that Confucianism is not old or irrelevant. The first reason for which a righteous person should make self-criticism of himself, as dictated by the *Analects*, is when he has compromised his credit, or failed to honor his word, in dealing with others.... A moral system does offer immense help to an economy.... When the rule of law is weak, and many rules that were made in the era of the planned economy are obsolete, a return to traditional teachings is a natural choice for many people.[11]

LIU HEDONG HAS taken on the task of convincing his fellow Chinese citizens to become more Confucian. The former government official is director of the China Confucian College, a nonprofit organization partially funded by the state that is trying to popularize Confucius through lectures and Internet-based education programs. His main targets are Chinese corporations, which he believes can help disseminate Confucian knowledge throughout the country by inculcating it in their employees. The institute operates out of the pavilions on the grounds of Beijing's Confucian Temple; across the street it is building what Liu calls "five-star" classrooms and other facilities. He considers his college a "model" institution to be replicated in major cities around the nation.

For Liu, Confucius can play the savior for modern Chinese society. The sage's ideas, Liu believes, can serve as a tonic for the evils that are a by-product of the country's rapid economic ascent and opening to the world. "There have been a lot of problems created by the market economy," Liu explains. "Only focusing on economic benefits has brought bad values and environmental degradation. That is why the government is reviving

Confucianism." He goes on to offer a long list of virtues Confucius could instill in today's China to counter the ills caused by China's economic reform. Confucianism promotes "humaneness, integrity, wisdom," and it teaches people "to discipline yourself, love others, to always be hard-working, have a good mental attitude, be more tolerant, sacrifice oneself." Moreover, "Confucianism advocates that we should not only think of the needs of the time but also of the long term and future generations. The objective is to learn to be a better person. We can care for the world, care for other people, and leave something good for future generations."[12]

"After three decades of reform, what Chinese society lacks are these core values," Liu says. "Our country is like a young person whose bones and muscles are growing too fast. The development of spiritual cultivation has not caught up to the physical growth." The result is a populace "who gets rich too fast and is not cultivated. The reform and opening up has built up the muscles; restoring core values will build up the mind." The goal of reviving Confucius "is to make the ordinary Chinese have more cultivated manners and to make them cultivated gentlemen, as opposed to those who only value money and consumerism."

What of the concerns that the government's renewed interest in Confucius is an attempt to preserve the political status quo? "This kind of attitude is reasonable," Liu concedes. "They are concerned that the government will make Confucianism a [state] religion. But they also don't understand that this time Confucianism is distinguished from the ruling party. Our [current] leaders are only temporary. They also have to think of the future. The value of Confucianism is that it helps make you deal with everybody in a different way. My assignment is to help people in the government, so we can form ties of trust between people in the economy, between the government and the people." Liu talks of a spiritual renewal in China that would be brought about by intensified Confucian education. The ultimate goal, he says, "is the realization of a revival of Confucianism in our generation to benefit the country and the world."

THE CHINESE GOVERNMENT is employing Confucius in a public relations campaign on an international scale as well. As the country's wealth has grown, many nations—including major trading partners like the United States and Japan—have become wary of China's expanding political influence, military might, and geopolitical ambitions. Beijing is counting on Confucius to smooth its relations with the rest of the world. By capitalizing on Confucius's reputation in the West for wisdom and pacifism, Beijing's leaders hope they can make China appear less threatening. Essentially, the government is enlisting him as a symbol of the nation. "Confucius and Confucianism have become China's 'brand,'" commented Professor Kam Louie.[13]

Beijing's true motives may have more to do with international geopolitics than with altruism. China's leaders see Confucius as an ambassador who can enhance its cultural and social clout—its "soft power." For centuries, as Confucianism spread around East Asia, it carried with it Chinese imperial influence. Today's leaders in Beijing intend to re-create that influence on a global scale by piggybacking on Confucius's international fame. The most notable aspect of that agenda is an active state program to promote knowledge of Chinese culture and language through a worldwide network of study centers called Confucius Institutes. A government agency known as Hanban, which is linked to Beijing's Ministry of Education, oversees the institutes and provides funding and other support to universities to establish and maintain them. Hundreds of Confucius Institutes have popped up since the program's launch in 2004. The list spans Afghanistan to Zimbabwe, with dozens of locations in the United States, including Stanford University and the University of California at Los Angeles.

Confucius Institutes, though, have little to do with Confucianism or the study of Confucius's doctrine. Their programs focus to a great degree on teaching the Chinese language. They are marked by a bit of irony as well. The Chinese Communists once tried to sway global affairs by exporting revolution; now they are using the much more traditional Confucius to translate China's economic might into a cultural pull. Most importantly, Confucius Institutes have become embroiled in controversy. Officially, the institutes' mission, as publicized by Beijing, is purely educational. The institutes "have provided scope for people all over the world to learn about Chinese language and culture," Hanban's website boasts, and they have acted "as a bridge reinforcing friendship and cooperation between China and the rest of the world." But some China experts and educators see the institutes as an attempt by the Chinese government to control global discourse on issues concerning the country. The project's bylaws, published on the Hanban website, give Beijing a heavy hand in the institutes' curriculum and management. The institutes "shall not contravene . . . the laws and regulations of China," and "shall not involve or participate in any activities that are not consistent" with their mission. In testimony before a US congressional hearing, Steven Mosher, president of the Population Research Institute, called the Confucius

Institutes "Trojan horses with Chinese characteristics." He feels that their "seemingly benign purpose" hides Beijing's intention of "sanitizing China's image abroad . . . and creating a new generation of China watchers . . . well-disposed towards the Communist dictatorship."[14]

The academic community, too, is becoming increasingly concerned that Beijing is using Confucius Institutes to try to control what universities worldwide teach about China. Confucius Institutes "function as an arm of the Chinese state and are allowed to ignore academic freedom," the American Association of University Professors warned in 2014. "Most agreements establishing Confucius Institutes feature nondisclosure clauses and unacceptable concessions to the political aims and practices of the government of China . . . North American universities permit Confucius Institutes to advance a state agenda in the recruitment and control of academic staff, in the choice of curriculum, and in the restriction of debate." The group recommended that US universities end their involvement with Confucius Institutes unless given full control over their activities. More than a hundred University of Chicago professors signed a petition in 2014 calling for termination of that institution's Confucius Institute, stating that the terms of its operation impinged on academic freedom. Later that year, the university decided to shutter its institute, dealing a serious blow to China's efforts to promote the program in America. A few days later, the Pennsylvania State University announced it too would close its institute. Beijing's attempts to capitalize on Confucius's image to enhance its "soft power" are facing mounting resistance from academics and others who don't trust Beijing's objectives and goals.[15]

WILL CHINA'S CONFUCIAN resurrection have any more success at home than abroad? So far, the government's effort to reintroduce Confucianism hasn't progressed beyond the superficial. Most schools provide only the most cursory instruction in Confucius's teachings. Government officials may occasionally trot out a phrase or two from Confucius, or toss out a few carefully chosen Confucian-sounding slogans, but they appear to have little intention of promoting a return to intensive Confucian education and practice. That caution is a reflection of the queasiness about Confucius that still exists within the regime and stems from the uncertainty about how the great sage's reintroduction will ultimately impact Communist rule. When Gu Mu said that China should "inherit the essence and discard the dross" of Chinese tradition, he meant that the Communists wish to restore the elements of Confucius's teachings (or, more accurately, the interpretations of those teachings) that they feel support the current political system while conveniently ignoring those that might pose a threat. However, in the process of resurrecting the Supreme Sage, China's leaders may not be able to control the version of Confucius that remerges. The Chinese citizenry, reawakened to traditional culture, might discover another of the many Confuciuses who have populated history—the Confucius who "remonstrated" with authority, or demanded that rulers uphold the highest principles of virtuous government. By reanimating Confucius, the government is taking a big risk. The Communist Party is potentially holding up a moral standard that its own senior leaders cannot meet. The dilemma facing China's leadership is whether their propagation of Confucianism will build support for the regime or foster a source of resistance to it.

Yet it would be wrong to assume that all the advocates of Confucianism in modern China are content with the current political system, or believe that Confucius should be a pillar of the status quo. There are others in China who see Confucius as a critical part of China's future—but not the same Confucius as the one being promoted by Beijing's Communists. Confucian literati Jiang Qing has crafted a new type of Confucian political order that he markets, appropriately enough, from a book-stuffed apartment in a modern tower in Shenzhen, the industrial enclave where China's economic miracle began. Much like Deng Xiaoping's economic reforms, which borrowed policies from the West and elsewhere in Asia to create "socialism with Chinese characteristics," Jiang's Confucianism infuses the philosophy of the Supreme Sage with Western political institutions, beliefs, and practices to forge a reformed system of governance that Jiang believes is the best option for modern China. "The world is changing," Jiang says. "Confucian theorists need to make an adaptation to accord with the times."[16]

The solution, Jiang believes, is to strike a careful balance between old and new, Chinese and foreign. It would be disastrous, in his view, for China to adopt ideas on government and society from the West wholesale. They simply would not fit with China's Confucian culture. "Confucianism is Chinese civilization," says Jiang. "The only way [forward] is to revive Confucianism." But Confucians should not be stuck in a bygone age, either. Jiang believes that Confucianism can't be revived in a "fundamentalist" movement—an effort to reestablish the Confucian practices of old without regard for the realities of the modern world. "We should use the principles of Confucianism and choose acceptable values from the West and current society," Jiang explains, sounding a lot like the controversial nineteenth-century reformer Kang Youwei. "We are against two trends, a separate Chinese culture from the rest of the world, or totally embracing Western culture. One is to absolutely refuse, the other is to absolutely accept. We need to use the basic values of Confucianism as a foundation and then absorb certain values from the West to create a new Confucianism."

The outgrowth of that process would be what Jiang calls a "constitutional Confucian political system" based on the "Way of the Humane Authority." Such a system would be centered on a tricameral legislature. One chamber would be a "House of Exemplary Persons," led by an eminent scholar and filled by people nominated by literati schooled in the Confucian classics. The house's members would prove their merit through a rigorous examination system, as in imperial days, and years of handling responsibilities within the civil service. A second chamber, the "House of the Nation," would be led by a direct descendant of Confucius and filled by relatives of other famous scholars and officials. The lawmakers in the third chamber, the "House of the People," would be elected, either by direct popular vote or through organizations representing different occupations.

Jiang believes that such a structure benefits from the checks and balances of the American democratic system—but with an important distinction. In usual Confucian fashion, Jiang does not trust ordinary folks to consistently make the right decisions for the nation. "Democracy is flawed in practice," he once wrote. "Political choices come down to the desires and interests of the electorate. This leads to two problems. First, the will of the majority may not be moral: it may favor racism, imperialism or fascism. Second, when there is a clash between the short-term interests of the populace and the long-term interests of mankind, as is the case with global warming, the people's short-term interests become the political priority."[17] Jiang thinks his Confucian constitutional government would avoid these failings by giving the common man a voice in governing while also allowing for oversight by the most educated and virtuous members of society. The House of Exemplary Persons would have veto power over decisions taken by the other two houses. In this way, the learned could counter unwise choices made by popularly elected officials.

Such a governing structure would provide legitimacy to China's rulers that they currently lack, according to Jiang. He compares today's leadership in China to Emperor Wu of the Han Dynasty, who also engaged in a quest for new ideas to improve the government—a quest that ended up with his embrace of Confucius. "The Chinese Communist Party wants to gain the legitimacy to rule China so they are looking for new theories," he says. "The party won't accept democracy and freedom. So the rulers have to accept Confucian culture and use it as a base; otherwise they can't rule China. If you want to rule China for a long time, you have to use Confucian culture." Jiang believes that the rapid turnaround in the government's attitude toward Confucius "shows the severity of the crisis of the legitimacy of the ruling party. You cannot only use the military, the police and the prisons to rule a country. You need a cultural foundation."

For China to overcome its current problems, however, the revival of Confucianism has to go much deeper than a few official speeches, Jiang says. The general public must reconnect with Confucius as well. To that end, he suggests the government borrow a page from Kang Youwei and establish Confucianism as a "state religion," which it would actively promote by a state-founded organization through Confucian temples modeled on the Christian churches of the West. "The issue is how to rebuild both the political system and the foundation at a popular level," Jiang explains. "It is the religious organizations in the West that have the churches where people with a similar faith get together. The government can create conditions to revive the cultural foundation among the general populace, but it cannot conduct religious activities itself."

Without such a large-scale Confucian revivalist movement, Jiang feels that China might be doomed. "The life and culture of Chinese people have reached a crisis, a crisis never seen before," he says. "Since China opened up to the world, the economy developed, but Chinese culture is still empty, China is the only country that achieved modernization that has been totally against its own culture. The moral benchmark has been lost. In the West, God sets up a moral benchmark for people. In China there is no God. There is no moral restraint on people's behavior. Can you believe what would happen in Western countries if people didn't believe in God anymore? China has a moral crisis, and it is the worst crisis in Chinese history."

Still, Jiang is not optimistic that his voice will be heard. "In the next twenty or thirty years, I have no hope that my ideas will be realized, because the rebuilding of Confucianism is still very superficial," he says. "It takes generations to make one idea happen. Rebuilding Confucianism is like a big building. Right now the building collapsed. What I am doing now is drawing the blueprint, the whole picture. It is a difficult task to draw up a new blueprint and get everyone to agree on it. The rebuilding of Confucianism cannot be done by one person."

JIANG, HOWEVER, IS not alone. The renewed interest in Confucius isn't merely a government propaganda exercise or limited to academic journals.

The emerging acceptance of Confucius at the highest levels of the Chinese Communist Party has fostered a more permissive attitude toward China's ancient philosophies and religions not seen before in the history of the People's Republic, and in response, some of the Chinese—such as Richard Kong, Confucius's descendant—are rediscovering their Confucian heritage. In a society in perpetual flux, without clear direction, and, as Jiang Qing put it, facing a moral crisis, the Chinese are turning to their own history and traditions—rather than those of the West—for guidance and spiritual nourishment. Inevitably, that quest is reintroducing them to Confucius.

This rediscovery of the sage is in full flourish at the Sihai Confucius Academy on the outskirts of Beijing. Here founder and schoolmaster Feng Zhe puts his 130 young students (ages three to thirteen) through the daily rigors of an old-fashioned Confucian education. Each morning at the crack of dawn, the children assemble and bow reverently to pictures of Confucius that are proudly hung on the walls. Soon after come three hours of intensive study of the Confucian classics. The youngsters read the *Analects*, *Mencius*, and *The Classic of Filial Piety*, among other texts, over and over again—three hundred times each, their teachers insist—until they have thoroughly memorized all of them, word by word. This type of hard-core education in the classics, reminiscent of the lost days of imperial examinations, has been practically nonexistent in China since the Communist conquest.

Feng opened the school after pursuing his own personal quest into China's ancient culture. After leaving college in his junior year, he started his own publishing company that distributed Chinese translations of the writings of Western philosophers, such as Kant and Hegel, among other foreign works. Around 1999, he began to question his purpose: Why was the company disseminating the works of all of these foreigners and not China's own philosophers? Few people in China possessed any significant knowledge of the Chinese classics at that time—after all, almost no one had given them serious consideration in the country in decades. He sought out the few elderly scholars who could teach him about the philosophies of antiquity, then began printing versions of them, including the most important works in the Confucian canon, first in Chinese and later in English.

Feng's discovery of Chinese tradition became much more than a sound business proposition. As he read through the ancient works, he believed he was finding within them the answers to the problems facing modern China. He came to see how the Chinese traditions—and, more specifically, Confucian traditions—could restore ethical behavior and order to a Chinese society lacking a moral foundation. "In order to save China, the people have to start with a cultural revival," Feng says. "There are so many people who don't behave morally, so there is no trust. In Confucianism, the most important aspect is to know how to treat other people. What will make China a strong country is to build a harmonious society for all—based on Confucianism." In 2006, Feng decided that simply publishing the classics wasn't enough. It was at that point that he founded the academy. "As an important part of the cultural renaissance of the people, we want to educate them when they are very young," Feng says.[18]

The parents who have enrolled their children in Feng's Confucian school share both his concern about Chinese society and his conviction that Confucius is just the man to fix it. For this new generation of Chinese parents, Confucius is no longer the oppressor of Maoist rhetoric, but an antidote to the failings of today's China. Li Xiaohua pulled her ten-year-old daughter, Fang Muzi, out of a regular Chinese state school and placed her into Feng's academy because "I wanted her to have a foundation in the Chinese classics," she says. "They can teach people how to relate well with others and how to be an ethical human being. If you don't know how to be a good human being, how can you be helpful to society?" Miao Ran, who enrolled her six-year-old daughter in Feng's school, sees Confucian study as a counterweight to the forces roiling modern China. "There is too much emphasis on money," Miao says. "The biggest gift you can give your child is not money but spiritual support, so when the kids grow up they can make the right decisions."[19]

Such enthusiasm aside, Feng, much like Jiang Qing, is a barely audible voice, drowned out by the earsplitting cacophony of modern China. Although his experiment is not unique—similar Confucian academies are surfacing throughout China—the number of youngsters receiving a classical education today hardly registers in a nation of nearly 1.4 billion people. Feng, however, believes his efforts are merely part of an emerging, and inevitable, Chinese cultural renaissance. As China grows wealthier and more confident, he believes, the nation will find its future in its past. "The ideas that Confucius taught—about how to interact with others, or find your place in society—will make Confucianism a living part of Chinese society again," Feng says.

STEVEN LUAN AND his friends are rediscovering Confucius for reasons that have nothing to do with politics, or educating their children, or stamping out corruption. It is entirely personal. Each month, the Bamboo for Living Culture Club convenes at the Wu Yu Tai Tea House in Beijing's bustling

Wangfujing shopping district to discuss Chinese classical philosophy and literature. Confucius and his followers figure prominently in these conversations. At one Sunday morning session, a dozen club members select the Song Dynasty Confucian activist Fan Zhongyan as their focus. They take turns reading passages from Fan's writings—one participant recites them with the dramatic flourishes of an ancient bard. Then Luan offers a lecture on Fan, his life, and his contribution to Chinese philosophy. Fan was a Confucian reformer who had grand ideas about altering the government's policies, but ultimately, much like Wang Anshi, he had little lasting impact. His experience clearly resonates with the club. "Just like today," one member remarks. "There is a lot of talk of reform but not a lot of action." Lei Bin, one of the club's leaders, later expounds on the lessons he learned from Fan. "Chinese people are idealistic and have good ideas and work hard to implement them," he says. "It makes me feel I am just wasting my life. Learning about Fan gives me something to aspire to."

Luan, an executive at a financial services firm, and Lei, an employee at a business association for automotive companies, had previously become friends at a public-speaking group, and when they discovered their common interest in the Chinese classics, they founded the Culture Club in 2005. Their motivation was a very Confucian search for self-improvement through learning. "It is important for me to learn new things and improve my knowledge both in quantity and quality," says Luan. He believes he has become a better person for it. "Treat others as you would have them treat you," Luan continues, paraphrasing one of Confucius's most famous proverbs. "I keep saying that in my mind. In the past, when I was in a disagreement with my wife, maybe I'd shout out. But now I stop myself. I try to accommodate her needs." Lei concurs. Studying traditional Chinese philosophy "helps me with my own personal life and in my relations with others at home and at work, and helps me spiritually as well," he says. "Chinese culture has let me become more tolerant. I act more rationally and have less stress. Learning all these new things helps me gain wisdom and solve problems."[20]

Luan and Lei believe that the Western influences pouring into the country can never be a substitute for China's own heritage. "To me, Chinese culture is more spiritually nourishing [than that of the West]," says Luan. "You try to make yourself better, and try to increase your knowledge, and you can improve society overall." Lei goes further, blaming Western ideas for contributing to the decay of ethics in modern China. "Right now people in China don't care about others. There has been a loss of compassion. There is no more self-cultivation," Lei observes. "The American dream has influenced

Chinese people to admire success. But the Chinese didn't learn the substance of the dream. They only learned to get things for yourself. There has been huge moral degradation. With the Western cultural bombardment, China has lost itself."

Zheng Wanlong, a hotel manager and another leading club participant, laments that the necessity of catching up to the West forced China to sacrifice its own traditions. "China felt pressured to learn from the West and adopt its technology, but the country's cultural progress has been more backward," he says. "There is not enough cultural development. It will take China a long time to regain what it has lost."[21]

Yet the Bamboo for Living Culture Club has hope. Confucius thought that the common man must be prosperous to be able to pursue the Way, and with China's rise from poverty, Lei and his friends believe that will now happen—that they are at the forefront of what will become a national movement to reconnect with Chinese traditions. "Now since the economy is better and people are living a better life, they can focus on culture," Lei says. "More people will join us. There will be a cultural renaissance."

And who will lead the way? "Confucius can guide China into the future," says Zheng.

Epilogue

Seeking the Real Confucius

Traveling to Confucius's hometown of Qufu, in Shandong Province in eastern China, was once a bit of a chore. Qufu isn't very close to any major urban centers, and with Confucius out of favor for much of the twentieth century, no one felt the need to smooth the process of getting there. But now that the Communist government is promoting the sage, the party cadres, always efficient when an opportunity to propagandize presents itself, have made the trip much more convenient. The latest high-speed trains zipping between Beijing and Shanghai now stop in Qufu, making the town a mere two-hour journey from the capital in a comfortable coach. There is perhaps no more obvious sign of Confucius's resurrection in China than Qufu's spiffy train station. Forty years ago, Beijing's Red Guards rushed to Qufu to ransack its historic Temple of Confucius. Today Beijing tourists are rushed to Qufu to rediscover the great sage in the temple's peaceful courtyards.

I made that trip myself in the summer of 2013. In my quest to discover Confucius in modern China, I figured there was no better place to find him than in his hometown. Qufu has been a center of Confucian study in China since the sage lived and taught in the town 2,500 years ago. When Sima Qian, the dedicated Han Dynasty historian, visited Qufu on a research trip, he found a community of scholars engrossed in the classics and absorbed in Confucius's teachings. The Communists had suppressed Qufu's Confucians during its assault on the great sage, but since the government has given Confucius official sanction once again, that community has been reborn.

One of its more prominent members is Duan Yanping. The Qufu native has spent most of his life teaching himself about Confucius. At the age of ten—just as the Communists' attitude toward Confucius was beginning to thaw—he began reading the *Analects* and other Confucian texts and became enthralled. Inside he discovered the ancient wisdom of China, which, he says, "helped me build up my own personal values." By the time he reached high school, he was staying up late into the night reading *Mencius*—and ignoring his regular studies. As a result, he failed to gain entrance to a university and ended up as a technician at his father's company, which services power generation equipment. As the government's attitude toward Confucius warmed, however, Duan realized he had an important opportunity. "Before Mao died, no one really dared to mention Confucius," Duan says. "But that kind of closed cultural attitude was not initiated by the common people. It was forced by the outside. After Mao died, the old memories started coming back and people started talking about Confucianism again. I set up my goal to expand Confucian culture."

To achieve that goal, Duan opened the Qufu Confucian Institute in 2009 in an old schoolhouse just inside the rebuilt walls of Qufu's old town, aiming to reintroduce Confucius to a population raised on Marx and Mao. Six days a week, the thirty teenagers who live at the institute memorize the Four Books, just as if they were cramming for the civil service examinations of China's imperial past. They can learn calligraphy and traditional painting, too. Desks in the classrooms are splattered with ink from their brushes. One closet houses the school's collection of ceremonial red and yellow robes.

The goal, Duan says, is to nurture a new generation of Confucian scholars and set China on the correct path—the Confucian Way. "In the future, China should rely on Confucian culture to expand and develop its prosperity," he tells me. "Confucian culture holds a lot of wisdom and it could foster the entire nation to be more competitive in the world. The development of Confucius will better serve as the guideline for China's political development." Nevertheless, Duan isn't certain Confucius will win the day. Western cultural influences have become stronger in society as the nation has grown richer. If the Chinese choose the West over Confucius, the country could be ruined. "The American democratic ideology is not compatible with the psychological conditioning that the Chinese people have been used to for a long time," Duan explains, sounding eerily like Lee Kuan Yew. Confucius, he believes, could act as a bulwark against such dangerous Western ideas. "Learning about Confucius could upgrade the wisdom of the Chinese people to better cope with globalization," he adds.

What, I ask him, is so terrible about Western culture? "Chinese people value morals and rules," he says. "At home the father is the authority, and for a country, the emperor is the core. Confucianism cherishes obedience and conformity. If there is democracy, the country may become chaotic. There is a materialistic Western culture, a nonconformist Western culture, that is not suitable for China's development." What, then, should the Chinese people do to avoid the dangers of Western liberalism? "Now we need to listen to the government and respect government officials," Duan continues. "Confucianism is supportive of authoritarian government. Since ancient times it has always been like this."

I step out of the institute's main gate onto the dark, muddy streets of Qufu feeling dismayed. Duan's Confucius is the Confucius that the old emperors wanted the public to know—the Confucius that was meant to keep them quiet and submissive, the Confucius that squashes challenges to those in control. Of the many Confuciuses who have lived throughout China's long history, I wonder, is this the Confucius who China needs today? Is this the Confucius who will take China into the glorious future the nation so deserves? Duan apparently thinks so. During our conversation, I ask Duan what he would tell a student who complained that the government was doing something the student thought was wrong. "I would tell him to stay in his studies and not engage in politics," Duan answers.

I rise the next morning hoping that day's meeting will lift my spirits. Kong Leihua, a Qufu-born descendant of the sage himself (the 76th generation), appropriately, manages the Analects of Confucius Recital Center, located outside the gate to Qufu's famous Temple of Confucius. There, anyone can test his or her knowledge of Confucius by regurgitating passages from the *Analects* before appointed officials. Recite thirty of them correctly and the center will grant you free access to the temple. My visit came only six weeks after the Qufu municipal government had opened the center, and 3,000 people had already tried their luck, with an impressive 80 percent winning their free tickets.

Kong, like Duan, believes that China needs Confucius in order to counteract the ills of modern society, especially the rampant materialism that has gripped the Chinese people. "Now in the country, where people's ideas are restless, they particularly need Confucian thought," Kong explains. "The uncivilized behavior in society is because people have too many desires. They cannot fulfill all of them. Confucianism requires people's words and behavior to be in line with rationality and morality. That is why it is important for us to advocate Confucian thought."

It is hard to argue with that. In today's China, money rules over duty, responsibility, and compassion. Yet few in Qufu seem to have gotten Kong's message, least of all the municipal government that funds his center. Local officials clearly have grand hopes that Confucius will translate into jobs and cash. Restaurants, shops selling calligraphy and other trinkets, and other tourist-related businesses have proliferated. A luxury Shangri-la hotel is being built. Local eateries advertise "Confucius food," a smattering of Shandong dishes that includes smoked bean curd with peppers in gravy and a crispy (and miserably dry) pancake filled with peanuts. Like everything else in China, Confucius has become big business. Rather than counteracting materialism in Qufu, Confucius is fueling it.

As my talk with Kong Leihua continues, I ask him what would happen if more of the Chinese begin to adhere to Confucian teachings. "The *Analects* could play a role in maintaining societal stability and order," Kong asserts. Rules and regulations would help as well, he adds, but "to order a society, laws alone are not enough. You also need tradition and culture to do that." So Kong, like Duan, is ultimately advocating that Confucius be employed to pacify the populace. Perhaps, in his own way, he means well—like all those countless imperial officials who were forced to compromise the lofty ideals of Confucius's teachings in order to serve a state that didn't adhere to them.

I retreat into the Temple of Confucius across the street, hoping to find some solace amid its quiet courtyards and aged trees. The finely carved and appropriately sedate wooden pavilions leading to the main shrine are all hundreds of years old. Yet the temple only adds to my growing cynicism. It still bears the scars of the vicious attack on Confucius perpetrated by the very regime that now upholds him. The paint and concrete splattered by the Red Guards onto the few tablets they didn't shatter renders them illegible. "Revolution is not a crime," reads a bit of graffiti scrawled onto one of them. The new statue of Confucius installed by the Communists—to replace the one burned by the Red Guards—doesn't portray the sage as we usually imagine him—as a saintly, bearded wise man. Here he is once again the "Uncrowned King" of the Chinese empire. His hat, with small balls hanging from the rim, is the same style once worn by the old emperors. An employee stands near the shrine, yelling in an authoritative voice: "Bow to Confucius! Bow for your family!"

That sums up what China's officials want Confucius to mean in modern China: bowing. Bowing to authority. Bowing to the status quo. Although I agreed to bow to my in-laws at my wedding, I still don't care much for bowing, and especially when it means bowing to oppression. That, after all, is what is really behind the Confucian resurrection in China. Today's dictators, Communist only in name, are abusing Confucius's reputation just as Emperor Wu and Ming Taizu had—to convince an uneducated public that China's greatest sage told them to be subservient and docile and accept a "harmony" imposed from above. Once again, a repressive government is draping itself in a colorful Confucian cloak to try to mask its corruption and brutality, and to fool the average Chinese citizen into thinking his ancient traditions teach that he is getting the government he wants and deserves. If that is the Confucius being revived today, isn't China better off without him?

Years ago, before I started my own investigation of Confucius, I would probably have answered that question with a resounding "yes." The Confucius I held in my mind was the one hated by democrats, reformers, and feminists—the Confucius of imperial repression, foot-binding, and parental tyranny. But now, after reading his words and studying his history, I think the Chinese—and, in fact, all of us—would be better off in a world with Confucius than without him. All doctrines and faiths founded so long ago have some ideas and practices that no longer fit into modern society. If we adhered strictly to the Bible, we would still own slaves. Proper Hindu wives were once expected to throw themselves onto their husbands' funeral pyres. Every faith at some point has been used to justify actions clearly at odds with the substance of its teachings. The Crusaders slaughtered in the name of Christ, Osama bin Laden in the name of Allah. Yet despite all of that, we haven't thrown out the Bible, the Koran, or the Vedas. The Vatican has been corrupt and greedy throughout much of its history; its pedophile priests go unpunished. Yet we don't discard Jesus or the Gospels. Confucianism is no different. Yes, Confucius believed in sage-kings and subservient sons. His teachings have been drafted to legitimize authoritarian regimes for centuries on end. But that doesn't mean Confucius holds no value for us today.

China may be a rising global power and a marvel of supersonic economic progress, but it is also a society adrift, without purpose, without a soul. That leaves China rotting from within, and vulnerable to aggressive bursts of violence that could destabilize the country or threaten peace in Asia. It is a China where people ignore a two-year-old dying in the street, or poison babies to turn a quick buck. It is a China where government officials amass great fortunes and stand above the law.

The Confucius I have come to know over the course of researching this book can provide what China is missing. That Confucius was not a pawn of autocrats or a tool of suppression. That Confucius, though far from perfect, was a voice of boundless humanity and unswerving determination. He was a man who refused to compromise his principles for fame, wealth, or status. He would not submit to the will of immoral men or abusive regimes. He told the most powerful people of his day that they were wrong, directly to their faces. He judged men not by their riches or birth, but on their sincerity and benevolence. He could laugh at himself. He envisioned a society in which everyone fulfilled their responsibilities and placed the welfare of their families and communities over their own. He strove to transform a world convulsed by selfishness and war into one of selflessness and peace. He thought our society could be perfected if we first improved ourselves. Most of all, he thought that any one of us who took the time and made the effort to become a better person held the power to change the world.

The great calamity of Confucius's long life story is how widely his reputation has diverged from his intent. He is attacked for being an advocate for injustice—an oppressor of women, an enemy of personal liberty, a devotee of autocracy. In fact, the mortal flaw in his teachings can be found elsewhere—in his undying and ultimately misplaced faith in humanity. Confucius believed in his heart in the inherent goodness of man, that we strive for self-perfection, that we wish to act with honor, decency, and wisdom. He based his entire philosophy on that conviction. And time and time again, during his own lifetime and for the 2,500 years since, mankind has disappointed him. The tragedy of Confucius is that so many people who have sworn to uphold his vision and mission have so often betrayed the sage's trust. They are still doing so today.

Perhaps, though, the upcoming generation of Chinese, or the generation after them, or the generation after that, once again studying their *Analects*, will gain more than a free ticket to a tourist site. What we can hope is that as they read the sage's ancient words they will discover their own Confucius, a Confucius who holds special meaning for them, a Confucius who opens their minds, a Confucius free of government slogans and petty purpose. Maybe they'll invent a new Confucius for a new age.

ACKNOWLEDGMENTS

I have almost as many people to thank for making this book possible as have commented on Confucius over the many centuries since he walked the earth. First and foremost I must thank my editors at *Time* magazine, Bobby Ghosh, Zoher Abdoolcarim, and the tragically now-deceased Jim Frederick. This book would never have happened without their support.

I next must express my sincere appreciation to Keith Knapp and Neil Weinberg, who donated their precious time and expertise to reading my manuscript, providing invaluable guidance and advice that greatly improved the book. So, too, did the thoughts and recommendations of my editors at Basic Books, Lara Heimert and Dan Gerstle.

There have also been several journalists and friends who have helped research and find sources for this book: in China, Zhao Xue, Haze Fan, Chen Xiaoni, and Lin Yang; in South Korea, Lina Yoon; and in Taiwan, Natalie Tso and Joyce Huang. I must also thank Roberto Ribeiro and Russell Moses at the Beijing Center for so generously granting me permission to conduct research in their exceptional Chinese studies library. Librarians Shan Yanrong and David Lyons were both tremendously patient in helping me navigate the stacks.

A host of academics who know a lot more about Confucian history than I do also lent their wisdom and insights to this project, including Li-hsiang Lisa Rosenlee, Alan Wood, Thomas Wilson, Herman Ooms, Madeleine Zelin, Sam Crane, David Jordan, and Licia Di Giacinto.

I am also grateful to my patient literary agent, Michelle Tessler, who worked her usual magic to sell this book in the middle of a major recession.

Numerous other people shared their thoughts or lent a hand in the preparation of this project, including Simon Elegant, Gady Epstein, Tzyy Wang, Jessie Jiang, Jeff Timmermans, and Sue Kim. Last, I cannot forget to thank my wife, Eunice Yoon, who put up with me through the stress of writing and publishing this book and also provided many valuable suggestions and insights of her own.

NOTES

Introduction: How Confucius Changed the World

1. James Legge, trans., *The Confucian Analects, The Great Learning, and The Doctrine of the Mean* (repr., New York: Cosimo, 2009), 97.

2. D. C. Lau, trans., *Analects* (New York: Penguin, 1979), VII:33.

3. Deborah Sommer, "Images for Iconoclasts: Images of Confucius in the Cultural Revolution," *East West Connections* 7, no. 1 (2007).

4. Lionel M. Jensen, *Manufacturing Confucianism: Chinese Traditions and Universal Civilization* (Durham, NC: Duke University Press, 1997), 5, 9.

5. Reginald Fleming Johnston, *Confucianism in Modern China* (Vancouver, BC: Soul Care Publishing, 2008), 59.

6. *Analects*, VII:21 (Legge translation); XI:12 (Lau translation).

7. Lee Dian Rainey, *Confucius and Confucianism: The Essentials* (West Sussex, UK: Wiley-Blackwell, 2010), 203; *The Doctrine of the Mean*, XXXIII:2.

8. Legge, trans., *The Confucian Analects, The Great Learning, and The Doctrine of the Mean*, 99; *Analects*, IX:5, XIV:35 (Lau translation).

9. Quoted in Wm. Theodore de Bary, ed., *Sources of Chinese Tradition*, 2nd ed, vol. 2. (New York: Columbia University Press, 2001), 578; *Analects* (Lau translation), 52.

10. Zhang Weiwei, "Eight Ideas Behind China's Success," *New York Times*, September 30, 2009.

Chapter One: Confucius the Man

1. Much of this opening story is from Chapter XI of *Zuo Commentary* on the *Spring and Autumn Annals*. Other details are from Sima Qian's narrative (*Records of the Historian*, 6–7, in the Yang and Yang translation). What I've presented here is just one version of the events of the Xiagu summit. I think it is the most likely and reliable of the versions. Sima Qian tells us a tale in which the duke of Qi hatched no kidnapping plot. This omission is curious, since the *Zuo Commentary*, which features that plot, predates his narrative, and Sima Qian was just the type of dramatic storyteller who would have gobbled up such a yarn. Yet Sima Qian's own version has Confucius

shaming the duke into a disadvantaged negotiating position merely by pointing out his breaches of ceremonial propriety, which seems a bit hard to believe.

2. This tidbit is from Sima Qian, *Records of the Historian* (unless otherwise noted, the references to this work are always to the Yang and Yang translation).

3. Ibid., 1.

4. The story about Shuliang He's heroism in battle is from the *Zuo Commentary* to Chapter IX of the *Spring and Autumn Annals*. The details of his marriage are from a text called the *Kongzi Jiayu* (School Sayings of Confucius), Chapter 39. The translation is from Lionel M. Jensen, "Wise Man of the Wilds: Fatherlessness, Fertility, and the Mythic Exemplar, Kongzi," *Early China* 20 (1995): 417.

5. On Confucius's conception, see Robert Eno, "The Background of the Kong Family of Lu and the Origins of Ruism," *Early China* 28 (2003): 2, among other sources; for Jensen's view, see Jensen, "Wise Man of the Wilds."

6. This tale is from Fung Yu-lan, *A History of Chinese Philosophy*, vol. 2, *The Period of Classical Learning*, translated by Derk Bodde (Princeton, NJ: Princeton University Press, 1983), 129. You can find some of the myths surrounding Confucius's birth in Michael Nylan and Thomas Wilson, *Lives of Confucius: Civilization's Greatest Sage Through the Ages* (New York: Doubleday, 2010), 91–93.

7. Sima Qian, *Records of the Historian*, 1.

8. *Analects*, II:4 (Lau translation).

9. *Analects*, IX:6 (Lau translation); Sima Qian, *Records of the Historian*, 2.

10. *Mencius*, translated by James Legge, online at the Chinese Text Project, http://ctext.org/mengzi, II:2.

11. Sima Qian, *Records of the Historian*, 2.

12. Ibid., 3.

13. Ibid., 4.

14. Ibid., 22; *Mencius*, II:3. See D. C. Lau's translation of the *Analects*, p. 196.

15. *Analects*, VI:3, V:9, XI:9 (Lau translation).

16. Ibid., V:12, 7.

17. Ibid., XVII:5.

18. Sima Qian, *Records of the Historian*, 8. There is some confusion in the historical record and debate among scholars over when Confucius might have taken the post as minister of crime.

19. Ibid.

20. Much of the section on the conflict between Confucius and the noble families is from the *Zuo Commentary* to the *Spring and Autumn Annals*, Chapter XI. For an interesting and detailed look at the possible origins of the plan, consult Annping Chin's *The Authentic Confucius: A Life of Thought and Politics* (New York: Scribner, 2007), esp. 29–31. Generally, Annping Chin's first chapter offers some very useful insights into Confucius's role in the politics of Lu at this point in his life.

21. Sima Qian, *Records of the Historian*, 9. Also see *Analects*, XVIII:4.

22. *Mencius*, VI:26.

23. The quotation about his wife's family is from the *Kongzi Jiayu*, Chapter 39, translated for this book by Lin Yang. The information about the son-in-law is from *Analects*, V:1 (Lau translation).

24. *Analects*, X:1, 2, 3, 6, 8, 12, 20 (Lau translation).

25. *Analects*, XIV:43 (Lau translation), XVII:20 (Legge translation).

26. *Analects*, VII:16, VII:19 (Lau translation), XI:26 (Legge translation).

27. *Analects*, XIX:24–25 (Legge translation).

28. *Analects*, VII:3 (Lau translation).

29. *Mencius*, V:13; Sima Qian, *Records of the Historian*, 19. Annping Chin makes a valiant effort to figure out Confucius's route. See Chin, *Authentic Confucius*, 85–87.

30. *Analects*, XVII:7 (Lau translation).

31. Sima Qian, *Records of the Historian*, 10.

32. *Analects*, VI: 28 (Lau translation); Sima Qian, *Records of the Historian*, 11.

33. Sima Qian, *Records of the Historian*, 11.

34. *Analects*, XV:2 (Lau translation); Sima Qian, *Records of the Historian*, 17.

35. *Analects*, XV:2 (Lau translation); quoted in Chin, *Authentic Confucius*, 106.

36. Sima Qian, *Records of the Historian*, 18.

37. Ibid., 19; *Analects*, XVIII:5 (Lau translation).

38. *Analects*, XVIII:6 (Lau translation).

39. *Analects*, XVI:2 (Legge translation).

40. Ibid., XIII:3.

41. *Analects*, II:20 (Lau translation).

42. Ibid., XII:2.

43. Ibid., XVII:6, XII:22, VII:26.

44. Ibid., XIII:1, XII:17, II:1.

45. Ibid., XV:1, XIII:20.

46. Sima Qian, *Records of the Historian*, 21.

47. *Zuo Commentary*, Chapter XII; *Analects*, XI:17 (Lau translation).

48. See Chin, *Authentic Confucius*, 138–141.

49. *Analects*, VII:1 (Lau translation).

50. Sima Qian, *Records of the Historian*, 22.

51. For a summary of views on Confucius's connection to the Five Classics, see Xinzhong Yao, *An Introduction to Confucianism* (New York: Cambridge University Press, 2009), 53–54. For a neat summary of the history of the Five Classics themselves, see pp. 57–63 in the same work.

52. Sima Qian, *Records of the Historian*, 25–26. A few other details are from Nylan and Wilson, *Lives of Confucius*, 1–3.

Chapter Two: Confucius the Sage

1. Sima Qian, *Records of the Historian*, 26; Legge, trans., *The Confucian Analects, The Great Learning, and The Doctrine of the Mean*, 90. Some scholars are convinced that the story of Duke Ai's sacrifices was written into history long after that time.

2. Sima Qian, *Records of the Historian*, 26.

3. *Mencius*, III:4.

4. *Mencius*, II:1; Sima Qian, *Records of the Historian*, 70.

5. *Mencius*, II:22.

6. Ibid., III:14, II:15; Sima Qian, *Records of the Historian*, 70.

7. *Mencius*, II:6.

8. *Mencius*, VI:7.

9. Fung Yu-lan, *A History of Chinese Philosophy*, vol. 1, *The Period of Philosophers*, translated by Derk Bodde (Princeton, NJ: Princeton University Press, 1983), 279.

10. Xunzi, *Xunzi: Basic Writings*, Burton Watson, trans. (New York: Columbia University Press, 2003), 130.

11. Ibid., 161, 162, 163–164.

12. *Mencius*, III:14.

13. *Mozi*, translated by W. P. Mei, online at http://ctext.org/mozi, Chapter 39, "Anti-Confucianism."

14. *Zhuangzi*, translated by Burton Watson, online at "The Complete Works of Chuang Tzu," Terebess Asia Online, http://terebess.hu/english/chuangtzu.html, Chapter 26, "External Things."

15. Zhuangzi, "The Robber Zhi" (Legge translation).

16. *Han Feizi*, translated by W. K. Liao, online at University of Virginia website *Traditions of Exemplary Women*, www2.iath.virginia.edu/saxon/servlet/Saxon Servlet?source=xwomen/texts/listtexts.xml&style=xwomen/xsl/dynaxml.xsl&chunk .id=d1.1&toc.depth=1&toc.id=0&doc.lang=bilingual, Chapter XLIX, "Five Vermin: A Pathological Analysis of Politics." I adapted the translation slightly for clarity.

17. *Han Feizi*, Chapter XLVII, "Eight Fallacies."

18. Sima Qian, in K. E. Brashier, ed., *The First Emperor: Selections from the Historical Records*, translated by Raymond Dawson (Oxford: Oxford University Press, 2009), 72–74.

19. Ibid., 29.

20. Ibid., 76–78.

21. Mark Edward Lewis, *The Early Chinese Empires: Qin and Han* (Cambridge, MA: Belknap Press, 2007), 53–54.

22. Sima Qian, in Brashier, ed., 47–49.

23. See Jack L. Dull, "Anti-Qin Rebels: No Peasant Leaders Here," *Modern China* 9, no. 3 (1983): esp. 309.

24. Wm. Theodore de Bary and Irene Bloom, compilers, *Sources of Chinese Tradition*, 2nd ed., vol. 1 (New York: Columbia University Press, 2000), 230.

25. Homer Dubs, *History of the Former Han Dynasty*, 2 vols. (Baltimore: Waverly Press, 1944). The quotations are from Dubs's introduction to Chapter 1 on Gaozu's reign; de Bary and Bloom, comps., *Sources*, 1:285.

26. Ibid., 1:288, 286–287.

27. Sima Qian, in Burton Watson, trans., *Records of the Grand Historian* (New York: Columbia University Press, 1961), 37.

28. Quoted in John K. Shryock, *The Origin and Development of the Cult of Confucius: An Introductory Study* (New York: Paragon, 1966), 40.

29. Sima Qian, in Watson, trans., *Records of the Grand Historian*, 410.

30. Alan T. Wood, *Limits to Autocracy: From Sung Neo-Confucianism to a Doctrine of Political Rights* (Honolulu: University of Hawaii Press, 1995), 55.

31. Fung Yu-lan, *History of Chinese Philosophy*, 2:72.

32. This translation is from de Bary and Bloom, comps., *Sources*, 1:299.

33. Chan Wing-tsit, *Sourcebook in Chinese Philosophy* (Princeton, NJ: Princeton University Press, 1989), 276, 285; de Bary and Bloom, comps., *Sources*, 1:298, 301.

34. Quoted in Shryock, *Cult of Confucius*, 51–53.

35. This translation of Dong's memorial is from Fung Yu-lan, *History of Chinese Philosophy*, 2:17.

36. Translated in de Bary and Bloom, comps., *Sources*, 1:311.

37. Fung Yu-lan, *History of Chinese Philosophy*, 2:17.

38. This figure is from Cai Liang, a professor at the University of Arkansas, who was kind enough to share an unpublished draft of a manuscript that later became the book *Witchcraft and the Rise of the First Confucian Empire*, published by the State University of New York Press in 2014.

39. Sima Qian, *Records of the Historian*, 26.

40. This is discussed in Keith Nathaniel Knapp, *Selfless Offspring: Filial Children and Social Order in Medieval China* (Honolulu: University of Hawaii Press, 2005), 22.

41. Fung Yu-lan, *History of Chinese Philosophy*, 2:17, 2:139; quoted in Keith Nathaniel Knapp, "The Confucian Tradition in China," in *The Wiley-Blackwell Companion to Chinese Religions*, Randall L. Nadeau, ed. (Oxford: Wiley-Blackwell, 2012), 157–158.

Chapter Three: Confucius the King

1. De Bary and Bloom, comps., *Sources*, 1:583–595.

2. Ibid., 1:570, 572.

3. Ibid., 1:600.

4. Historian Dieter Kuhn makes this case in *The Age of Confucian Rule: The Song Transformation of China* (Cambridge, MA: Belknap Press, 2009), esp. 29.

5. Quoted in ibid., 31.

6. Ibid., 1.

7. Translation in Shryock, *Cult of Confucius*, 154.

8. De Bary and Bloom, comps., *Sources*, 1:638; quoted in Wm. Theodore de Bary, *The Trouble with Confucianism* (Cambridge, MA: Harvard University Press, 1996), 51.

9. Kuhn, *Age of Confucian Rule*, 121; Peter K. Bol, *Neo-Confucianism in History* (Cambridge: Harvard University Press, 2008), 125–126.

10. For a detailed discussion of the ideological differences between Wang and Sima, see Peter K. Bol, *"This Culture of Ours": Intellectual Transitions in T'ang and Sung China* (Stanford, CA: Stanford University Press, 1992), esp. Chapter 7.

11. De Bary and Bloom, comps., *Sources*, 1:609.

12. Ibid., 1:614.

13. Ibid., 1:613.

14. Patricia Buckley Ebrey, *Chinese Civilization: A Sourcebook*, 2nd ed. (New York: Free Press, 1993), no. 35.

15. De Bary and Bloom, comps., *Sources*, 1:668.

16. Chan, *Sourcebook in Chinese Philosophy*, 588, 591.

17. Kuhn, *Age of Confucian Rule*, 103.

18. De Bary and Bloom, comps., *Sources*, 1:702.

19. Ibid., 1:729.

20. Ibid., 1:669.

21. Ibid., 1:733; quoted in Kuhn, *Age of Confucian Rule*, 105.

22. De Bary and Bloom, comps., *Sources*, 1:777.

23. Ibid., 1:778.

24. For a good summary of Confucianism's history in early Korea, see Key P. Yang and Gregory Henderson, "An Outline History of Korean Confucianism: Part I. The Early Period and Yi Factionalism," *Journal of Asian Studies* 18, no. 1 (1958).

25. Peter H. Lee and Wm. Theodore de Bary, eds., *Sources of Korean Tradition*, vol. 1, *From Early Times Through the Sixteenth Century* (New York: Columbia University Press, 1997), 253.

26. Quoted in Martina Deuchler, *The Confucian Transformation of Korea: A Study of Society and Ideology* (Cambridge, MA: Harvard University Press, 1992), 17.

27. My summary of the Confucianization of Korea is based on Martina Deuchler's work.

28. Deuchler, *Confucian Transformation*, 128.

29. Herman Ooms, "Neo-Confucianism and the Formation of Early Tokugawa Ideology: Contours of a Problem," in *Confucianism in Tokugawa Culture*, Peter Nosco, ed. (Honolulu: University of Hawaii Press, 1997), 28–29.

30. Wm. Theodore de Bary, Carol Gluck, and Arthur E. Tiedemann, eds., *Sources of Japanese Tradition*, vol. 2, *Part One* (New York: Columbia University Press, 2006), 46.

31. For more, see Ooms, "Neo-Confucianism," esp. 32, 59.

32. See Kiri Paramore, "The Nationalization of Confucianism: Academism, Examinations, and Bureaucratic Governance in the Late Tokugawa State," *Journal of Japanese Studies* 38, no. 1 (2012): 26.

33. Quoted in Conrad Totman, *Early Modern Japan* (Berkeley: University of California Press, 1993), 470.

34. The description of the imperial ceremony is from Legge, trans., *The Confucian Analects, The Great Learning, and The Doctrine of the Mean*, 91–92.

Chapter Four: Confucius the Oppressor

1. This translation is from Teng Ssu-yu and John King Fairbank, *China's Response to the West: A Documentary Survey, 1839–1923* (New York: Atheneum, 1963), 152–153.

2. Liang Ch'i-ch'ao, *Intellectual Trends in the Ch'ing Period*, translated by Immanuel C. Y. Hsu (Cambridge, MA: Harvard University Press, 1959), 98.

3. Simon Winchester, *The Man Who Loved China: The Fantastic Story of the Eccentric Scientist Who Unlocked the Mysteries of the Middle Kingdom* (New York: Harper, 2008), 57.

4. Joseph Needham, *Science and Civilization in China*, vol. 2, *History of Scientific Thought* (Cambridge, UK: Cambridge University Press, 1956), 1, 15.

5. *Analects*, VII:21, XIII:4 (Legge translation).

6. See, for instance, John K. Fairbank, Alexander Eckstein, and L. S. Yang, "Economic Change in Early Modern China: An Analytic Framework," *Economic Development and Cultural Change* 9, no. 1 (1960): 6 (Part 1). Also see Justin Yifu Lin. "The Needham Puzzle: Why the Industrial Revolution Did Not Originate in China," *Economic Development and Cultural Change* 43, no. 2 (1995): 269–292.

7. De Bary, ed., *Sources*, 2:238–239.

8. Ibid., 2:240.

9. Ibid., 2:248, 253.

10. Ibid., 2:261.

11. Ibid.

12. Ibid., 2:268–269.

13. *Book of Rites*, translated by James Legge, online at University of Virginia website *Traditions of Exemplary Women*, www2.iath.virginia.edu/saxon/servlet/SaxonServlet ?source=xwomen/texts/listtexts.xml&style=xwomen/xsl/dynaxml.xsl&chunk. id=d1.1&toc.depth=1&toc.id=0&doc.lang=bilingual; Chan, *Sourcebook in Chinese Philosophy*, 735.

14. De Bary, ed., *Sources*, 2:273; Chan, *Sourcebook in Chinese Philosophy*, 733.

15. De Bary, ed., *Sources*, 2: 266–67; Liang Ch'i-ch'ao, *Intellectual Trends*, 95.

16. De Bary, ed., *Sources*, 2:282.

17. Liang Ch'i-ch'ao, *Intellectual Trends*, 94.

18. De Bary, ed., *Sources*, 2:277–278.

19. Ibid., 2:278–280.

20. Ibid., 2:270.

21. Teng and Fairbank, *China's Response*, 177–178.

22. De Bary, ed., *Sources*, 2:286.

23. Chow Tse-tsung, *The May 4th Movement: Intellectual Revolution in Modern China* (Cambridge, MA: Harvard University Press, 1964), 300; de Bary, ed., *Sources*, 2:355–356; quoted in Chow, *May 4th*, 59; translation from Teng and Fairbank, *China's Response*, 242–244.

24. All quotations and other details from Lu Xun's short stories are from *Selected Stories of Lu Hsun*, translated by Yang Hsien-yi and Gladys Yang (Beijing: Foreign Languages Press, 1972).

25. Lin Yutang, "Confucius as I Know Him," *China Critic* 4, no. 1 (1931): 5–9, online at www.chinaheritagequarterly.org/features.php?searchterm=030_confucius .inc&issue=030.

26. Mao Zedong, *On New Democracy*, 1940, online at www.marxists.org/reference /archive/mao/selected-works/volume-2/mswv2_26.htm.

27. Hung Kwangszu, "Criticize the Doctrines of Confucius and Mencius to Consolidate the Dictatorship of the Proletariat," *Peking Review*, April 18, 1975.

28. Much of the tale of the Red Guards' attack on Qufu is summarized from a detailed account by a Chinese journalist, Wang Liang, which can be found in a chapter called "The Confucian Temple Tragedy of the Cultural Revolution" in Thomas A. Wilson, *On Sacred Grounds: Culture, Society, Politics, and the Formation of the Cult of Confucius* (Cambridge, MA: Harvard University Press, 2003). I also drew from Joseph Esherick, Paul Pickowicz, and Andrew George Walder, *The Cultural Revolution as History* (Stanford, CA: Stanford University Press, 2006), 84–92.

29. Wang Liang, "Confucian Temple Tragedy," 377–378.

30. Ibid., 378.

31. Ibid., 379.

32. Ibid., 383.

33. Mao Zedong, "Speeches at the Second Session of the Eighth Party Congress: The First Speech, May 8, 1958," www.marxists.org/reference/archive/mao/selected-works /volume-8/mswv8_10.htm.

34. De Bary, *Trouble with Confucianism*, ix.

Chapter Five: Confucius the Father

1. The title of Part Two is my play on Book XXV of *The Book of Rites*, which is called "Confucius at Home at Ease." The estimate of Vincent Lo's fortune is from *Forbes*, March 2013.

2. All quotes from Vincent and Adrian Lo are from author's interview, June 2013.

3. Lin Yutang, *My Country and My People* (London: William Heinemann, 1936), 167.

4. Francis L. K. Hsu, *Under the Ancestors' Shadow: Kinship, Personality and Social Mobility in China* (Stanford, CA: Stanford University Press, 1971), 265.

5. Knapp, *Selfless Offspring*, 3. I am greatly indebted to Dr. Knapp's work on filial piety, which has heavily influenced the historical perspective presented in this chapter.

6. Quote from Kam Louie, *Critiques of Confucius in Contemporary China* (Hong Kong: Chinese University Press, 1980), 8.

7. For a history of the early development of the *xiao* concept, see Keith Nathaniel Knapp, "The *Ru* Reinterpretation of *Xiao*," *Early China* 20 (1995): 195–222. The quotations from Confucius are from *Analects*, II:7, 6, and 5 (Lau translation).

8. *Classic of Filial Piety*, translated by James Legge, online at Chinese Text Project, http://ctext.org/xiao-jing, Chapters X, VI; *Analects*, IV:19 (Lau translation).

9. *Analects*, I:11, XVII:21 (Lau translation).

10. *Book of Rites*, Chapter X, Section I.

11. *Twenty-Four Filial Exemplars*, translated by David Jordan, http://pages.ucsd .edu/~dkjordan/chin/shiaw/shiaw00.html, No. 14, "He Strangled a Tiger to Save His Father"; No. 11, "He Let Mosquitoes Consume His Blood"; and No. 16, "He Tasted Dung with an Anxious Heart."

12. Ibid., No. 1, "The Feeling of Filial Piety Moved Heaven," and No. 13, "He Buried His Son for His Mother."

13. Ibid., No. 23, "He Wept Until the Bamboo Sprouted."

14. Ibid., No. 6, "He Sold Himself to Bury His Father."

15. Much of this analysis of the development of the Asian family and Confucianism is from Knapp, *Selfless Offspring*, esp. 14–24.

16. De Bary and Bloom, comps., *Sources*, 1:790.

17. *Classic of Filial Piety*, Chapters I, IX.

18. Ibid., Chapters X (p. 30), II (p. 18), I (p. 16).

19. Ibid., Chapters V (p. 21), I, XIII.

20. Legge, trans., *The Great Learning*, in *The Confucian Analects, The Great Learning, and The Doctrine of the Mean*, IX:3; *Classic of Filial Piety*, Chapter XI; *Analects*, I:2 (Lau translation).

21. *Classic of Filial Piety*, Chapter XV (p. 33).

22. *Analects*, IV:18 (Lau translation); *Book of Rites*, Chapter X, Section I; *Analects*, IV:26 (Legge translation).

23. *Analects*, XIII:18 (Lau translation); Chin, *Authentic Confucius*, 111–112.

24. *Han Feizi*, Book 19, Chapter 49.

25. *Analects*, XV:24, 37, VI:30 (Legge translation); *Great Learning*, IX:1.

26. Bertrand Russell, *The Problem of China* (London: George Allen and Unwin, 1922).

27. Yutang, *My Country and My People*, 167, 172–173.

28. Ibid., 169; de Bary, ed., *Sources*, 2:353–354.

29. Wesley Yang, "Paper Tigers," *New York Magazine*, May 8, 2011.

30. All quotes from Wang are from author's interview, June 2013.

31. All quotes from Woon are from author's interview, January 2013.

32. You can watch the video on YouTube at www.youtube.com/watch?v=ybxNkp S5q-g.

33. All quotes from Lee are from author's interview, May 2013.

34. "New Filial Piety Law Takes Effect to Much Criticism in China," *South China Morning Post*, July 1, 2013.

35. "A Look Back at China's Filial Piety Culture," *People's Daily*, May 16, 2012.

36. All quotes from Feng Wang are from author's interview.

37. "Challenges of Population Aging in China: Evidence from the National Baseline Survey of the China Health and Retirement Longitudinal Study," May 2013, 11.

38. All quotes from Na are from author's interview, June 2013.

39. All quotes from Zhang are from author's interview, June 2013.

40. All quotes from Wang are from author's interview, September 2013.

Chapter Six: Confucius the Teacher

1. All quotes from Oh are from author's interview, May 2013.

2. All quotes from Lee are from author's interview, May 2013.

3. Amy Chua, *Battle Hymn of the Tiger Mother* (New York: Penguin, 2011), 5.

4. Allison Pearson, "Why We All Need a Tiger Mother," *Telegraph*, January 13, 2011.

5. *Analects*, XIX:7, XVII:8 (Lau translation).

6. Xunzi, *Xunzi: Basic Writings*, Watson, trans., 162, 15.

7. *Analects*, IV:17, XV:30 (Lau translation).

8. *Great Learning*, introduction.

9. *Doctrine of the Mean*, XX:10; *Great Learning*, introduction.

10. *Analects*, XV:31, 21 (Lau translation).

11. *Analects*, VIII:12 (Legge translation).

12. *Analects*, V:28, VII:2 (Lau translation); Sima Qian, *Records of the Historian*, 22.

13. Sima Qian, *Records of the Historian*, 11–12.

14. Fung Yu-lan, *History of Chinese Philosophy*, 1:48.

15. *Analects*, VII:7 (Lau translation); Fung Yu-lan, *History of Chinese Philosophy*, 1:49.

16. Ebrey, *Chinese Civilization*, No. 54.

17. Ibid., No. 30.

18. Ichisada Miyazaki, *China's Examination Hell: The Civil Service Examinations of Imperial China*, translated by Conrad Schirokauer (New Haven, CT: Yale University Press, 1981), 13.

19. Ibid., 17.

20. Quotes from author's interviews with Wang, Zhao, Liu, and Lin, June 2013.

21. All quotes from Kim Jong Hun are from an interview by Lina Yoon for this book in 2013.

22. Author's interview with Jeon, May 2013.

23. De Bary and Bloom, comps., *Sources*, 1:615; the quotation from Morris Chang is from my interview with him in 2009, which appeared in *Time*, "Rebooting the Dragon," July 27, 2009.

24. All quotes from Kim Eun Sil are from author's interview, May 2013.

25. *Analects*, VII:8 (Lau translation).

26. All quotes from Chen are from author's interview, 2011.

27. The translation from the *Liberty Times* is from a blog post on the *Wall Street Journal*'s website, "Debate Swarms Around Taiwan Confucius Requirement," posted

April 7, 2011. The Crane quotation is from "Confucius in the Schools . . . Taiwan Schools," *The Useless Tree*, April 10, 2011.

28. Quote from Lai is from author's interview, 2011.

Chapter Seven: Confucius the Chauvinist

1. All quotes from Pae are from author's interview, May 2013.

2. Chad Steinberg, "Can Women Save Japan (and Asia Too)?" October 2012, International Monetary Fund, www.imf.org/external/pubs/ft/fandd/2012/09/steinberg.htm.

3. All quotes from Bae are from author's interview, May 2013.

4. Julia Kristeva, *About Chinese Women*, translated by Anita Barrows (New York: Marion Boyars, 1986), 66; de Bary, ed., *Sources*, 2:392; Li-hsiang Lisa Rosenlee, *Confucianism and Women: A Philosophical Interpretation* (Albany: State University of New York Press, 2006), 1.

5. *Analects*, II:20 (Lau translation).

6. *Analects*, XVII:25 (from de Bary and Bloom, comps., *Sources*, vol. 1).

7. *Analects*, VIII:20 (Lau translation).

8. Ibid., IX:18, XVI:7 (Lau translation).

9. *Book of Rites*, VII:18.

10. *Mencius*, III:4.

11. *Book of Rites*, Book X, Section I; quoted in Patricia Ebrey, "Women in Traditional China," Asia Society, http://asiasociety.org/countries/traditions/women-traditional-china.

12. Speech delivered by Hu Shi in 1933 entitled "Social Disintegration and Readjustment," which can be found online at http://csua.berkeley.edu/~mrl/HuShih/.

13. *Mencius*, III:7.

14. *Book of Rites*, Book IX, Section III.

15. Chan, *Sourcebook in Chinese Philosophy*, 277.

16. *Discussions in White Tiger Pavilion*, translated by Tjan Tjoe Som, published by Hyperion Press, 1973, online at University of Virginia website *Traditions of Exemplary Women*, www2.iath.virginia.edu/saxon/servlet/SaxonServlet?source=xwomen/texts/list texts.xml&style=xwomen/xsl/dynaxml.xsl&chunk.id=d1.1&toc.depth=1&toc .id=0&doc.lang=bilingual, Chapter XXIX. I altered the original translation slightly in this narrative for clarity.

17. Tu Wei-Ming, "Probing the 'Three Bonds' and 'Five Relationships' in Confucian Humanism," in *Confucianism and the Family*, Walter H. Slote and George A. De Vos, eds. (Albany: State University of New York Press, 1998), 122.

18. Tu, "Probing the 'Three Bonds,'" 122–123.

19. De Bary and Bloom, comps., *Sources*, 1:830; Ebrey, *Chinese Civilization*, No. 17.

20. De Bary and Bloom, comps., *Sources*, 1:828–829.

21. *Book of Rites*, Book I, Section I; de Bary and Bloom, comps., *Sources*, 1:828.

22. *Book of Rites*, Book X, Section I; de Bary and Bloom, comps., *Sources*, 1:829.

23. *Mencius*, IV:26.

24. De Bary and Bloom, comps., *Sources*, 1:826–827.

25. Ibid., 1:822; Patricia Buckley Ebrey, *The Inner Quarters: Marriage and the Lives of Chinese Women in the Sung Period* (Berkeley: University of California Press, 1992), 186; Susan Mann and Cheng Yu-yin, eds., *Under Confucian Eyes: Writings on Gender in Chinese History* (Berkeley: University of California Press, 2001), 151–152.

26. *Biographies of Exemplary Women*, in Albert Richard O'Hara, *Position of Women in Early China* (Hong Kong: Orient Publishing, 1946), 39–42.

27. Ibid., 117.

28. Howard S. Levy, *Chinese Footbinding: The History of a Curious Erotic Custom* (New York: Bell, 1967), 225–226. Levy shares many such tales of horror.

29. Lin, *My Country and My People*, 160; *Classic of Filial Piety*, Chapter I; C. Fred Blake, "Foot-Binding in Neo-Confucian China and the Appropriation of Female Labor," *Signs* 19, no. 3 (1994): 695, 708.

30. Quoted in Ebrey, *Inner Quarters*, 199.

31. Ebrey, *Chinese Civilization*, No. 56.

32. De Bary, ed., *Sources*, 2:354.

33. Kristeva, *About Chinese Women*, 75.

34. De Bary, ed., *Sources*, 2:392, 394.

35. Ibid., 2:395.

36. All quotes from Rosenlee are from emails sent to the author in 2013, except where otherwise noted.

37. Ibid., 154, 149, 159. For a full explanation of Rosenlee's analysis, see Chapter 7 of her book.

Chapter Eight: Confucius the Businessman

1. All quotes from Jin are from author's interview, June 2013.

2. All quotes from Lu are from author's interview, 2013.

3. Dale Carnegie, *How to Win Friends and Influence People* (New York: Pocket Books, 1998), 12. Quote from Yanai is from author's interview April 2013.

4. *Great Learning*, X:19.

5. *Analects*, I:5, XX:2 (Legge translation).

6. Ibid., XII:7, XIII:9; *Great Learning*, X:9.

7. *Mencius*, I:7.

8. *Analects*, XII:9 (Legge translation).

9. *Mencius*, I:3.

10. De Bary and Bloom, comps., *Sources*, 1:357.

11. Ibid., 1:362, 360.

12. Ibid., 1:363.

13. *Analects*, I:14, IV:9 (Lau translation).

14. Ibid., IV:16, IV:5; *Great Learning*, X:7.

15. De Bary and Bloom, comps., *Sources*, 1:361.

16. Ibid., 1:357–358.

17. Quote from Zelin is from author's interview, May 2013. See Albert Feuerwerker, "The State and the Economy in Late Imperial China," *Theory and Society* 13, no. 3 (1984), 305, 308.

18. Angus Maddison, "The West and the Rest in the World Economy: 1000–2030: Maddisonian and Malthusian Interpretations," *World Economics* 9, no. 4 (2008): 87, 170.

19. Max Weber, *The Religion of China: Confucianism and Daoism*, translated by Hans H. Gerth (New York: Macmillan, 1951), 248.

20. Ibid., 229, 237, 242.

21. Ibid., 244–245.

22. Fairbank et al., "Economic Change in Early Modern China," 15.

23. Roderick MacFarquhar, "The Post-Confucian Challenge," *The Economist*, February 9, 1980, 68.

24. Ibid., 71.

25. Ibid.

26. Ezra F. Vogel, *Japan as Number One: Lessons for America* (Bloomington, IN: iUniverse, 1999; originally published by Harvard University Press, 1979), 226, 254.

27. Min Chen, *Asian Management Systems* (London: Thomson Learning, 2004), 25.

28. Fareed Zakaria, "A Conversation with Lee Kuan Yew," *Foreign Affairs*, March/April 1994.

29. Barbara Crossette, "Western Influence Worries Singapore Chief," *New York Times*, January 4, 1987.

30. Habibullah Khan, "Social Policy in Singapore: A Confucian Model?" World Bank, 2001, 20.

31. Tan Chwee Huat, "Confucianism and Nation Building in Singapore," *International Journal of Social Economics* 16, no. 8 (1989): 9.

32. Han Fook Kwang, Warren Fernandez, and Sumiko Tan, *Lee Kuan Yew: The Man and His Ideas* (Singapore: Times Editions, 1998), 196.

33. Mortimer Zuckerman, "Japan Inc. Unravels," *U.S. News & World Report*, August 9, 1998.

34. "Poll: 'Young Chinese Use 'Daddies' to Get Ahead," WSJ.com, August 20, 2013.

35. See Bruce Stanley, "Korean Air Bucks Tradition to Fix Problems," *Wall Street Journal*, January 9, 2006.

36. All quotes from Yoo are from author's interview, May 2013.

37. All quotes from Liu are from author's interview, December 2009, except where noted. Portions of this section also appeared in an article written by the author in *Time* magazine, "Lenovo's Legend Returns," May 10, 2010.

38. These quotations are from an email sent to the author by Liu Chuanzhi. Small changes have been made for grammar and clarity.

Chapter Nine: Confucius the Politician

1. The transcript of the interview can be found on the website of the Prime Minister of Singapore, www.pmo.gov.sg/content/pmosite/mediacentre/speechesninterviews /primeminister/2010/April/transcript_of_primeministerleehsienloongsinterviewithus televisi.html.

2. "Confucian Ethics for Schools," *Straits Times*, February 4, 1982, 1.

3. Government of Singapore, White Paper on Shared Values, 1991, graph 41.

4. "Singapore: A Most Un-Confucian Government," November 28, 2005, *Useless Tree*, http://uselesstree.typepad.com/useless_tree/2005/11/singapore_a_mos.html.

5. *Analects*, VIII:9, 21 (Lau translation); *Doctrine of the Mean*, XX:12.

6. J. Mason Gentzler, ed., *Changing China: Readings in the History of China from the Opium War to the Present* (New York: Praeger, 1977), 172.

7. *Analects*, XII:11 (Lau translation).

8. Samuel P. Huntington, *The Third Wave: Democratization in the Late Twentieth Century* (Norman: University of Oklahoma Press, 1993), 300.

9. *Analects*, XIII:15 (Lau translation).

10. Ibid., XIII:6, II:19.

11. *Analects*, II: 3; XII:19, XX:2 (Lau translation); *Doctrine of the Mean*, XXXIII:4; *Mencius*, II:3.

12. Francis Fukuyama, "Confucianism and Democracy," *Journal of Democracy* 6, no. 2 (1995): 26.

13. Sun Yat-sen, *San Min Chu I: The Three Principles of the People*. Frank W. Price trans. L. T. Chen ed. (Shanghai: China Committee Institute of Pacific Relations, 1927), 169, 171.

14. *Analects*, XV:25 (Lau translation); *Great Learning*, X:5.

15. *Mencius*, VII:60, I:6.

16. Ibid., V:5, IV:2.

17. Ibid., I:15.

18. Sun Yat-sen, *San Min Chu I,* 170; Kim Dae Jung, "Is Culture Destiny? The Myth of Asia's Anti-Democratic Values," *Foreign Affairs*, November/December 1994.

19. De Bary et al., *Sources of Japanese Tradition*, 48–49.

20. Quoted in Bol, *Neo-Confucianism in History*, 133; Fung Yu-lan, *History of Chinese Philosophy*, 2:565.

21. Quoted in Wood, *Limits to Autocracy*, 113, 96, 120. I made a slight adjustment for clarity in the first quotation.

22. The details of Liu Ji's and Song Lian's ideas are from John W. Dardess, *Confucianism and Autocracy: Professional Elites in the Founding of the Ming Dynasty* (Berkeley: University of California Press, 1983), 134–139, 165–166.

23. Zhengyuan Fu, *Autocratic Tradition and Chinese Politics* (Cambridge, UK: Cambridge University Press, 1993), 58–59; Wood, *Limits to Autocracy*, 111.

24. Dardess, *Confucianism and Autocracy*, 216.

25. Ibid., 5, 132–133, 184–185.

26. Ibid., 209, 223, 240.

27. *Analects*, VIII:13 (Lau translation).

28. United Nations, "Capital Punishment and Implementation of the Safeguards Guaranteeing Protection of the Rights of Those Facing the Death Penalty," December 2009.

29. Kim Dae Jung, "Is Culture Destiny?"; Han Fook Kwang et al., *Lee Kuan Yew*, 380, 383; Zakaria, "A Conversation."

30. Han Fook Kwang et al., *Lee Kuan Yew*, 89; "Government's Hard-Nosed Approach Defended," *Straits Times*, April 20, 1987.

31. Zakaria, "A Conversation"; Han Fook Kwang et al., *Lee Kuan Yew*, 147, 407–409.

32. Eric X. Li, "Democracy Is Not the Answer," *Huffington Post*, May 16, 2012, www.huffingtonpost.com/eric-x-li/democracy-is-not-the-answ_b_1520172.html.

33. Chris Patten, *East and West: The Last Governor of Hong Kong on Power, Freedom, and the Future* (London: Macmillan, 1998), 155; Fukuyama, "Confucianism and Democracy," 30.

34. Text of speech printed in the *Straits Times*, February 8, 1982, 14.

35. "Confucian Ethics for Schools," *Straits Times*, February 4, 1982, 1; *Straits Times*, February 8, 1982.

36. Quoted in Eddie C. Y. Kuo, "Confucianism as Political Discourse in Singapore: The Case of an Incomplete Revitalization Movement," in Tu Wei-ming, *Confucian Traditions in East Asian Modernity: Moral Education and Economic Culture in Japan and the Four Mini-Dragons* (Cambridge, MA: Harvard University Press, 1996), 300.

37. Quoted in Kuo, "Confucianism as Political Discourse," 299; *Straits Times*, March 10, 1982, 43.

38. Tan Chwee Huat, "Confucianism and Nation Building," 5.

39. Government of Singapore, "White Paper on Shared Values," graphs 2, 39.

40. Ibid., graphs 24, 26, 25, 28.

Chapter Ten: Confucius the Communist

1. "Xi Underlines Morality During Confucius Site Visits," *Xinhua*, November 28, 2013.

2. Abigail Lamberton, "The Kongs of Qufu: Power and Privilege in Late Imperial China," in Thomas A. Wilson, *On Sacred Grounds*, 328. Lamberton's article goes into great detail about the wealth and influence of the Kongs during the imperial age.

3. All quotes from Kong are from author's interview, September 2011.

4. De Bary, ed., *Sources*, 2:576, 578.

5. The selections from Gu Mu's speech are from Wm. Theodore de Bary, "The New Confucianism in Beijing," *American Scholar* 64, no. 2 (1995): 181–182.

6. Ibid.

7. Quoted in Daniel A. Bell, "China's Leaders Rediscover Confucianism," *International Herald Tribune*, September 14, 2006.

8. Francis Fukuyama, "China Is Looking to Its Dynastic Past to Shape Its Future," *Financial Times*, July 12, 2011.

9. Daniel A. Bell and Eric Li, "In Defense of How China Picks Its Leaders," *Financial Times*, November 11, 2012.

10. Zhang Wei Wei, "Eight Ideas Behind China's Success," *New York Times*, September 30, 2009.

11. "Modern China Needs Some Old Thinking," *China Daily*, July 31, 2006.

12. All quotes from Liu are from author's interview, July 2013.

13. Kam Louie, "Confucius the Chameleon: Dubious Envoy for 'Brand China,'" *Boundary* 2 38, no. 1 (2011): 77–78.

14. Website of Hanban, http://english.hanban.org/index.html. The bylaws are published on the Hanban website. Mosher's testimony, originally presented to the US House of Representatives' Committee on Foreign Affairs, Subcommittee on Oversight and Investigations, can be found at Steven W. Mosher, "Confucius Institutes: Trojan Horses with Chinese Characteristics," March 28, 2012, Population Research Institute website, http://pop.org/content/confucius-institutes-trojan-horses-chinese-characteristics.

15. The statement from the American Association of University Professors can be found at http://www.aaup.org/report/confucius-institutes.

16. All quotes from Jiang are from author's interview, April 2012, except where noted.

17. Jiang Qing and Daniel A. Bell, "A Confucian Constitution for China," *New York Times*, July 10, 2012.

18. All quotes from Feng are from author's interview, March 2012.

19. All quotes from Li and Miao are from author's interviews, March 2012.

20. All quotes from Luan and Lei are from author's interviews, July 2013.

21. All quotes from Zheng are from author's interview, July 2013.

BIBLIOGRAPHY

Classical Texts and Historical Records

The Analects: The most famous of Confucian texts, the *Analects* probably contains more original material from Confucius than any other (although he did not compile the book himself). I employed several different translations: The one I used most often was translated and analyzed by D. C. Lau; the version I read was published in 1979 by Penguin Books. I also used a translation by the patron saint of Chinese studies in the West, James Legge, which was reprinted in 2009 by Cosimo Classics in New York in a compilation entitled *The Confucian Analects, The Great Learning, and The Doctrine of the Mean*. You can also find the Legge translation online, kindly placed there by the Chinese Text Project, at http://ctext .org/analects.

Biographies of Exemplary Women: Albert Richard O'Hara included a translation of these biographies in his book *Position of Women in Early China*, published by Orient Publishing in Hong Kong in 1946.

The Book of Rites: I used James Legge's translation from 1885, which the University of Virginia has kindly placed on the Internet at the *Traditions of Exemplary Women* website at http://www2.iath.virginia.edu/saxon/servlet/SaxonServlet ?source=xwomen/texts/listtexts.xml&style=xwomen/xsl/dynaxml.xsl&chunk .id=d1.1&toc.depth=1&toc.id=0&doc.lang=bilingual.

The Classic of Filial Piety: For this highly influential text, I used a translation by James Legge. The full text is online at the Chinese Text Project, http://ctext.org /xiao-jing.

Discussions in White Tiger Pavilion: This Han-era text has also been placed on the University of Virginia website (see *The Book of Rites* above). The original was translated by Tjan Tjoe Som and published by Hyperion Press in 1973.

The Doctrine of the Mean: I used James Legge's version, reprinted by Cosimo Classics in 2009, in *The Confucian Analects, The Great Learning, and The Doctrine of the Mean.*

The Great Learning: I used James Legge here, too, in the same 2009 Cosimo Classics compilation, *The Confucian Analects, The Great Learning, and The Doctrine of the Mean.*

Han Feizi: The 1936 translation of his collected works, completed by W. K. Liao, can be found at the University of Virginia website cited above (see *The Book of Rites*).

The Hanshu, or *History of the Han Dynasty:* Once again, I am indebted to the University of Virginia for placing the translation of Homer Dubs on the website listed above (see *The Book of Rites*). The original was published by Waverly Press, Baltimore, in 1944. The site also includes explanations and introductions to the actual annals, which are very useful.

Mencius, or *Mengzi:* James Legge's translation of Mencius's works can be found online at the Chinese Text Project, http://ctext.org/mengzi.

Mozi: A partial translation of the works of Mozi is available online at the Chinese Text Project, http://ctext.org/mozi. This English version is from *The Ethical and Political Works of Motse* by W. P. Mei (1929).

Records of the Historian: Sima Qian's historical opus contains the first attempt at a full narrative biography of Confucius. I had to employ a mix of different translations of this text. For much of the material on Confucius himself, I used a translation by Yang Hsieh-yi and Gladys Yang, which was published in Hong Kong by the Commercial Press in 1975. Sima Qian's records of the Qin Dynasty come from a translation by Raymond Dawson, edited by K. E. Brashier, entitled *The First Emperor: Selections from the Historical Records,* published by Oxford University Press in 2009. For the material on Emperor Wu and the Han Dynasty, I used Burton Watson's classic translation, *Records of the Grand Historian,* published by Columbia University Press in 1961.

The Spring and Autumn Annals and the Zuo Commentary: This text adds some flesh onto the bare bones of the *Annals.* I used James Legge's 1872 translation, which can also be found on the University of Virginia website cited above (see *The Book of Rites*). The transliteration of Legge's original has been adjusted in this version.

The Twenty-Four Filial Exemplars: I used a translation of this collection from David Jordan, a professor at the University of California at San Diego, who has kindly placed his work on his website at http://weber.ucsd.edu/~dkjordan/chin/shiaw /shiaw00.html.

Xunzi: Burton Watson's translation of some of Xunzi's writings was published by Columbia University Press in 2003.

Zhuangzi: Most of the quotations used in my text are from the James Legge translation (1891), which appears online at the Chinese Text Project, http://ctext.org /zhuangzi. I also read a bit of the Burton Watson translation, which is available at "The Complete Works of Chuang Tzu," *Terebess Asia Online,* http://terebess.hu /english/chuangtzu.html.

Compilations of Original Texts and Records

I also used several collections of translations of Chinese philosophical treatises and historical documents:

Chan, Wing-tsit, trans. *A Sourcebook in Chinese Philosophy*. Princeton, NJ: Princeton University Press, 1989.

de Bary, Wm. Theodore, ed. *Sources of Chinese Tradition*, 2nd ed., vol. 2. New York: Columbia University Press, 2001.

de Bary, Wm. Theodore, and Irene Bloom, compilers. *Sources of Chinese Tradition*, 2nd ed., vol. 1. New York: Columbia University Press, 2000.

Ebrey, Patricia Buckley. *Chinese Civilization: A Sourcebook*, 2nd ed. New York: Free Press, 1993.

Gardner, Daniel K. *The Four Books: The Basic Teachings of the Late Confucian Tradition*. Indianapolis: Hackett, 2007.

Gentzler, J. Mason, ed. *Changing China: Readings in the History of China from the Opium War to the Present*. New York: Praeger, 1977.

Teng Ssu-yu and John King Fairbank. *China's Response to the West: A Documentary Survey, 1839–1923*. New York: Atheneum, 1963.

Other Sources

Ackerly, Brooke A. "Is Liberalism the Only Way Toward Democracy? Confucianism and Democracy." *Political Theory* 33, no. 4 (2005): 547–576.

Bell, Daniel A. *China's New Confucianism: Politics and Everyday Life in a Changing Society*. Princeton, NJ: Princeton University Press, 2008.

Blake, C. Fred. "Foot-Binding in Neo-Confucian China and the Appropriation of Female Labor." *Signs* 19, no. 3 (1994): 676–712.

Bodde, Derk. "The Idea of Social Classes in Han and Pre-Han China." In W. L. Idema and E. Zurcher, eds., *Thought and Law in Qin and Han China: Studies Dedicated to Anthony Hulsewe on the Occasion of His Eightieth Birthday*. Leiden: E. J. Brill, 1990, 26–41.

Bol, Peter K. *"This Culture of Ours": Intellectual Transitions in T'ang and Sung China*. Stanford, CA: Stanford University Press, 1992.

———. *Neo-Confucianism in History*. Cambridge, MA: Harvard University Press, 2008.

Chang, Carsun. *The Development of Neo-Confucian Thought*. London: Vision, 1958.

Chang, Wonsuk, and Leah Kalmanson, eds. *Confucianism in Context: Classic Philosophy and Contemporary Issues, East Asia and Beyond*. Albany: State University of New York Press, 2010.

Chen, Min. *Asian Management Systems*. London: Thomson Learning, 2004.

Chin, Annping. *The Authentic Confucius: A Life of Thought and Politics*. New York: Scribner, 2007.

Chow Tse-tsung. *The May 4th Movement: Intellectual Revolution in Modern China*. Cambridge, MA: Harvard University Press, 1964.

Chua, Amy. *Battle Hymn of the Tiger Mother*. New York: Penguin, 2011.

Clements, Jonathan. *Confucius: A Biography*. Stroud, UK: Sutton, 2004.

Csikszentmihalyi, Mark. "Confucius and the Analects in the Han." In Bryan W. Van Norden, ed., *Confucius and the Analects: New Essays*. New York: Oxford University Press, 2002.

Dardess, John W. *Confucianism and Autocracy: Professional Elites in the Founding of the Ming Dynasty*. Berkeley: University of California Press, 1983.

De Bary, Wm. Theodore. "The New Confucianism in Beijing." *American Scholar* 64, no. 2 (1995): 175–189.

_____. *The Trouble with Confucianism*. Cambridge, MA: Harvard University Press, 1996.

_____. *Asian Values and Human Rights: A Confucian Communitarian Perspective*. Cambridge, MA: Harvard University Press, 2000.

de Bary, Wm. Theodore, Carol Gluck, and Arthur E. Tiedemann, eds. *Sources of Japanese Tradition*, vol. 2, Part 1. New York: Columbia University Press, 2006.

Deuchler, Martina. *The Confucian Transformation of Korea: A Study of Society and Ideology*. Cambridge, MA: Harvard University Press, 1992.

Dotson, John. "The Confucian Revival in the Propaganda Narratives of the Chinese Government." Staff Research Report for the US-China Economic and Security Review Commission, July 2011.

Dubs, Homer H. "The Victory of Han Confucianism." *Journal of the American Oriental Society* 58, no. 3 (1938): 435–449.

Dull, Jack L. "Anti-Qin Rebels: No Peasant Leaders Here." *Modern China* 9, no. 3 (1983): 285–318.

Ebrey, Patricia Buckley. *The Inner Quarters: Marriage and the Lives of Chinese Women in the Sung Period*. Berkeley: University of California Press, 1992.

Elman, Benjamin A. *A Cultural History of Civil Examinations in Late Imperial China*. Berkeley: University of California Press, 2000.

Elstein, David. "Why Early Confucianism Cannot Generate Democracy." *Dao* 9 (2010): 427–443.

Englehart, Neil A. "Rights and Culture in the Asian Values Argument: The Rise and Fall of Confucian Ethics in Singapore." *Human Rights Quarterly* 22, no. 2 (2000): 548–568.

Eno, Robert. "The Background of the Kong Family of Lu and the Origins of Ruism." *Early China* 28 (2003).

Esherick, Joseph, Paul Pickowicz, and Andrew George Walder. *The Cultural Revolution as History*. Stanford, CA: Stanford University Press, 2006.

Fairbank, John K., Alexander Eckstein, and L. S. Yang. "Economic Change in Early Modern China: An Analytic Framework," Part 1. *Economic Development and Cultural Change* 9, no. 1 (1960): 1–26.

Fairbank, John King, and Liu Kwang-ching, eds. *The Cambridge History of China*, vol. 11, *Late Qing, 1800–1911*, Part 2. Cambridge, UK: Cambridge University Press, 1980.

Feuerwerker, Albert. "The State and the Economy in Late Imperial China." *Theory and Society* 13, no. 3 (1984): 297–326.

Fingarette, Herbert. *Confucius: The Secular as Sacred.* Long Grove, IL: Waveland Press, 1998.

Fu, Zhengyuan. *Autocratic Tradition and Chinese Politics.* Cambridge, UK: Cambridge University Press, 1993.

Fukuyama, Francis. "Confucianism and Democracy." *Journal of Democracy* 6, no. 2 (1995): 20–33.

Fung, Yu-lan. *A History of Chinese Philosophy,* vol. 1, *The Period of Philosophers,* translated by Derk Bodde. Princeton, NJ: Princeton University Press, 1983.

_____. *A History of Chinese Philosophy,* vol. 2, *The Period of Classical Learning,* translated by Derk Bodde. Princeton, NJ: Princeton University Press, 1983.

Gao, Xiongya. *Pearl S. Buck's Chinese Women Characters.* Cranbury, NJ: Associated University Presses, 2000.

Goldin, Paul. R. *Confucianism.* Berkeley: University of California Press, 2011.

Goossaert, Vincent. "1898: The Beginning of the End for Chinese Religion?" *Journal of Asian Studies* 65, no. 2 (2006): 307–336.

Gregor, A. James. "Confucianism and the Political Thought of Sun Yat-Sen." *Philosophy East and West* 31, no. 1 (1981): 55–70.

Han, Fook Kwang, Warren Fernandez, and Sumiko Tan. *Lee Kuan Yew: The Man and His Ideas.* Singapore: Times Editions, 1998.

Harrell, Stevan. "Why Do the Chinese Work So Hard? Reflections on an Entrepreneurial Ethic." *Modern China* 11, no. 2. (1985): 203–226.

Hicks, G. L., and S. G. Redding. "The Story of the East Asian 'Economic Miracle': Part 1: Economic Theory Be Damned." *Euro-Asia Business Review* 2, no. 3 (1983). 24–32.

_____. "The Story of the East Asian 'Economic Miracle': Part 2: The Culture Connection." *Euro-Asia Business Review* 2, no. 4 (1983): 18–22.

Hill, John S. "Confucianism and the Art of Chinese Management." *Journal of Asia Business Studies* 1, no. 1 (2006).

Hofstede, Geert, and Michael Harris Bond. "The Confucius Connection: From Cultural Roots to Economic Growth." *Organizational Dynamics* 16, no. 4 (1988): 5–21.

Holzman, Donald. "The Place of Filial Piety in Ancient China." *Journal of the American Oriental Society* 118, no. 2 (1998): 185–199.

Hsiao, Kung-chuan. *A Modern China and a New World: K'ang Yu-wei, Reformer and Utopian, 1858–1927.* Seattle: University of Washington Press, 1975.

Hsu, Francis L. K. *Under the Ancestors' Shadow: Kinship, Personality and Social Mobility in China.* Stanford, CA: Stanford University Press, 1971.

Huang, Chun-chieh. *Taiwan in Transformation: The Challenge of a New Democracy in an Old Civilization.* New Brunswick, NJ: Transaction, 2006.

Huang, Yong. "Government by Propriety: Why the Political Is Also Personal," in Lin Jianfu, ed., *The Kingly Culture, Social Renovation, and the Sustained Development in a Global Age.* Taipei: National Taiwan University Press, 2013, 101–165.

Huntington, Samuel P. *The Third Wave: Democratization in the Late Twentieth Century.* Norman: University of Oklahoma Press, 1993.

Hutton, Eric L. "Han Feizi's Criticism of Confucianism and Its Implications for Virtue Ethics." *Journal of Moral Philosophy* 5 (2008): 423–453.

James, Harold. "Family Values or Crony Capitalism?" *Capitalism and Society* 3, no. 1 (2008).

Jensen, Lionel M. "Wise Man of the Wilds: Fatherlessness, Fertility, and the Mythic Exemplar, Kongzi." *Early China* 20 (1995): 407–437.

———. *Manufacturing Confucianism: Chinese Traditions and Universal Civilization.* Durham, NC: Duke University Press, 1997.

Johnston, Reginald Fleming. *Confucianism in Modern China.* Vancouver, BC: Soul Care Publishing, 2008.

Kahn, Herman. *World Economic Development: 1979 and Beyond.* Boulder, CO: Westview Press, 1979.

Kaizuka, Shigeki. *Confucius: His Life and Thought,* translated by Geoffrey Bkownas. Mineola, NJ: Dover Publications, 2002.

Khan, Habibullah. "Social Policy in Singapore: A Confucian Model?" World Bank, 2001.

Kim Dae Jung. "Is Culture Destiny? The Myth of Asia's Anti-Democratic Values." *Foreign Affairs,* November/December 1994.

Knapp, Keith Nathaniel. "The *Ru* Reinterpretation of *Xiao.*" *Early China* 20 (1995): 195–222.

———. *Selfless Offspring: Filial Children and Social Order in Medieval China.* Honolulu: University of Hawaii Press, 2005.

———. "The Confucian Tradition in China," in Randall L. Nadeau, ed., *The Wiley-Blackwell Companion to Chinese Religions.* Oxford, UK: Wiley-Blackwell Press, 2012, 147–170.

Kristeva, Julia. *About Chinese Women,* translated by Anita Barrows. New York: Marion Boyars, 1986.

Kuhn, Dieter. *The Age of Confucian Rule: The Song Transformation of China.* Cambridge, MA: Belknap Press, 2009.

Kuhn, Philip A. *Chinese Among Others: Emigration in Modern Times.* Lanham, MD: Rowman and Littlefield, 2009.

Kwong, Luke S. K. "Chinese Politics at the Crossroads: Reflections on the Hundred Days Reform of 1898." *Modern Asian Studies* 34, no. 3 (2000): 663–695.

Lee, Peter H., and Wm. Theodore de Bary, eds. *Sources of Korean Tradition,* vol. 1, *From Early Times Through the Sixteenth Century.* New York: Columbia University Press, 1997.

Levy, Howard S. *Chinese Footbinding: The History of a Curious Erotic Custom.* New York: Bell Publishing, 1967.

Lew, Seok-Choon, Woo-Young Choi, and Hye Suk Wang. "Confucian Ethics and the Spirit of Capitalism in Korea: The Significance of Filial Piety." *Journal of East Asian Studies* 11, no. 2 (2011): 171–196.

Lewis, Mark Edward. *The Early Chinese Empires: Qin and Han*. Cambridge, MA: Belknap Press, 2007.

Liang, Ch'i-ch'ao. *Intellectual Trends in the Ch'ing Period*, translated by Immanuel C. Y. Hsu. Cambridge, MA: Harvard University Press, 1959.

Lin, Justin Yifu. "The Needham Puzzle: Why the Industrial Revolution Did Not Originate in China." *Economic Development and Cultural Change* 43, no. 2 (1995): 269–292.

Lin, Yutang. "Confucius as I Know Him." *China Critic* 4, no. 1 (1931): 5–9. Reproduced at www.chinaheritagequarterly.org/features.php?searchterm=030_confucius.inc& issue=030.

_____. *My Country and My People*. London: William Heinemann, 1936.

Long, Roderick T. "Austro-Libertarian Themes in Early Confucianism." *Journal of Libertarian Studies* 17, no. 3 (2003): 35–62.

Louie, Kam. *Critiques of Confucius in Contemporary China*. Hong Kong: Chinese University Press, 1980.

_____. *Theorizing Chinese Masculinity: Society and Gender in China*. Cambridge, UK: Cambridge University Press, 2002.

_____. "Confucius the Chameleon: Dubious Envoy for 'Brand China.'" *Boundary* 2 38, no. 1 (2011): 77–100.

Lu, Xun. *Selected Stories of Lu Hsun*, translated by Yang Hsien-yi and Gladys Yang. Beijing: Foreign Languages Press, 1972.

MacFarquhar, Roderick. "The Post-Confucian Challenge." *The Economist*, February 9, 1980.

Maddison, Angus. "The West and the Rest in the World Economy, 1000–2030: Maddisonian and Malthusian interpretations," *World Economics* 9, no. 4 (2008) 75–99.

Mahbubani, Kishore. "The Pacific Way." *Foreign Affairs*, January/February 1995.

Mann, Susan, and Cheng Yu-yin, eds. *Under Confucian Eyes: Writings on Gender in Chinese History*. Berkeley: University of California Press, 2001.

Miyazaki, Ichisada. *China's Examination Hell: The Civil Service Examinations of Imperial China*, translated by Conrad Schirokauer. New Haven, CT: Yale University Press, 1981.

Nathan, Andrew. *Chinese Democracy*. Berkeley: University of California Press, 1986.

Needham, Joseph. *Science and Civilization in China*, vol. 2, *History of Scientific Thought*. Cambridge, UK: Cambridge University Press, 1956.

_____. *The Grand Titration: Science and Society in East and West*. Toronto: University of Toronto Press, 1979.

Nosco, Peter, ed. *Confucianism in Tokugawa Culture*. Honolulu: University of Hawaii Press, 1997.

Nylan, Michael. "Confucian Piety and Individualism in Han China." *Journal of the American Oriental Society* 116, no. 1 (1996): 1–27.

Nylan, Michael, and Thomas Wilson. *Lives of Confucius: Civilization's Greatest Sage Through the Ages*. New York: Doubleday, 2010.

O'Brien, Patrick K. "The Needham Question Updated: A Historiographical Survey and Elaboration." *History of Technology* 29 (2009): 7–28.

O'Dwyer, Shaun. "Democracy and Confucian Values." *Philosophy East and West* 53, no. 1 (2003): 39–63.

Oldstone-Moore, Jennifer. *Confucianism: Origins, Beliefs, Practices, Holy Texts, Sacred Places*. Oxford, UK: Oxford University Press, 2002.

Paradise, James F. "China and International Harmony: The Role of Confucius Institutes in Bolstering Beijing's Soft Power." *Asian Survey* 49, no. 4 (2009): 647–669.

Paramore, Kiri. "The Nationalization of Confucianism: Academism, Examinations, and Bureaucratic Governance in the Late Tokugawa State." *Journal of Japanese Studies* 38, no. 1 (2012): 25–53.

Park, Chung Hee. *To Build a Nation*. Washington, DC: Acropolis Books, 1971.

Patten, Chris. *East and West: The Last Governor of Hong Kong on Power, Freedom, and the Future*. London: Macmillan, 1998.

Rainey, Lee Dian. *Confucius and Confucianism: The Essentials*. West Sussex, UK: Wiley-Blackwell, 2010.

Ramírez, Luis Felipe. "Culture, Government and Development in South Korea." *Asian Culture and History* 2, no. 1 (2010): 71–81.

Reid, T. R. *Confucius Lives Next Door: What Living in the East Teaches Us About Living in the West*. New York: Vintage, 2009.

Rosenlee, Li-hsiang Lisa. *Confucianism and Women: A Philosophical Interpretation*. Albany: State University of New York Press, 2006.

Russell, Bertrand. *The Problem of China*. London: George Allen and Unwin, 1922.

Schuman, Michael. *The Miracle: The Epic Story of Asia's Quest for Wealth*. New York: HarperBusiness, 2009.

Sellmann, James D., and Sharon Rowe. "The Feminine in Confucius." *Asian Culture Quarterly* 26, no. 3 (1998).

Shryock, John K. *The Origin and Development of the Cult of Confucius: An Introductory Study*. New York: Paragon, 1966.

Shun, Kwong-loi, and David B. Wong, eds. *Confucian Ethics: A Comparative Study of Self, Autonomy, and Community*. Cambridge, UK: Cambridge University Press, 2004.

Slote, Walter H., and George A. De Vos, eds. *Confucianism and the Family*. Albany: State University of New York Press, 1998.

Sommer, Deborah. "Images for Iconoclasts: Images of Confucius in the Cultural Revolution." *East West Connections* 7, no. 1 (2007): 1–23.

Spence, Jonathan. "Confucius." *Wilson Quarterly*, Autumn 1993.

Sun Yat-sen. *San Min Chu I: The Three Principles of the People*. Frank W. Price, trans. L. T. Chen, ed. Shanghai: China Committee Institute of Pacific Relations, 1927.

Tan, Charlene. "'Our Shared Values' in Singapore: A Confucian Perspective." *Educational Theory* 62, no. 4 (2012): 449–463.

Tan, Chwee Huat. "Confucianism and Nation Building in Singapore." *International Journal of Social Economics* 16, no. 8 (1989): 5–16.

Tan, Soo Kee. "Influence of Confucianism on Korean Corporate Culture." *Asian Profile* 36, no. 1 (2008): 9–20.

Tan, Sor-hoon. "Authoritative Master Kong (Confucius) in an Authoritarian Age." *Dao* 9 (2010): 137–149.

Tay, Wei Leong. "Kang Youwei: The Martin Luther of Confucianism and His Vision of Confucian Modernity and Nation." In Haneda Masashi, ed., *Secularization, Religion and the State*. Tokyo: University of Tokyo Center for Philosophy, 2010.

Taylor, Rodney Leon. *Confucianism*. New York: Chelsea House, 2004.

Thompson, Mark R. "Pacific Asia After 'Asian Values': Authoritarianism, Democracy, and 'Good Governance.'" *Third World Quarterly* 25, no. 6 (2004): 1079–1095.

Tillman, Hoyt Cleveland. *Confucian Discourse and Chu Hsi's Ascendancy*. Honolulu: University of Hawaii Press, 1992.

Totman, Conrad. *Early Modern Japan*. Berkeley: University of California Press, 1993.

Tu, Wei-ming. "The Rise of Industrial East Asia: The Role of Confucian Values." *Copenhagen Papers in East and Southeast Asian Studies*, no. 4 (1989): 81–97.

_____. *Confucian Traditions in East Asian Modernity: Moral Education and Economic Culture in Japan and the Four Mini-Dragons*. Cambridge, MA: Harvard University Press, 1996.

Twitchett, Denis, and Michael Loewe, eds. *The Cambridge History of China*, vol. 1, *The Qin and Han Empires, 221 BC–220 AD*. Cambridge, UK: Cambridge University Press, 1996.

Vogel, Ezra F. *Japan as Number One: Lessons for America*. Bloomington, IN: iUniverse, 1999. (Originally published by Harvard University Press in 1979.)

Weber, Max. *The Religion of China: Confucianism and Daoism*, translated by Hans H. Gerth. New York: Macmillan, 1951.

Whyte, Martin King. "The Social Roots of China's Economic Development." *China Quarterly*, no. 144 (1995): 999–1019.

_____. "The Chinese Family and Economic Development: Obstacle or Engine?" *Economic Development and Cultural Change* 45, no. 1 (1996): 1–30.

Wilson, Thomas A. *On Sacred Grounds: Culture, Society, Politics, and the Formation of the Cult of Confucius*. Cambridge, MA: Harvard University Press, 2003.

Winchester, Simon. *The Man Who Loved China: The Fantastic Story of the Eccentric Scientist Who Unlocked the Mysteries of the Middle Kingdom*. New York: Harper, 2008.

Winckler, Edwin A., and Susan Greenhalgh, eds. *Contending Approaches to the Political Economy of Taiwan*. Armonk, NY: M. E. Sharpe, 1988.

Woo, Terry. "Confucianism and Feminism." In Arvind Sharma and Katherine K. Young, eds., *Feminism in World Religions*. Albany: State University of New York Press, 1999.

Wood, Alan T. *Limits to Autocracy: From Sung Neo-Confucianism to a Doctrine of Political Rights.* Honolulu: University of Hawaii Press, 1995.

Yang, Key P., and Gregory Henderson. "An Outline History of Korean Confucianism: Part I: The Early Period and Yi Factionalism." *Journal of Asian Studies* 18, no. 1 (1958): 81–101.

Yao, Xinzhong. *An Introduction to Confucianism.* New York: Cambridge University Press, 2009.

Yi Il Cheong. "Formulation of Confucianism in the Social Welfare Systems of East Asia." *KATHA*, no. 1 (2005).

Yu, Dan. *Confucius from the Heart: Ancient Wisdom for Today's World,* translated by Ester Tyldesley. London: Pan Books, 2010.

Zakaria, Fareed. "A Conversation with Lee Kuan Yew." *Foreign Affairs*, March/April 1994.

Zelin, Madeleine. *The Merchants of Zigong: Industrial Entrepreneurship in Early Modern China.* New York: Columbia University Press, 2005.

Zhang Tong and Barry Schwartz. "Confucius and the Cultural Revolution: A Study in Collective Memory." *International Journal of Politics, Culture and Society* 11, no. 2 (1997).

INDEX

Admonitions for Women (Ban Zhao), 153

Age of Great Peace (Kang), 84–85

Ai, duke of Lu, 28, 33, 172, 196–197

Amelio, William, 188–189

American Association of University Professors, 228

An Hyang, 70

Analects
  origins, 6, 30, 34
  hidden in walls of Kong family home, 43
  included in the Four Books, 68
  official curriculum for civil service exams, 137
  as primary source on Confucius's life and ideas, 13, 18–19, 34
  studied for education and government, 30–31, 64, 74, 232
  See also references throughout text

The Analects for Women (Song Ruozhao), 153–155

Analects of Confucius Recital Center, 239

Ancestor worship, 72, 103, 106

Anti-Confucianism
  after collapse of Qing Dynasty, 89–91
  becomes state policy under Mao, 91–97, 217–219
  of Chen Duxiu, 124, 195

Asian values
  challenge Western political ideology, 192–194, 212–213
  criticism of, 209, 213
  role in Asian economic development, 185–186, 225
  of Singapore's Lee Kuan Yew, 183, 185–186, 192, 205–206

Authoritarianism
  Confucius's views on autocracy, 196–197, 209
  vs. democracy and Confucianism, 213
  and modern China's revived Confucius, 217, 222–223
  perceived as Confucian, xxi–xxii, 200, 239–241

Avatar film, 216

Bae, Fiona, 145

Bamboo for Living Culture Club, 233–235

Ban Zhao, 153, 155–156

Battle Hymn of the Tiger Mother (Chua), 130–131

Bell, Daniel, 223–224

Benevolence
  Confucius's views on, 26–27, 40, 112, 206, 241
  required of rulers and gentlemen, 26, 149, 175, 197
  role in ideal Confucian government, 50, 194, 197

The Bible, 85, 212, 241